RHETORIC AND CHANGE

William E. Tanner
J. Dean Bishop
editors

Contributors:

*Jacques Barzun
J. Dean Bishop
Kenneth Burke
Edward P. J. Corbett
Frank J. D'Angelo
Kay Parkhurst Easson
Wilbur Samuel Howell
Richard L. Larson
Gerald J. Prince
Thomas O. Sloane
Martin Steinmann, Jr.
William E. Tanner
Winston Weathers
W. Ross Winterowd
Richard E. Young*

D1596789

Mesquite

Ide House

1982

Ide House, Inc., Publishers
4631 Harvey Drive
Mesquite, Texas 75150 U.S.A.

ⓒ Rhetoric Committee
of the Federation of North Texas Area Universities
1982

Library of Congress Cataloging in Publication Data

Main entry under title:

Rhetoric and change.

  Bibliography: p.
  1. Rhetoric—Addresses, essays, lectures.
I. Tanner, William Edward, 1937-   .
II. Bishop, J. Dean (Jimmy Dean), 1933-
III. Barzun, Jacques, 1907-
P301.R44   808   82-6190
ISBN 0-86663-900-4   AACR2
ISBN 0-86663-901-2 (pbk.)

Permission to reprint articles appearing in the publications of the Rhetoric
Committee of the Federation of North Texas Area Universities granted by the edi-
tors. Articles include: Jacques Barzun, "The Rhetoric of the Arts," *Rhetoric of
the Arts* (in press); Kenneth Burke, "Motion, Action, and the Human Condition,"
a lecture delivered before the Federation, and which appeared in modified form in
Critical Inquiry, vol. 4, no. 4 (Spring, 1978), pp. 809-33; Edward P. J. Corbett,
"Rhetoric, Whether Goest Thou?" *A Symposium in Rhetoric* (1975), pp. 44-57;
Frank J. D'Angelo, "Up Against the Wall, Mother! The Rhetoric of Slogans,
Catchphrases, and Graffiti," *A Symposium in Rhetoric* (1976), pp. 41-50; Kay
Parkhurst Easson, " 'Description as Cosmos': Blake's Settings in *Milton*,"
Rhetoric of the Arts (in press); Wilbur Samuel Howell, "Peter Ramus, Thomas
Sheridan, and Kenneth Burke: Three Mavericks in the History of Rhetoric,"
Retrospectives and Perspectives (1978), pp. 91-105; Richard L. Larson, "The
Rhetoric of the Written Voice," *A Symposium in Rhetoric* (1976), pp. 22-32;
Gerald J. Prince, "Questions, Answers, and Narrative Legibility," *Retrospectives
and Perspectives* (1978), pp. 75-90; Thomas O. Sloane, "Beauty's Spouse's Odd
Elysium: Barth's *Funhouse*," *Retrospectives and Perspectives* (1978), pp. 57-74;
Martin Steinmann, Jr., "Speech Acts and Rhetoric," *Retrospectives and Per-
spectives* (1978), pp. 3-8; Winston Weathers, "The Value of Rhetoric to the
Creative Artist," *A Symposium in Rhetoric* (1975), pp. 25-33; W. Ross Win-
terowd, "The Three R's: Reading, Reading, and Rhetoric," *A Symposium in
Rhetoric* (1976), pp. 51-63: all published at Denton, Texas, by Texas Woman's
University Press. The essay by the editors is a new contribution to rhetoric
studies and scholarship: copyright 1982 by William E. Tanner and J. Dean Bishop.

TABLE OF CONTENTS

PART ONE

A New Awareness

By the 1970s rhetoric appeared to many a Galahad in a struggle to conquer a national malaise, a decline in literacy skills. This new awareness initiated yet another awareness— the validity of an ancient tradition, the art of rhetoric. This introductory essay, "Reform Amid the Revival of Rhetoric," chronicles the circumstances which opened new frontiers and explores the discoveries which directed the recent renascence of rhetoric.

Challenged by a new awareness, the contributors of the subsequent essays delineate the concerns of the past decade, promote a reevaluation of rhetoric, present new rhetorical theories, refine traditional rhetorical concepts and theories, and demonstrate applications of particular theories.

WILLIAM E. TANNER
J. DEAN BISHOP

REFORM AMID THE REVIVAL OF RHETORIC

For the first decade following the mid-point of the twentieth century, the lack of organized instruction in the discipline of writing became obvious. During this ten-year interval, those concerned began to sow seeds which would sprout in the decade of the sixties and mature in the seventies. The recognition in the 1950s that instruction in writing had dwindled into prescriptive "grammatical etiquette" comprised of a list of *dos* and *don'ts* (which Francis calls Grammar Three) inspirited educators to harrow the fields for planting seeds for revival and reform in rhetoric, once the center of schooling.

When in the nineteenth century the purview of rhetorical studies expanded to incorporate literary and philological concerns, classical rhetorical training slipped to a secondary position. In the first half of the nineteenth century the shift in traditional studies was reflected in the practices instituted by Edward T. Channing, then Boylston Professor of Rhetoric at Harvard. Associating rhetoric and literary studies and shifting emphasis away from the oratorical mode toward the written mode, Channing departed from the decidedly classical tradition of his predecessors. The shift from the classical orientation was further widened by Channing's successor, Francis James Child, who saw the office of rhetorical studies assigned to his assistant. With the relegation of composition reduced to a secondary position, rhetoric as it had been known for centuries was becoming old fashioned. And indeed, by the beginning of the twentieth century, rhetoric had fallen from grace: the term *rhetoric* gave way to *composition*; the old rhetoric texts moved to the library stacks; and literature became a model for teaching composition. Thus, under the influence of Adams Sherman Hill as Boylston Professor of Rhetoric from 1876-1904, imitation replaced the theoretical concept of rhetoric, and grammatical correctness substituted for the canon of style.

In addition, Hill's revised edition of *The Principles of Rhetoric* (1895) helped to cement into place the paradigm shift from the bellestristic aim of rhetoric to the modal concept of composition. A time-honored tradition stemming from Blair and other eighteenth-century rhetoricians, the bellestristic classification of forms—letters, treatises, essays, biographies, fiction—gave way as America sought to meet the demands for a different kind of education following the Civil War. Admittedly, the modes, generally limited to narration, description, argument, and exposition, had earlier advocates who attempted to promote these four modes as organizing principles for classifying discourse as well as means for teaching composition. As early as 1827, Samuel Newman, a professor at Bowdoin College, used similar terms in *A Practical System of Rhetoric*; Alexander Bain, a Scottish logician, in his 1866 *English Composition and Rhetoric* urged the adoption of the modes "to inform the understanding." In 1885 John Genung's *The Practical Element* accelerated the movement toward an acceptance of the modal concept over the bellestristic model. By 1895, with the new edition of Hill's *The Principles of Rhetoric*, the modes for all practical purposes reigned absolute.

While the decline of the rhetorical sphere here indicated the particular biases of a few men, these attitudes toward the classical orientation also reflected a tendency that was prevalent throughout the nation, not just the east coast, and although some semblances of the system of rhetoric remained, especially in the retention of the classical topics as modes of paragraph development and the emphasis upon structured unity—the tripartite unity-coherence-emphasis, the classical rhetorical concept of writing had vanished from the classroom, and handbooks were introduced to dictate the correct usage of language.

Inherited thus from the nineteenth-century masters, the stress placed upon error-free writing and upon the modal approach to composition prevailed virtually unchallenged until the 1940s when again a cultural and political climate necessitated a change in allegiances. Actually, a further dilution of these already narrowed rhetorical principles emerged in the 1920s with a growing tendency to reduce the modes to a single approach, particularly exposition, which seemed especially functional in a trade-oriented society. Although the modal approach continued to assert its virtues, it tended to fragment along functional lines. Exposition dominated the composition classroom; description and narration became the core of creative writing classes; argument found sanctuary in speech departments where it re-assumed its oral heritage. Throughout the 1930s and 1940s this fragmentation persisted, and by the mid-forties the modes lost their power to define the forms of discourse as well as the means for composition. The single mode assumed authority, that is, exposition with an emphasis upon a composed product adhering to the rules of grammatical correctness.

Even though the classical tradition was abandoned by the teachers of composition, it was nurtured by the speech teachers, who held on to the rhetorical tradition. In fact, the Speech Department at Cornell University holds claim to the revival of classical rhetoric in the twentieth century. In 1920 Alexander Durmond and Everett Hunt established a seminar where students studied Aristotle's *Rhetoric*, Cicero's *De Oratore*, and Quintilian's *Institutio Oratoria*. The impact of this study became apparent when these students accepted positions at universities throughout the nation. Thus scholarly work in rhetoric was ongoing in departments of speech and journals devoted to speech studies, such as *Quarterly Journal of Speech* and *Speech Monographs*, now changed to *Communication Monographs*. In the succeeding decades of the thirties and forties a renewed interest in rhetoric appeared imminent. An additional boost to this interest was fostered by theoreticians like I. A. Richards, C. K. Ogden, Kenneth Burke, and even the New Critics, who applied rhetorical techniques to the study of literature, but the new impulse toward a revival of classical rhetoric remained aloof from the classroom and from the practical concerns of composition.

Adding to the continued attention to the rhetorical concept was a trend toward composition texts with a decided bias or focus. These single-focus texts emphasized a central thesis or controlling idea which governed the principles included in the rhetoric. Such texts grew out of a disillusionment with current practices. When placed under a microscope, the modal approach with its emphasis on correctness yielded no evidence of usefulness. Grammar fell into disfavor as a means to composition skills, and new intellectual systems were invoked to produce the product the modes failed to achieve. In the forefront of the intellectual movements in the 1940s, general semantics rushed to aid the ailing composition teacher. S. I. Hayakawa's *Words in Action* (1940), based on the work of Alfred Korzybski, was influential for the next decade. Another resource came from the general education movement which emphasized communication skills—reading, writing, speaking, listening. Reflecting Dewey's interest in "English for Life Skills," the movement led to the creation of the communications course in colleges throughout the country and the founding of the Conference on College Composition and Communication (1948). Both of these intellectual movements provided theses urging practical usefulness, but disaffection was not long in coming. Like other untested propositions when subjected to scrutiny, communications and semantics lacked theoretical validity and ultimately failed as strategies for writing.

In the long line of panaceas which have followed, few avoided the dangers of *a priori* thought. Single-focus texts continued to follow contemporary intellectual currents, but none could replace the center once occupied by classical rhetoric. If the 40s relied upon communications and semantics theory, the 50s and 60s applied propositions derived from structural linguistics and transformational grammar as well as behavioral modification. The work of Paul Roberts, W. Nelson Francis, and Sumner Ives provided objective criteria for describing language that would significantly alter the use of the written language. By the late 50s the structuralists came under attack from the exponents of transformational grammar. Initially introduced by Chomsky in *Syntactic Structure* (1957), the "new" grammar sought an objective, reliable structure for describing language. In turn, this base could generate a stable foundation for composition theory. The widely acclaimed essays of Francis Christensen on a generative rhetoric of the sentence in 1963 and the paragraph in 1965 called attention to some processes by which writing is generated.

Concurrent with the development in transformational and structural theory was the advocacy of programmed instruction based on behavioral psychology. Using the methods of B. F. Skinner, programmed instruction relied on teaching machines to modify unwanted habits and to enforce the behavior desired. Although such programs succeeded in achieving the goals of traditional prescriptive workbook grammar and usage, they failed when attempting to program a course in composition. As with other schemes which depend heavily upon linear processes, programmed instruction in composition was incapable of processing and communicating the active principles actually involved in the composing process.

The attempts of programmed instruction, transformational grammar, structural linguistics, general semantics, and communications to alter the decay in prose writing suffered the same fate as the modal approach to composition. All possessed the same weakness. Each claimed to be a functional tool. In reality, each, though interesting in theory, had little effect on the product produced in the writing class. When educators and theorists alike ceased to be intimidated by the authority imposed by textbooks and questioned the effectiveness of the methods to achieve the aims desired, the schemes were found wanting, for the procedures of the last hundred years had focused on the product of writing, ignoring or minimizing the importance of the purpose of writing. As James Kinneavy points out, this procedure "is actually a substitution of means for ends." It lays undue emphasis "on 'what' is being talked about rather than on 'why' a thing is talked about" (*A Theory of Discourse*, pp. 28-29).

With a general dissatisfaction over the state of the profession growing throughout the country, another change was in the wind, a change that would attempt to correct the imbalance of past generations. By the late 50s, the seeds were already sprouting and the phrase "new rhetoric" sounding through academe. The forces contributing to a surge of new intellectual pursuits can be attributed to the curriculum reform movement which began in 1958 at Dartmouth College, when under a grant from the Carnegie Corporation of New York, Dartmouth undertook a project to study the writing of college students. A second conference at Dartmouth in 1966, the Anglo-American Seminar on the Teaching of English, then urged a shift in curriculum priorities, from an emphasis on the grammatical conventions to an emphasis on the writing process. Additional support for reconsideration of a system that no longer worked came from the Projects English of the U. S. Office of Education, which funded the establishment of curriculum centers. On April 1, 1962, three curriculum centers began operation. Eight others were to follow. Of these first centers, Carnegie Institute of Technology set out to reform curricula for grades ten to twelve; Northwestern University, seven to fourteen. Both stressed composition. The Nebraska Center, however, sought a major revision of composition strategies. Among its aims were the development of materials which related "composition to the relevant portions of classical rhetoric" and "the devising of a 'new rhetoric' based on recent research in linguistics, philosophy, and psychology" (*College English*, 28 [1962], 677-79). Cognizant of the need for reform, Albert

Kitzhaber, director of the Oregon Curriculum Center, in *Themes, Theories, and Therapy* (New York: McGraw-Hill, 1963), summarized the malaise that plagued English programs:

> Confusion in purpose, content, and organization; inexpert teaching; poor textbooks: these criticisms will have a strangely familiar sound. . . . The most exciting educational development of the last half dozen years has been the widespread effort to improve the quality of instruction in several of the basic academic subjects, mainly by identifying and concentrating more directly upon their central principles and by bringing their content more nearly into line with current knowledge of the particular disciplines . . . one finds little evidence that the people who plan and run freshman English courses, or those who write textbooks for these courses, have been at all conscious of this movement or of its bearing on their own concerns. Most of them are still doing business in the same old way at the same old stand. Freshman English in the nation's colleges and universities is now so confused, so clearly in need of radical and sweeping reforms, that college English departments can continue to ignore the situation at their own increasing peril. (pp. 10, 26)

Indeed, solutions to resolve the anarchy were not long in coming. The plea for a "new rhetoric" came from all quarters. Drawing upon insights gleaned from linguistics, anthropology, philosophy, psychology, and other disciplines, the pieces of a new rhetoric began to fall into place, aided by Marshall McLuhan's edicts on the electronic age and the increasing presence of non-verbal rhetoric or "body rhetoric" as in marches and sit-ins. Kenneth Burke's *A Rhetoric of Motives* (1950), Chaim Perelman's *La Nouvelle Rhetorique: Traité de l'Argumentation* (1958), Daniel Fogarty's *Roots of a New Rhetoric* (1959) had already sounded a clarion. Wayne Booth's "The Revival of Rhetoric" (1964), Richard Ohmann's "In Lieu of a New Rhetoric" (1964), and Corbett's *Classical Rhetoric for the Modern Student* (1965) reflected the growing trend toward reviving the principles of classical rhetorical theory. Martin Steinmann's *New Rhetorics* (1967) collected key statements and led the way for extended treatises, and in 1968 *Philosophy and Rhetoric*, a journal founded at Pennsylvania State University, was established to promote rhetorical studies. By 1970 the land had been harrowed for planting a new rhetoric with the forces for a revolution in composition theory.

During the next ten years, from the early 1970s until now, significant changes occurred in rhetorical theory. These changes may have been made more rapidly because of the National Development Project on Rhetoric, sponsored by The Speech Communication Association in 1970. The project had three parts. In January 1970, twelve scholars presented position papers at the Johnson Foundation's Wingspread Conference at Racine, Wisconsin, in which they attempted to delineate ". . . a conception of rhetoric useful in the second half of the twentieth century" (*The Prospect of Rhetoric*, p. v). Four months later at a second meeting held at St. Charles, Illinois, May 1970, twenty-three scholars read the essays and reports from the Wingspread Conference. Each participant was assigned to three committees, each of which was charged with synthesizing and refining the materials of the Wingspread Conference, with evaluating the state of scholarship in a particular area, and with drafting specific resolutions addressed to the profession about scholarly rhetorical research, undergraduate and graduate training in rhetoric, and social impact from these activities.

A survey of the developments in the following ten years will help to assess the impact of the Wingspread Conference and to chart the unfolding of the plan set forth. First a review of rhetorical activities outside of the classroom will focus on forces that will in turn influence classroom instruction.

Following the lead of the Wingspread Conference, other conferences and symposia on rhetoric were sponsored by professional organizations and universities. In November 1973, Edward P. J. Corbett chaired a session at the Midwest Modern Language Association in Chicago at which Richard Young shared his research on invention based on the linguistic concept of tagmemics. The following month at the New York meeting of the Modern Language Association, a special interest group on rhetoric was addressed by Richard Young, Edward P. J. Corbett, and others. The year 1974 saw special interest groups chaired by Tommy Boley at Rocky Mountain Modern Language Association and by J. Dean Bishop at South Central Modern Language Association. The Federation of North Texas Area Universities in cooperation with the Department of English of the Texas Woman's University sponsored symposia in rhetoric from 1974 to 1980 at which prominent rhetoricians were engaged. Martin Steinmann, Jr. in 1978 organized an interdisciplinary conference on the theory of rhetoric. In 1979 Carnegie-Mellon along with Indiana University and the University of Michigan under the auspices of the Speech Communications Association Re-search Board sponsored a doctoral seminar in rhetoric that featured graduate students and James J. Murphy. Thus the forces set into motion at the Wingspread Conference at the beginning of the decade expanded and grew in intensity throughout the 1970s.

Longer rhetoric conferences or symposia sponsored by professional organizations such as Conference on College Composition and Communications and universities such as the University of Minnesota were modified and expanded in-to the two-week seminar devoted exclusively to rhetoric such as Current Theories of Teaching Composition begun in 1975 by Janice M. Lauer at the University of Detroit, but now held at Purdue University, or the week seminar Writing as Process organized by Forrest D. Burt of Texas A & M University at which nationally recognized rhetoricians instructed teachers of writing in recent developments in rhetorical theory and applications of those theories. Other opportunities for study of rhetoric were the NEH Summer Seminars, led by such rhetoricians as Gary Tate and Edward P. J. Corbett, and the year-long NEH Seminars of Richard Young. In addition to seminars that dealt exclusively with rhetoric, other seminars such as the one at Laramie, Wyoming, incorporated rhetorical theory and application into programs. Such inclusion of rhetoric indicates that rhetorical theory was reaching into the mainstream of compositional studies.

These rhetorical activities at symposia and conferences encouraged participants to initiate changes in traditional literary curricula, changes which had been advocated at the Wingspread Conference. Ten years later, responses to a national survey of colleges and universities in the United States and Canada that offer graduate work in English show that seventy-five percent of these departments have added at least one or two new graduate courses in rhetoric and com-position between 1976 and 1980. Graves and Solomon (*Freshman English News*, Spring 1980) have conveniently classified these graduate courses in rhetoric into six categories: (1) The Teaching of Rhetoric and Composition (by and large these courses emphasize the application of rhetorical theory for classroom teaching); (2) Theory of Rhetoric and Composition (courses in this category usually survey twentieth-century rhetorical theories and/or particular single-focus texts); (3) Advanced Writing (such courses most often address writing problems peculiar to a particular profession such as business and industry or a discipline "other than English"; (4) Basic Writing (with few exceptions, Mina Shaughnessy's *Errors and Expectations* serves as a text and justification for this course); (5) Research in Rhetoric and Composition (this kind of course, offered at only a few schools, stresses empirical research); (6) Stylistics (this category most frequently indicates a rhetorical approach instead of a linguistic one). These courses may suggest that some of the resistance to change by teachers who at one time felt comfortable with a static system that ignored scholarly investigation and research that revolutionized language study may be lessening. To accomplish the goals set forth at the Wingspread Conference, instruction in rhetoric and composition must be grounded in current knowledge about language and the composing process instead of on a prescriptive attitude toward correct usage. For the next decade these courses in rhetoric and composition should provide teachers sufficiently trained in the principles of writing, of the composing process, of psycho-cognitive development, and of socio-linguistics to insure that instruction in writing centers on the principles of rhetoric.

Further evidence of the revival of rhetoric is the significant number of graduate degree programs developed during the decade of the seventies. Perhaps the first doctoral program in rhetoric is the one W. Ross Winterowd planned and still directs at the University of Southern California. Certainly, it was among the first to gain national recognition. By the end of the 70s, a sufficient number of doctoral programs had been established that alternatives existed within the discipline of rhetoric for satisfying a range of professional needs: for instance, the Ph.D. in rhetoric for those wishing to teach rhetoric and conduct research or the interdisciplinary doctorate for those with interest outside of academe.

At the March 1980 Rhetoric Society of America meeting held in Washington, D.C., a survey of the two hundred participants established that there are both masters and doctoral degrees and that at least thirty universities offer a concentration in rhetoric as a requirement and/or option within doctoral programs.

Not only have graduate studies in rhetoric, especially graduate degree programs, established the validity of the discipline for the twentieth century, but they have also fostered the publication of rhetorical research. One avenue for dissemination of rhetorical scholarship is the serial, and during the decade of the 70s several appeared either as the official publication of an organization or for a particular audience. The Rhetoric Society of America, organized in 1968 for the advancement of the study of rhetoric, began to publish a newsletter which in 1976 became *Rhetoric Society Quarterly*. Founded in 1977, the International Society for the History of Rhetoric issued its first volume of *Rhetoric Newsletter* (June 1978). Among publications for particular audiences started in this period are *Freshman English News* (1971), which publishes articles about the teaching of writing and related topics; *Pre/Text: An Inter-disciplinary Journal of Rhetoric* (1980), which publishes scholarship in process; *The Writing Instructor* (1981), which publishes pedagogical research; *Rhetoric Review* (announced for 1982), which will be devoted to theory and application. Much research and scholarship on rhetoric found its way into print in places other than these, especially in those publications sponsored by NCTE. The number of serials and the variety among them attest to the revival of rhetoric.

Perhaps the most innovative contribution to the discipline of rhetoric in this century, and certainly the most influential, is Gary Tate's *Teaching Composition: 10 Bibliographical Essays* (Fort Worth: Texas Christian University Press, 1976). This essential resource contains ten essays written by authorities who stress the teaching of writing at the college level. This volume now has an *Index* compiled by Barbara McDaniel (Blaine, Wa.: Verlaine Books, 1982); her *Index* augments the usefulness of Tate's collection as a reference resource.

Five years before Tate's volume, Jame L. Kinneavy's *A Theory of Discourse: The Aims of Discourse* (Englewood Cliffs, N.J.: Prentice-Hall, 1971) appeared, and its impact on rhetorical studies has been considerable. Kinneavy organizes his modes of discourse into static categories and ignores rhetorical processes because he planned for his treatise to provide an ordered approach to the study of discourse. Unfortunately, Kinneavy has failed to supply a consistent, uniform theory, and the lack of order results in fragmented insights and contributions. He intended to construct a paradigm to aid in the understanding and teaching of discourse "within a framework suggested by modern philosophy and linguistics." While he did not achieve his stated goal, his *A Theory of Discourse* has mapped a path toward order in rhetorical studies by having served as a catalyst for additional rhetorical scholarship and investigation of discourse theory. A third book of importance was published the year after Tate's: E. D. Hirsch, Jr., *The Philosophy of Composition* (Chicago: University of Chicago Press, 1977). Hirsch's organizing principle is measurable readability. In *The Philosophy of Composition*, though, Hirsch offers an incomplete and inconsistent explanation of his principles, and rhetoricians agree that his contribution to rhetorical studies rests in his having stimulated dialogue in print and at professional meetings. A fourth book that deserves mention in this representative list is James Britten's *The Development of Writing Abilities (11-18)* (London: Macmillan Education Ltd., 1975) in which he applies the concept of distance developed by James Moffett in *Teaching the Universe of Discourse* (Boston: Houghton Mifflin Co., 1968). In a five-year study completed in 1971, Britten studied the developmental stages in the writing of British school children ages 11-18. Convinced that rhetorical modes are non-existent, he applied Moffett's scales of distance to classify writing samples based on the processes the student writers used. Britten argues that by "concerning ourselves with writing as process, we are suggesting that such a perspective is of major importance in understanding how children's writing develops. . . ." He continues by emphasizing the relationships between the writer and the audience: ". . . the interaction of writers with readers, pupils with teachers, children with parents and other adults, and children with each other, influences and promotes the development of writing in all its functions" (p. 20). A final entry in this brief survey must be a bibliography: Winifred Bryan Horner, editor, *Historical Rhetoric: An Annotated Bibliography of Selected Sources in English* (Boston: G. K. Hall & Co., 1980), which contains five chronologically arranged bibliographies from the classical period through the nineteenth century.

While these works document the growth and activity in rhetorical research, one important impact of these activities may be seen in the modification of theory applied in textbooks for use in schools. The reforms result in the teaching of composition according to rhetorical principles, principles which now dominate the making of textbooks.

Though publishers have not abandoned prescriptive handbooks, increased awareness of the value of rhetoric among teachers of composition has caused them to print specialized texts based on rhetorical principles. Edward P. J.

Corbett in *Classical Rhetoric for the Modern Student* (1965) was the first twentieth-century rhetorician to author a codified, systematic rhetoric text. Several textbooks based on new theories of invention followed. Richard E. Young, Alton L. Becker, and Kenneth L. Pike utilized tagmemic theory for their *Rhetoric: Discovery and Change* (1970); modifying Kenneth Burke's five key terms of dramatism. William F. Irmscher advanced the pentad format by having writers explore the ratios among agent, agency, act, purpose, and scene in *The Holt Guide to English* (1972). W. Ross Winterowd included three inventional guides derived from tagmemics, prewriting, and the pentad in *The Contemporary Writer* (1975). In the same year, Frank J. D'Angelo published *A Conceptual Theory of Rhetoric* on which he patterned his textbook *Process and Thought in Composition* (1975). Cognitive research in composition and in other disciplines, particularly cognitive psychology, provided Linda Flower a theoretical basis for her *Problem-Solving Strategies for Writing* (1981). Combining the concepts of tagmemics, prewriting, and cognitive psychology, Janice M. Lauer, Gene Montague, Andrea Lunsford, and Janet Emig designed their *Four Worlds of Writing* (1981). These textbooks focus mainly on generative and process rhetoric and sentence-combining in the 1970s and cognition and problem-solving at the end of the decade and early 1980s.

Even though these rhetorical activities suggest that a revival of rhetoric has been achieved, rhetorical activities continue. Although the need for rhetoric had been identified in the 1950s, little was accomplished toward its revival, but in the 1960s several important events contributed to a steadily growing resurgence that became a groundswell by the 1980s. Interestingly, the revival of rhetoric had its early planting on the great plains in America, and from these fertile fields rhetoric appears to be recapturing a part of its once supreme position.

Texas Woman's University

PART TWO

Voices of Change

The government curriculum centers operated during the 1950s initiated curricular innovations which improved instruction in composition. Once launched, these early innovations opened a new frontier for the teaching of composition in the twentieth century, and from these launch pads the new frontiers expanded during the 1960s and early 1970s as the voices of change urged extensive curricular revisions in the teaching of composition. These voices stressed that changes should develop codified or systematic processes derived from the classical rhetorical tradition and rhetorical research. Edward P. J. Corbett and Winston Weathers stand out as two of the most influential voices of change. Corbett, whose Classical Rhetoric for the Modern Student *(1965) translated Aristotelian rhetoric into the twentieth-century idiom, in "Rhetoric, Whether Goest Thou?" assesses the state of rhetoric in the early seventies. He records, documents, and evaluates the significant rhetorical research produced during this time, and prevails upon the academic community caught in an electronic age to become engaged in the pursuit of rhetorical studies. In "The Value of Rhetoric for the Creative Artist," Weathers, whose* The Strategy of Style *(1967) codified his rhetorical principles, calls for the restitution of rhetoric and for the development of a "rhetorically oriented creative-writing textbook." He admonishes the developing artist to learn traditional rhetoric and thus avoid "creative-writing tragedies." These two voices of change sound the call for the re-establishment of traditional rhetoric.*

EDWARD P. J. CORBETT

RHETORIC, WHETHER GOEST THOU?

When I chose the title "Rhetoric, Whether Goest Thou?"—an obvious variation on the *quo vadis* motif—what I had in mind was posing the question, not about the *whither*, the direction, that rhetoric will take in the coming years, but about the *whether*, the capability of rhetoric to adjust to the growing volume and variety of rhetorical activities in our time. Whether rhetoric can adapt will, of course, have some influence on whither it goes in the future. But *whether* poses a more crucial question, it seems to me, than *whither* or *whence* or *wherefore*. With apologies to one of our panelists, let me say that if rhetoric cannot Weather the storm, it will Winstonly wither on the vine. I presume that the toilers in the vineyard would prefer to harvest the fruit of the vine and bring it to an intoxicating ferment. If it is true that the Kobler is worthy of her hire, all of us should Bennett-fit if rhetoricians Tate their burden.[1]

Now that I have purged my system of those dyspeptic puns, I can settle down to less serious business.

Unless my observations have been egregiously myopic, the current scene exhibits a greater abundance and variety of what can be regarded as rhetorical activities than I ever witnessed before in my lifetime. Watergate alone has presented a three-ring, three-tired circus of rhetorical activities. But there are many other arenas under the Big Top of contemporary life, and in each of those arenas prodigious acts are being performed, which contribute in their own way to the divertissement or the heart-stopping of the spectators. The ring-masters are scurrying about, frantically trying to keep the acts in bounds, and the peanut galleries are howling for more bread or more circuses.

At this point, I should define what I mean by "rhetorical activity." From the stock of available definitions of rhetoric, I choose one from *The Prospect of Rhetoric* (Englewood Cliffs, N.J.: Prentice-Hall, 1971), a report of the National Developmental Project on Rhetoric, which held its first conference at the Johnson Wingspread Center in Racine, Wisconsin, in January of 1970. Using the definition of rhetoric provided in that book, I regard as a *rhetorical activity* any activity in which "man uses or is used by symbols of inducement" (p. 210). By accepting the term *symbols* rather than the term *words*, I have broadened the purview to include not only verbal utterance or discourse, the traditional province of rhetoric, but also such non-verbal media as icons—to use Marshall McLuhan's term for a variety of pictorial images—and sounds, whether musical or cacophonous. I realize that by expanding the province of rhetoric to embrace the non-verbal as well as the verbal, I run two risks: (1) making rhetoric so all-inclusive that it loses its distinctness as a discipline and (2) alienating those teachers who, by disposition or training, feel uncomfortable in any media other than the *logos*.

Tempermentally, I too feel more comfortable in the verbal medium. I feel that I am in my element when I am poring over a printed page; on the other hand, I often feel a bit spooked when I listen to music that is totally divorced from words or when I watch the pictorial images on a television screen after the sound has been turned down to an inaudible level. Icons and sounds are languages too, but I am still at the stage where I frequently have to resort to a dictionary in order to read those languages. For my students, however, icons and sounds are native languages, languages they learned, not at their mother's knees but from those endless hours they have spent at the side of their stereo sets and their TV boxes. They need another kind of dictionary to read the printed pages that I delight in, and I am beginning to suspect that when left to their own volition, they are going less and less to the printed page and to Webster's word-hoard.

If they have a library, it is more likely to be a library of record albums. Nor is it students alone who are neglecting the printed page. I urge you to read George Steiner's ominous essay "The Retreat from the Word" in his collection entitled *Language and Silence*. In that essay, he paints a gloomy picture of how academically respectable disciplines °such as chemistry, physics, biology, history, and economics are recording and transmitting their knowledge, not in articulated sentences but in the mathematical modes of the chart, the graph, the curve, and the statistical table. What has happened, Steiner says, is that "the sum of realities of which words can give a necessary and sufficient account has sharply diminished" (p. 25). Steiner is as unhappy about this noticeable retreat from the word as I or anybody else who cherishes the word must be. But because I too have observed the retreat from the word and have recognized the pre-emptive incursion of other media of communication, I am prepared to run the risks of blurring the confines of rhetoric and of alienating my reluctant colleagues. I want to become more polyglot than I am. I want to learn all the dialects of the twentieth century so that in the years that remain to me in this vale of tears, I won't have to sit in the corner like a dumb thing, mumbling my familiar quotations and fingering my first editions. We teachers can still reserve our primary allegiance for the spoken and written word, but we can enhance our literacy and certainly enhance our efficacy as rhetoricians if we are willing to study how words interact with, and serve as an adjunct to, other media of communication.

After all that indulgence in plaintive apologia, let me return to the definition that I adopted from *The Prospect of* °*Rhetoric*: rhetoric is the study of how "man uses and is used by symbols of inducement." Somehow that definition makes me optimistic about the future of rhetoric. And it makes me less doubtful about whether rhetoric will go. In the great Monopoly game among the other disciplines, rhetoric can confidently laugh off the injunction, "Go directly to jail. Do not pass Go. Do not collect two hundred dollars." Rhetoric can afford to be temporarily arrested. Rhetoric can collect its thoughts, assess its resources, and calculate its risks before it has to make its next perilous career toward the grand pay-off at Go. And judging from some of the impressive prose and poetry that have been issuing from behind iron bars recently, the jailhouse is not a bad place for a rhetorician to spend a few days in.

From my listening post as an editor of a journal, as a reviewer for several publishers of prospectuses and manuscripts of new rhetoric texts, as an attendant at several conferences, seminars, and symposia on rhetoric, I have gathered ample evidence that many contemporary rhetoricians are collecting their thoughts, assessing their resources, calculating their risks—and going for broke or the $200 pay-off. I would like to lay some of that evidence on the board so that you can decide whether rhetoric is a piece of property in which you would care to make an investment.

One area of rhetoric that I find to be in a very healthy state is the area of style. Ever since the appearance of rhetoric texts by such Greeks as Aristotle, Isocrates, Gorgias, Hermogenes, and Longinus, the study of style has been a major preoccupation of rhetoricians. In fact, the study of style became such a preoccupation with some of them that they neglected the study of the other canons of rhetoric— invention, arrangement, memory, and delivery—with the consequence that rhetoric was substantially impoverished and was saddled with the adhesive reputation of being mere "sound and fury, signifying nothing." But it seems to me that in our time, professional linguists and electronic computers have enlivened and enriched the study of style.[2]

Noam Chomsky's theory, for instance, about deep structure and surface structure has served to prevent contemporary students of style from divorcing meaning from expression, and visa versa. J. L. Austin's theories about utterances as "speech acts" may help to discourage the notion of a dichotomy between thought and expression. In one of the issues of *College Composition and Communication* this fall, I will be publishing an article by Alan Lemke, in which he argues that we teachers of composition should move away from the expression theory of writing and adopt the action theory of writing as the rationale of our composition courses. The expression theory, Lemke says, "sees writing as a process through which a writer more or less adeptly puts thoughts into words." The action theory, on the other hand, is "one which holds that a writer thinks and then translates thought into overt verbal acts." Teachers committed to the expression theory are likely to write on a student's paper, "Your ideas are good, but your expression is poor." Lemke maintains, however, that when a person thinks one thing and then writes something slightly different, "he has not expressed himself poorly; he has simply completed two speech acts with different meanings"–the meaning of the thought and meaning of the overt verbal act. The "speech act" theory should be of interest to rhetoricians, for if to write or to speak is *to do* something rather than *to express* something, we may be influenced to regard utterances as completions of actions in the real world of events– acts such as warning, complimenting, reprimanding, urging, promising, pledging, thanking, affirming, informing, correcting. And when we look at what Austin calls the perlocutionary aspects of utterances, we are into the rhetorician's heartland, because we are studying the effects of utterances on the thoughts, feelings, or actions of the audience.[3] I think it significant that one of our more prominent new rhetoricians, Richard Ohmann, has written extensively not only about the usefulness of transformational grammar in the analysis of style, but also about the rhetorical dimensions of J. L. Austin's "speech act" theory.[4]

The computer too has made a helpful contribution to the study of style. Not only has the computer facilitated the collection of data for complete and accurate concordances and word-lists, but it has also facilitated descriptive studies of lexical and syntactical patterns in prose and poetic texts. The computer-assisted gathering of hard evidence about the stylistic features that actually appear in printed pages has helped to confirm or to correct the impressionistic and subjective characterizations of style that we have had in the past. Does Ernest Hemingway write predominantly in short, simple sentences?–an impression we may get from simply reading him. The computer can answer that question–and others like it. (I can assure you that the computer will turn up many surprises about Hemingway's style.) As an example of what an industrious, intelligent, sensitive student of language and literature can do with the aid of the computer, let me recommend to you Louis Milic's *A Quantitative Approach to the Style of Jonathan Swift* (The Hague: Mouton, 1967). We will get more studies of this kind as our graduate students, desperate to find unworked topics for their dissertations, turn to this relatively unplowed field.

As further evidence of the healthy state of stylistic studies today, I would point to the many collections of essays on style now available for classroom use and to the existence of Richard Bennett's journal *Style*, now in its seventh year of publication. I would point to the many impressive articles in that journal that explore theories of style or apply theories to the analysis of specific texts, and I would also point to the astonishingly extensive annual bibliography of stylistic studies in that journal. Because the study of style concentrates on *verbal* discourse, it should be congenial to teachers of English, whether their primary interest is literature or linguistics or rhetoric or composition. Intensive study of style may be unfamiliar territory for many of them, but at least it is not alien territory.

Another healthy area of rhetorical studies at present, one that assures me that rhetoric will indeed go with the march of events, is that of invention—what has lately been referred to as prewriting, all those processes that we engage in before we sit down to inscribe words on a blank sheet of paper. Invention is unquestionably the most crucial area in the whole composition process, but unfortunately it is—or has been—the most mysterious area. Invention gets us into this misty mid-region of epistemology, the branch of philosophy that deals with cognition, with the question of how the human mind comes to know. That rhetoricians since the time of Aristotle have been vitally interested in the problem of invention is evident from the preponderant attention they accorded it in their rhetoric texts. Those who did not find the system of topics devised by the classical rhetoricians to be of much help in cracking the mystery of invention turned hopefully to the disquisitions of creative writers. Surely the poets, novelists, dramatists would be able to give us an illuminating exposition of the composing process, from conception to final execution. Coleridge tried his hand at such an exposition in the *Biographia Literaria*, but unfortunately, he never got down out of the abstract level of talking about the imagination and the fancy. Perhaps the most illuminating exposition that we have had from a creative writer is to be found in Henry James's *Notebooks* and in the Prefaces for the New York edition of his novels and stories. But even that "most" was not enough. James was able to tell us what the "germ" was for many of his stories and then show us what that "germ" matured into after it had been drawn up out of the "deep well of the unconscious." But even a self-conscious artist like James was not able to explain fully just how the idea evolved from germ to maturation.

Nor have I found that any of the new rhetoricians has given us the ultimate key to unlocking the mystery of how we discover something to say on any given subject. But by appropriating some of the findings and insights of physical scientists, psychologists, psycholinguists, and cultural anthropologists like Claude Levi-Strauss, some of the contemporary rhetoricians have provided us with some new heuristic procedures that can aid the stymied writer in finding something to say. Richard L. Larson, who has himself published some valuable articles on invention, has conveniently summarized several of the recent heuristic systems in an article published in the December 1973 issue of *Kansas English* ("Invention: Discovering One's World," pp. 18-24).

One of the most innovative of the recent systems of invention is one that Richard Young, Alton Becker, and Kenneth Pike developed from tagmemics and presented in their rhetoric text *Rhetoric: Discovery and Change* (New York: Harcourt, Brace, Jovanovich, 1970). Combining the perspectives of particle, wave, and field—notions that they appropriated from physics—with the perspectives of contrast, variation, and distribution—notions that they appropriated from linguistics—Young, Becker, and Pike have devised a heuristic procedure that, as actual classroom experiments have shown, students find useful in generating ideas for papers they have to write. Running the themes of variation, contrast, and distribution successively through particle, wave, and field, the student is provided with a set of nine questions that he can apply as a heuristic probe of virtually any subject. So, for instance, he can look at the contrastive features of an object, idea, or experience (how does it differ from other objects, ideas, or experiences that are like it?), at its range of variation (how much can the object, idea, or experience be changed and still be recognizable as what it is?), and at its distribution (how are the components organized in relation to one another? More specifically, how are they related by class, in class systems, in temporal sequence, and in space?). Once the student gets a firm grasp of the differentiation among the nine questions, he finds the questions as useful for generating something to say about a subject as journalists find the formulaic questions *who? what? when? where? how?* when they are writing a news story.

Similarly, William Irmscher in his *The Holt Guide to English* took Kenneth Burke's dramatistic pentad of *action, agent, scene, means,* and *purpose* and subdivided those five topics into fifteen basic questions that are capable of generating kernel propositions, which in turn can be expanded, supported, and evaluated.[5] Richard Larson devised a much longer list of questions that can be asked when one is writing about single items, about a completed event or an ongoing process, about abstract concepts, about collections of items or events, or about propositions.[6] From my own experience in the composition classroom, I find that sets of formulaic questions serve the students better in generating ideas than do the inert classical topics that I have presented in my text.

Lately, Richard Larson and Richard Young have been exploring the possibility of using the technique of problem-solving as a heuristic device. Larson has written about the problem-solving process in his article "Problem-Solving, Composing, and General Education" (*College English*, 34 [March, 1972], 628-35), and I won't summarize that article here. Under a grant from the National Endowment for the Humanities, Richard Young has been experimenting with the problem-solving technique in a rhetoric class for seniors in the College of Engineering at the University of Michigan. Young reported on this experiment in a paper "Problems and the Rhetorical Process" that he prepared for a forum on rhetoric that I chaired at the Midwest Modern Language Association convention in Chicago in November of 1973 and in a published summary report entitled *The Tagmemic Discovery Procedure: An Evaluation of Its Uses in the Teaching of Rhetoric* (University of Michigan, 1973). The problem-solving approach can help the student generate ideas for a piece of writing, Young contends, if he can be trained to recognize and analyze a problem and then to articulate clearly what the problem is and what the "unknown" is—that is, what it is that will eliminate or mitigate the problem or the "felt difficulty." Another dividend of the problem-solving technique is that if the student is dealing with something that is really a problem for him—and Young insists that his students deal with real, not invented or putative, problems—the genuine quest for a solution can lead to the kind of purposeful writing that many of our assigned topics often cannot produce.

In an article in the May 1970 issue of *College English*, Ross Winterowd purposed another set of inventional topics.[7] He argued that the seven basic relationships that exist among sentences or, more accurately, among what Kellogg Hunt calls T-units can serve as topics to generate units of discourse larger than the sentence. Those seven basic relationships, which are the source of coherence in collocation of clauses, Winterowd classifies as (1) coordinate, (2) obversative, (3) causative, (4) conclusive, (5) alternative, (6) inclusive, and (7) sequential. Winterowd says,

> Any set of topics is merely a way of triggering the process. Thus the student, say, who has difficulty with the invention of arguments, can use the seven-item list to tell him what might come next—not what content, to be sure, but what relation his next unit must take to the previous one. There are only seven possibilities. (pp. 834-35)

I see immense possibilities for the fruitful application of Winterowd's seven-item list in the composition process, because the seven relationships that he outlines seem to me to designate, as the classical topics do, the characteristic ways in which the human mind operates when it is operating deliberatively. Having seen the manuscript of the rhetoric text that Winterowd is doing for Harcourt, Brace, I can tell you that in that forthcoming text, he demonstrates the practical applications of his system of topics—as well as other systems of topics--to the composition process.[8] Having seen the manuscript of a book to be called *A Theory of Conceptual Rhetoric* and the manuscripts of some forthcoming articles, I can also inform you that Frank D'Angelo of Arizona State University has formulated his own set of generating devices that could be helpful to students who have trouble finding something to say.

The upshot of this review of some of the recent work in inventional theory is that I find the current thinking about the most crucial state of the composition process to be in a vigorous and promising state and that if we teachers of composition do not entirely abandon the cognitive approach in the classroom, in response to the current vogue for the affective and the turn-on-the-spigot approaches, we will be able to make use of these new heuristic procedures to provide genuine help for our floundering students.

Another encouraging development is the attempt by contemporary rhetoricians to devise new ways of classifying modes or genres of discourse. The classical rhetoricians dealt primarily with persuasive discourse, and partly on the basis of the kind of audience that listened to the discourse and partly on the basis of whether the discourse dealt with the past, the present, or the future, they distinguished three species of persuasive discourse: judicial, deliberative, and ceremonial. Late in the nineteenth century Alexander Bain proposed the "four forms of discourse" that remained the staple of school texts for over seventy-five years: exposition, narration, description, and argumentation. But in the last ten years, some interesting new rationales for classifying kinds of discourse have been proposed.

In 1964 Leo Rockas, in his *Modes of Rhetoric* (New York: St. Martin's Press, 1964), classified the types according to the means of procedure: the static modes (description and definition); the temporal modes (narration and process); the mimetic modes (drama and dialogue); and the mental modes (reverie and persuasion). Winston Weathers and Otis Winchester, after having proposed in their 1968 text *Prevalent Forms of Prose* (Boston: Houghton Mifflin) the more conventional types of the popular article, the professional article, the personal essay, the formal essay, and the critical essay, in 1970, in their text *The Attitudes of Rhetoric* (Englewood Cliffs, N.J.: Prentice-Hall), came up with a much more interesting and fruitful way of classifying discourses according to the writer's attitude toward his subject and his audience. Arguing that attitude constitutes a significant part of the writer's message and influences the choice of strategies that carry the message to the audience, they presented nine different kinds of discourse according to attitude: confident, judicious, quiet, imperative, impassioned, compassionate, critical, angry, and absurd.

James Moffett and James Kinneavy have also done some astute rethinking about the modes of discourse. Viewing rhetorical interaction in pronominal terms of *I, you,* and *it,* Moffett in his *Teaching the Universe of Discourse* (Boston: Houghton Mifflin, 1968) proposed two ways of classifying discourse according to a time/space perspective. In terms of the distance in time and space between speaker and listener, between first person and second person in the rhetorical interaction, Moffett classified four kinds of discourse:

Reflection—Intrapersonal communication between two parts of one nervous system (as in a journal or an interior monologue)

Conversation—Interpersonal communication between two people in vocal range

Correspondence—Interpersonal communication between remote individuals or small groups with some personal knowledge of each other

Publication—Impersonal communication to a large anonymous group extended over space and/or time.(p. 33)

Moffett then proposes another classification according to the increasing distance between the speaker and his subject, between the *I* and the *it* of the rhetorical interaction:

What is happening—drama, recording

What happened—narrative, reporting

What happens—exposition, generalizing

What may happen—argumentation, theorizing. (p. 35)

In his *A Theory of Discourse: The Aims of Discourse* (Englewood Cliffs, N.J.: Prentice-Hall, 1971), James L. Kinneavy viewed rhetorical interaction in terms appropriated from communications theory—encoder, decoder, signal, reality—and he distinguished the types of discourse according to which element in this four-part interrelationship received the predominant emphasis. If the emphasis is on the encoder (the speaker or writer), we get Expressive Discourse; if on the decoder (the audience), we get Persuasive Discourse; if on the signal (the message, the work, the artifact), we get Literary Discourse; if on the reality (the universe, "the world out there"), we get Reference Discourse. Reference Discourse in turn is subdivided into three distinct species: Informative, Scientific, and Exploratory. Each of these aims of discourse, Kinneavy claims and demonstrates, has its own system of logic, its own organizational structure, and its own stylistic characteristics.

All of these attempts to invent a new terminology and rationale for kinds of discourse may have been sparked by Northrop Frye's concern for reorienting and redefining genres in his influential *The Anatomy of Criticism* (Princeton, N.J.: Princeton University Press, 1957). In any case, all this serious reworking of the theories about modes of discourse has inspirited me about the future of rhetorical studies, because it opens the way to our considering a broader spectrum of discourse than we have traditionally dealt with in our classrooms.

What else do I see on the current scene that makes me optimistic about the future of rhetorical studies? Many things, really, but I can only mention some of them here and hope you will pursue those developments or suggestions that interest you particularly.

For one thing, I was much impressed by the prize-winning essay by Richard Coe, which Gary Tate will publish in the next issue of *Freshman English News.*[9] In this essay, Coe contends that we have to develop a new rhetoric to fit the changed consciousness of our computer age. The kind of mechanistic, linear consciousness that has prevailed until recent years is a heritage of Newtonian physics and Cartesian epistemology and is built on a set of analogies with energy systems—the billard-ball model of the universe. Cybernetic consciousness, on the other hand, is built on a set of analogies with information systems and operates, Coe maintains, on an entirely different logical order than energy systems do.

So we will have to modify and supplement our thinking and our teaching on such matters as causality, summativity (the axiom that the whole is equal to the sum of all its parts), and the duality of all phenomena (those dichotomies that we are so fond of—mind/body, heredity/environment, man/nature, thought/expression). We can get our retraining for the computer age, Coe proposes, from such disciplines as quantum physics, gestalt psychology, cybernetics, and general-systems theory—not from formal study of these disciplines, of course, but from what filters down from these disciplines in terms that the layman can understand. This was a very exciting essay for me, and I urge you to read it when it is published. Chaim Perelman's great book *The New Rhetoric: A Treatise on Argument* is also a revolt against the positivistic mode of thinking that the Western world inherited from Descartes, as is Wayne Booth's forthcoming book ₒ *Modern Dogma and the Rhetoric of Assent.* (As an aside, I hope that Wayne Booth will find an outlet for his paper "B. F. Skinner's Rhetorical Theory" that he prepared for my forum on rhetorical theory at the Midwest MLA meeting last November.)

You may have noted that I have not said anything yet about "symbols of inducement" other than the verbal ones. One reason for that silence is that the contemporary rhetoricians I have been talking about have not said much directly, in their books and articles, on the other media of communication. But I see no reason why much of the new theory they have developed could not be applied to the study of films, cartoons, comic strips, records, and advertising. For the theory about these other media of inducement, we have to go to that maverick rhetorician of the twentieth century, Marshall McLuhan. And if one is to judge from the articles in their journals, speech teachers seem to be doing more theorizing about the rhetoric of the audio-visual media than English teachers are. Where I get the hint that English teachers may be dealing in the classroom with the rhetoric of the audio-visual media is from some of the freshman readers that have been appearing recently, such as *Popular Writing in America: The Interaction of Style and Audience,* ed. Donald McQuade and Robert Atwan (New York: Oxford University Press, 1974) and *The Age of Communication,* ed. William D.

Lutz (Pacific Palisades, Calif.: Goodyear Publishing Co., 1974). In addition to prose essays, anthologies like these carry cartoons, comic strips, ads, photographs, paintings, collages, and the musical stories, as well as the lyrics, of popular songs.

And there is evidence too that English teachers are leading their students to study the rhetoric of the small units of the language of inducement. No NCTE committee in recent years has received as much notice in the public press as the Committee on Public Doublespeak has received lately. Several of the more active members of this committee have been directing their attention mainly to the exposure of jargon, the euphemism, or the deceptiveness to be found in phrases or single sentences from public utterances. Two anthologies of public doublespeak have already appeared, Robert Cirino's *Power to Persuade: Mass Media and the News* (New York: Bantam, 1974) and Mario Pei's *Double-Speak in America* (New York: Hawthorn Books, 1973), and at least two more are in preparation. The mood of young people has been so soured by events connected with the Vietnam War and the Watergate affair that the time may be propitious for us to lead them to a serious and intensive study of how language is being used to falsify and to obfuscate. But before we can do that, we will have to clean our own house of some of the worst examples of academic English.

In the May 1974 issue of *College Composition and Communication*, I am publishing an article by Frank D'Angelo in which he analyzes current examples of graffiti from the point of view of the classical schemes and tropes.[10] The lead article in the May 1974 issue of *Esquire* is Norman Mailer's "The Faith of Graffiti" in which the author discusses the social significance of the flamboyant graffiti painted on walls, buses, and subway cars in New York City. I know of teachers who are having fun studying campaign buttons, bumper stickers, advertising slogans, and the drawings and slogans on T-shirts. That some teachers are giving attention in the classroom to these one-liners may indicate that they have been convinced by Marshall McLuhan's claim that in this electronic age a good deal of persuasion is being con-ducted, not in the discursive, linear, protracted monologue of former years, but in the fragmentary, non-sequential, mosaic modes of discourse.

When one is disposed to see will-o-the-wisps, he will see will-o-the-wisps. And I do not dismiss the possibility that I see a good deal of significant rhetorical activity on the current scene because I am disposed to see it. Someone else, oriented in a different way, might view the same phenomena as social or political or religious or cultural movements. But while I grant sociologists, psychologists, philosophers, and anthropologists the right to view these phemonena from their persepective, I want also to be granted the privilege to view these phenomena from the point of view of a rhetorician— that is, as instances of how man uses and is used by symbols of inducement. That is an honorable occupation for the only symbol-using creature on the face of the earth to be engaged in. And I hope I have presented some evidence that a number of honorable, intelligent, serious-minded symbol-using crea- tures are engaged in this honorable occupation. Because the quality of the men and women currently engaged in rheto- rical studies—many of them working in nooks and crannies, far from the madding crowd—and the quality of thought that is emerging from those studies, I am confident that rhetoric will make a go of it in the coming years. The crucial, un- answered question at the moment is whether the great masses of our citizens are prepared to go along with rhetoric. We must induce them to come along for the exciting ride.

Ohio State University

NOTES

[1] The participants in the Symposium in Rhetoric, besides Profes- sor Corbett, were Winston Weathers, Turner Kobler, James R. Bennett, and Gary Tate. [The Editors]

[2] See the two recent articles in *College English*, 35 (April, 1974): Tim Shopen, "Some Contributions from Grammar to the Theory of Style," pp. 775-98; Eugene R. Kintgen, "Is Transformational Stylistics Useful?" pp. 799-824.

[3] See Paul Newell Campbell, "A Rhetorical View of Locution- ary, Illocutionary, and Perlocutionary Acts," *Quarterly Journal of*

Speech, 59 (October, 1973), 284-96.

[4]See for instance the following articles by Richard Ohmann: "Generative Grammars and the Concept of Literary Style," *Word*, 20 (1964), 424-39; "Literature as Sentences," *College English*, 27 (1966), 261-67; "Speech Acts and the Definition of Literature," *Philosophy and Rhetoric*, 4 (1971), 1-19; "Speech Action and Style," in *Literary Style: A Symposium*, ed. Seymour Chatman (New York: Oxford University Press, 1971), pp. 241-54; "Instrumental Style: Notes on the Theory of Speech as Action," in *Current Trends in Stylistics*, ed. Braj Kachru and Herbert F. W. Stahlke (Champagne, Ill.: Ling. Research, Inc., 1972), pp. 115-41.

[5]See Chapter 4, "The Subject: Generating a Topic," in *The Holt Guide to English: A Contemporary Handbook of Rhetoric, Language, and Literature* (New York: Holt, Rinehart and Winston, 1972), pp. 27-38.

[6]"Discovery Through Questioning: A Plan for Teaching Rhetorical Invention," *College English*, 30 (November, 1968), 126-34.

[7]"The Grammar of Coherence," *College English*, 31 (May, 1970), 828-35.

[8]Professor Corbett refers to *The Contemporary Writer: A Practical Rhetoric* (New York: Harcourt, Brace, Jovanovich, Inc., 1975). [The Editors]

[9]"Rhetoric 2001," *Freshman English News*, 3 (Spring, 1974). [The Editors]

[10]See Frank D'Angelo's "Up Against the Wall, Mother: The Rhetoric of Slogans, Catchphrases, and Graffiti" herein. [The Editors]

WINSTON WEATHERS

THE VALUE OF RHETORIC
TO THE CREATIVE ARTIST

If we define rhetoric simply to mean "persuasion," then I'm not sure that rhetoric will be of great value to the creative artist. But if we define rhetoric in a more detailed way, it can perhaps be proposed as a meaningful discipline for the creative minded. By more detailed definition, I mean something like this: "Rhetoric is a sharable systematic knowledge of the ways a communicator can most effectively present what he has to say to a particular audience in order to persuade that audience to give him a hearing, accept him as a communication-intending speaker, recognize and agree to the value of the communication, and respond to the communication in a meaningful way."

Even with that definition, however, rhetoric will not be accepted wholeheartedly by creative people. There is an inevitable resistance on their part to anything that boasts the characteristics of "sharable" and "systematic." Creative persons have a natural aversion to a sharing of their tricks and to a codifying of their habits. To the creative person, rhetoric can look suspiciously like an exposure and an imprisonment, all at once.

The creative person is not simply being perverse, however. On the one hand he usually does have a desire to make some sort of contact with an audience; on the other, he has a desire to express himself in his own terms. And he's caught in a struggle characteristic of all imaginative efforts: to move from the private into the public, from the personal, subjective atmosphere in which the magic of creativity takes place into the community "out there" where the products of creativity must finally exist.

Taking a dim view of rhetoric—retreating fearfully from public artistry in an increasingly materialistic and vulgar age—many artists have in our time developed aesthetics that are blatantly anti-rhetorical. Certainly in the last two hundred years, many creative artists have argued that art must exist and be evaluated in complete disassociation from audiences; that rather than the artist making accommodations to audiences, audiences must make accommodations to the artist; that the artist's first loyalty is to his own integrity, sincerity, and naturalness, and certainly not to the needs and expectations of audiences; and that any artistry that does not attempt to participate in a "sharable systematic knowledge of the ways" is simply to be dismissed as popular, formulaic, and commercial—not to be dealt with in academe or literary-land.

This does not mean, of course, that no rhetoric at all is practiced by creative artists. Even in this generally anti-rhetorical age, some do seriously seek audience reaction—in fact, we sometimes see the artist jabbing, pounding, manhandling audiences in an attempt to manipulate and force-feed. But most of the time any "rhetoric" that is practiced is denied or unacknowledged. Mention the very word "rhetoric"—and the artist will, ninety-nine per cent of the time, deny any such considerations on his part; he will talk about himself and his creative resources or about the art work he has created, but he is not too likely to talk about audiences he is trying to reach. Sometimes, yes. But most of the time, no. And because of the artist's refusal to subscribe openly to a "sharable and systematic knowledge" about reaching audiences, the rhetoric he does occasionally practice is usually inadequate, and marked by ignorance; limited to fellow craftsmen whom he is trying to impress or please, or disastrously diluted to reach some great indistinguishable mass of "people out there." By refusing to recognize rhetoric as a legitimate part of artistry, the creator handicaps himself and, alas, compromises the very role of art in our society.

I, for one, would like to see the restitution of rhetoric into the creative experience—and by restitution, I mean the public acknowledgement of rhetoric and the identification of it as a part of the artist's apprenticeship and training. For rhetoric to be of value to the artist it must be brought out in the open, and our task as rhetoricians is, surely, the publication of rhetoric in that area of discourse—imaginative, creative writing—in which we too often seem to be self-effacing strangers—letting creative writing rest exclusively in the hands of those who maintain it as a mystery cult. Our task as rhetoricians is to convince the artist that he really does have rhetorical intentions the moment he hands his work to someone else to read; that he really does make rhetorical gestures in his work, even nowadays, uncertain and rough as those gestures may be; and that he has nothing to fear by acknowledging rhetoric as a part of his expertise or by accepting a "sharable and systematic knowledge" as part of his creative competence.

What I would really like to do, of course, is to convince the young, talented writer—standing at the beginning of his career—to use traditional rhetoric as a foundation for his entire creative effort, to study traditional rhetoric in school, prior even to his study of creative writing. I'd like to say something like this to him:

> One, if you study traditional rhetoric and grasp its fundamental concern with audiences, you'll be committed to the most productive and meaningful path that a creative writer can follow. With such a commitment, you'll be saved from the alternative—that of circling around and around in the wilderness of your own moods, sensations, joys, and pains; a circling around in which the tremendous energy of your own creativity, unyoked from rhetoric, will lead you into the swamps of solipsism and into the inevitable cult of personality; will lead you finally to the frustrating discovery that audiences, whom you expect to applaud you but with whom you have refused to cooperate, will no longer be listening to anything you have to say but will respond to you only when you dangle your personality in front of them—dangle your life-style, costumes, vital statistics, secret vices; will respond to you only when you parade

your wife, children, mistresses, and political comrades in front of them; and will respond to you only as an extra-literary *objet de théâtre*, not as a writer, thinker, or serious spokesman of any sort.

A commitment to rhetoric will save you from that and will help you maintain an effective relationship with audiences who—because of your very practice of rhetoric—will be encouraged to enter into intellectual and emotional transactions with your works of art. Nor will those transactions mean that you are having to say things that audiences want to hear and with which they agree and that you don't want to say. Some writers resist rhetoric because they fear it means producing, contrary to their own desires, "happy endings," "pat solutions," "false emphases" upon sex or patriotism or such. But actually rhetoric means none of that—rather it is a discipline used, frequently, to make palatable the very things audiences don't want to hear and don't agree with. Rhetoric will be your greatest weapon when you do wish to tell the truth as you see it in the face of what you consider to be the misconceptions of your readers.

Two, if you study traditional rhetoric you will involve yourself in the history of that rhetoric and, as in all studying of history, you will be helped to escape the provincialism of your own particular time and place. Simply by grasping the concern—from ancient Greece to modern America—that man has had for the mysterious relationship of speaker and audience, you will see that your activity as a creative writer is related to and rooted in a tradition, an awareness of which may keep you from wasting a great deal of time in achieving your own delicate balance with reality and the world. It was Reed Whittemore, I believe, who said, in his book *From Zero to the Absolute*, that the greatest mistake of the contemporary artist, especially the contemporary writer, is his insistence upon isolation from the past, in his terrible imprisoning of himself in the present moment, and his subsequent struggle, out of self-maintained ignorance, to re-enact the last three thousand years of civilization, having to discover the word all over again, having to run language, literature, and discourse through all the laboratory experiments again, to insist upon shutting his eyes to everyone from Gorgias to I.A. Richards and saying, "I'm going to figure this all out myself."

The trouble with figuring it all out yourself is that you will stray into all the old booby traps and dead ends of discourse, all the clichés and stereotypes and banalities that have long been charted and identified in rhetorical history.   You will write a great deal more bad literature than you ever imagined you would—paying the inevitable price for making your own discoveries about man and the word.

You may argue, of course, that your study of literary history will effect an adequate historical perspective, that your study of Virgil and Shakespeare and Milton and Pope will rescue you from the provincialism just as well as the study of traditional rhetoric can. And I would agree. Yet in literary history you will surely discover that, until very recent times, rhetoric was the very preparation for literature and that for you to grasp the real quality of literature you will need to grasp its rhetorical dimensions and bases.

When you realize that out of the total number of creative writers in the history of Western civilization, seventy-five per cent were either trained in rhetoric or lived in societies in which rhetoric was the major educational subject, then you may begin to see that in the larger scheme of things literature and rhetoric are inseparable.   Indeed, the study of rhetoric can rescue you from a limited notion of what literature is all about, what part it plays in the social order, and what expertise produces it.

Three, if you do escape the solipsistic and provincial attitude of the non-rhetorical writer, you will have achieved a critical liberation that will be of tremendous value to you.   You will discover that you have stronger, more realistic criteria for the judgment of literature—not only the literature written by others, but also that which you attempt to write yourself.

You will judge literature—not in terms of authorial personality and mystique, or in terms of the isolated work of art—but in terms of audience reception and reaction.   You will discover that the question is not, Is this a good novel? but, Is this a good novel for this audience? or For what audience will this novel best work?   You will reject that criticism—prevalent in our times certainly—that re-enacts the fairy tale, "The Emperor's New Clothes," in its insistence that what we really see, or feel, or think as audiences has nothing to do with an evaluation of what is there.   You will reject the criticism that says a work of literature can be evaluated prior to its presentation to an audience.   Rather your criticism will consider how a work of literature reaches its readers, how it proceeds to talk with its readers, how it relates to or negotiates with its readers. And you will realize, in your striving to meet critical standards, that while your non-rhetorical fellow student is spending his energies discovering and establishing his "voice"—you can perhaps more profitably spend your energies discovering the psychological and emotional dimensions of readers, the nature of their "ears," their literary capacities, so that you can adapt your voices to their ability to listen and understand. Nor will you—once you have your own critical eyes set upon the critical goal of audience reaction—be diverted by artificial and alien standards maintained somewhere aloft in heaven or the *New York Times* or the University of So-and-so's English department—standards that might make your work acceptable to certain audiences but would divert you from the real and viable audiences to whom you can most meaningfully speak.

And, finally, four: If you, young writer, study rhetoric first, before specializing in creative writing, you will gain expertise in the basic skills of discourse upon which all subsequent discourse must rest. In your study of rhetoric you will come to realize that the difference between expository non-fiction and imaginative writing is a difference in degree and that the skills of invention, arrangement, and style are applicable to all discourse, regardless of the discourse's origin in fact or fancy and regardless of its intentions to entertain or inform. Though the particular problems of fiction may differ from those of legal defenses, there are some amazing generalities about language that unite all communication efforts.

You will, of course, learn a great deal about language communication in other disciplines—linguistics, semantics, history of the language—yet it is rhetoric that puts all those disciplines into motion, and it is rhetoric that carries those disciplines into the front-line production of discourse—speeches, letters, philosophical tracts; poems, stories, plays.

This is not to say that in rhetoric you will learn all there is to know about the technique of creative writing. The craftsmanship of writing is a life-long concern—a constant adaption of general principles to particular circumstances. But the adaption must be of "something"—and that "something" is a knowledge of rhetoric, a technical expertise that, at its best, is broad and flexible, providing a repertoire of skills and a system of options. Enthymemes work in poems as well as in prose; metaphors are a part of scientific exposition as well as a part of fiction; beginnings and endings and the problems thereto are not exclusive to any kind of discourse; illustrations, examples, comparisons, and contrasts are standard fare in the most technical of articles and the most delicate of haiku; the sequential orders—climactic, chronological—are found in political harangues as well as in the recitations of imaginary love affairs.

If you will study rhetoric first, you will be saved the agony of plunging—as some students of creative writing do—into the details of the creative forms without a sound knowledge of fundamentals. You will be saved the building of your work upon the shifting sand of unintended fallacies, non sequiturs, incoherence, lack of unity, confused order, erratic stylistics. And you will be spared the embarrassment of attempting to juggle a flashing display of original images while sliding on the slippery floor of poor sentence structure, inadequate development of ideas, sloppy transitions from thought to thought.

And there is an ancillary expertise to be gained from rhetoric that should be mentioned: the increased capacity for perceiving human discourse. You, as a creative writer, will make much of your insight into human behavior, your close and analytical observation of human beings; thus you will be glad to find—as your understanding of rhetorical techniques increases—that your understanding also increases of how people communicate or fail to communicate, relate or fail to relate. In the imitation of discourse, in your bringing characters together in dialogues and conversations, your knowledge of rhetoric will improve your comprehensions and articulation of the motives, intentions, procedures, even the convolutions of what human beings say to each other.

So I would talk to the young creative writer about attitude, perspective, evaluation, and expertise. But let's send him out of the room now and talk just a moment with each other, professionally, about the status of rhetoric in creative writing teaching today.

We can distinguish, it seems, between the study of traditional rhetoric as prelude to the study of creative writing, and the incorporation of certain aspects of rhetoric into the teaching of creative writing itself. The incorporation, I have to admit, involves a certain transformation of traditional rhetoric if it is to be truly serviceable. For instance, rhetoric's ultimate goal of moving an audience to some action probably gives way in creative writing to moving an audience into a community of feeling and perception with the author.°
And whereas in traditional rhetoric one seeks to convince an

audience of the reasonableness of the communication, in creative writing the goal may rather be to effect verisimilitude or an emotional intensity. Whereas in traditional rhetoric, communication—in a rather strict sense—is a *sine qua non*, in creative writing communication may sometimes bend to sheer experientialism: giving the reader a sense of denotationless beauty via patterns, sounds, rhythms, progressions, and the like.

Making such transformations, we can conceivably achieve a rhetoric of creative writing analogus to and developing from traditional rhetoric. We don't quite have that separate rhetoric of creative writing yet, but I believe something like it is emerging in the academic world, at least in a few of our writing programs.

If we were to go into the creative-writing classroom today we would find, I think, three basic modes of instruction—and there would be no great difficulty in recognizing the class in which rhetoric is viable. In one classroom we'd find the instruction going on according to the "method" school of acting—the student is stimulated, but is left to his own technical devices, encouraged only to express himself from his own depths. His creative products are to be judged by the criteria of his own involvement in their creation; by his sincerity and honesty. His work is to be considered successful to the extent that he has poured into the work his own passions and pains. In a second classroom, we'd find instruction focused primarily upon the construction of literary works; the student is taught to write the poem or story as absolute forms—that is, in a Platonic way—with the products judged in the light of ideal examples of the genres. This kind of teaching is most consonant with the old "New Criticism" and is essentially concerned with literary works divorced altogether from both conception and reception. In the third classroom, we'd find the instruction centered upon helping the writer reach his audience: teaching the student a repertoire of skills, but evaluating those skills in relationship to readers; teaching the student to write a sonnet—but asking him to write it several times, in consideration of one audience this time, another audience another. The creative-writing classroom—in which rhetoric is a major consideration—is primarily a workshop in which a student can present his work and be given feedback by representatives of various life-styles in our society today, a workshop in which the student will be forced to realize that he can't reach everyone and that what he "intends" is not what his auditors always "get"; he will be forced into an identification of the people he wants most to reach and the rhetoric it will take to reach them.

I think the rhetorically oriented creative-writing classroom is developing. And, at the same time, there is a very special pedagogical need that—to my knowledge at least—has not yet been satisfied. And that is the need for a rhetorically oriented creative-writing textbook. We must either incorporate more creative-writing matters into our general rhetorics, or we must prepare special rhetorics dealing with the special goals of creative-writing students. I don't, of course, mean that we don't have good books in the general area of rhetoric and creativity, but even such a fine book as Wayne Booth's *Rhetoric of Fiction* is not really the sort of book in which a student can find anything like specific writing advice. We need a text that sets forth actual writing practices drawn from a wide range of contemporary literature. We need a text that will show us all the different ways to bring a character through a door and into a room and that will advise us which way would be best—given our audience, our subject, and so on. We do have some excellent preliminary studies of literature that I think can make such a text increasingly possible: Herman Meyer's *The Poetics of Quotation in the European Novel*, for instance, or Barbara Herrnstine Smith's *Poetic Closure: A Study of How Poems End*. But I call such works preliminary because the information they contain has not yet been incorporated into a practical rhetoric, into a systematic and sharable knowledge that can be used by the artist to create his own rhetorically successful writing.

Rhetoric as a prelude to creative writing; rhetoric as an attitude and methodology in the teaching of creative writing. Both of these could change the complexion of literary artistry here at the end of the twentieth century. And I speak with great sincerity when I say that the call for a restitution of rhetoric is more than the self-serving admonition of the rhetorician himself. I have, in my teaching career at least, seen too many "creative-writing tragedies"—the tragedies of talented people denied their creative fulfillment because they

40

never experienced the baptism of rhetoric. I've seen young students, older men and women wanting to express themselves, visiting poets reading their work—failing because of an inability or unwillingness to consider the nature of their audience and to make any accommodations to it. How tragic to see the talented creative person uttering his words blindly into the void with no one listening. Or, almost as tragic, hearing him misdirect his words—speaking to one audience, but speaking the language of another. I think such is a sad waste, and if I were the god of literature for a day, I think I'd take my lightning bolts—or rose petals—or whatever—and shatter through the romantic myths of creativity that hang over our heads. I would illuminate the creative experience with the rigors and liberations of rhetorical knowledge.

University of Tulsa

PART THREE

Aristotle Astray

Sometimes the early voices of change which desired a return to traditional rhetoric met resistance to their pleas and encountered instead various theories and concepts splintered from classical rhetoric. *These departures tended to shunt the focus away from traditional rhetoric toward alternative stances formed by blending together rhetoric and poetics. As a percursor of the revival of rhetoric, Kenneth Burke in his essay "Rhetoric—Old and New" (1951) distinguishes between the two rhetorics: traditional or persuasion and new or identification. Since Burke extends rhetoric to encompass both verbal and nonverbal human behavior, his conception of rhetoric illuminates various casuistries which underlie nonsymbolic motions and symbolic actions. In "Motion, Action, and the Human Condition," Burke views all language as metaphorical and illustrates the correspondences which exist between the* res *(thing) and the* verba *(word for things). Both Wilbur Samuel Howell and Jacques Barzun react to Burke's conception of rhetoric because each holds concepts which limit the parameters of rhetoric. Barzun declares in "The Rhetoric of the Arts" that it is not possible to have a single rhetoric which will serve the various arts; he insists that terminology and critical vocabularies are "pedantic and faddish." He concludes that critics must invent for each art a proper descriptive and evaluative rhetoric. Howell concurs with Barzun's objections to an open-ended rhetoric. He wants to maintain the traditional canons of rhetoric, and in "Peter Ramus, Thomas Sheridan, and Kenneth Burke: Three Mavericks in the History of Rhetoric," Howell isolates three rhetoricians whom he identifies as having attenuated rhetoric by making the substance too narrow (Ramus and Sheridan) or too broad (Burke).*

JACQUES BARZUN

THE RHETORIC OF THE ARTS

The first thing that strikes the mind when one stops to consider the subject of rhetoric is that the word itself denotes something good or something bad, depending on what the speaker chooses to make it mean. He may use the word as a criticism, saying: "This piece of writing is not true literature, it is only rhetoric." Or he may use the word to name an essential element of art, saying: "You have failed to express your thought: your rhetoric is defective."

This contradiction is typical of the present state of discourse about rhetoric as a serious subject long recognized to be important. Here today we are supposed to deal with the rhetoric of the arts. What exactly may we understand by such an assignment? Rhetoric is often defined as "the art of expressive speech" or "the art of literary composition." Clearly, rhetoric relates to the use of words. Textbooks for the college course in English composition are often called a rhetoric of one sort or another. In the medieval curriculum, rhetoric was one of the three indispensable arts together with grammar and logic. And in ancient times, the *rhetor* was the teacher or practioner of oratory. In a culture that depended for its legal or political acts much more on the spoken than on the written word, oratory was a great art, taught and learned like a profession, and used for frequent public performance. The ultimate root of *rhetoric* means *word* or *I say*.

These multiple antecedents and connections may help explain some of the confusion now prevailing about rhetoric. The variety of meanings for the term is even greater now than it was fifty years ago, because lately there has been a revival of interest in the subject, and writers with different aims— linguists, psychologists, and philosophers; educators, grammarians, and so-called experts in communication; literary critics, art critics, and estheticians: all have proposed as "rhetoric" schemes of analysis, or of teaching, or of fundamental theory. If you glance at a collection of essays published a few years ago called *New Rhetorics*, you will find that one man works up a rhetoric of his own to explain what a paragraph really is, and another—the inimitable Kenneth Burke—manages, for an undisclosed purpose, to touch upon: symbolism, anthropology, Longinus and Demetrius on the Sublime, Castiglione on the Courtier, Machiavelli on the Prince, Gertrude Stein on the Americans, Marcel Proust and Mark Twain on stratagems, and finally Aristotle on rhetoric.

If you should still doubt that our subject is a jungle full of booby-traps, let me remind you that in addition to the rhetorics I have referred to there are several flourishing schools of literary criticism which could also be called rhetorics--notably the Structuralists and their enemies, the Post-Structuralists, also known as Deconstructivists. Some Marxist critics, moreover, are concerned with rhetoric as much as with substance; and beyond all these, of course, are the numerous writers who deal with the arts other than literature and sometimes speak of the rhetoric of painting, sculpture, architecture, music, or the dance. One should perhaps add theatre and drama, since their obvious relation to literature is often submerged in technical differences.

There! I have casually spoken the word that may prove a thread to lead us through the jungle—the technical. Rhetoric was originally a technique of oratory, then of written composition. And for three hundred years after the Renaissance, the "philosophy of rhetoric" was the name given to many works we should now call theories of literary composition and criticism. So it would seem that by extension one might speak of the rhetoric of any art, or portion of each art, including the solitary paragraph. The revival of rhetoric, the profusion of rhetorics and of critical schools in this century, could then be explained by the strong scientific, technological interest of our time. We want to know how everything is put together, from the atom to Blake's *Songs of Innocence*. Thus also, the critic who says of a work that it is "mere rhetoric" is saying that he perceives technique but no feeling or truth or wisdom. Like Hamlet's mother speaking to the pussyfooting Polonius, he wants: "more matter with less art."

But on second thoughts, things are not so simple as the

Queen suggests. Polonius cannot regulate the proportion of material and craftsmanship as if he were mixing a martini. In judging and understanding art more is needed than an awareness of technique. Surely what moves us and what we admire in a work of art is not the handling by itself, nor is it substance without shape or polish. It is the happy conjunction—the fusion, rather—of skill and material; and because the two are fused, it is difficult if not impossible to pry them apart again. So the task of the critic or rhetorician is how to describe the shaping and refining and ordering of substance without at the same time implying that manner can produce fine work apart from matter—and vice versa.

To put this differently, anyone can list and describe the forms, the formulas, the devices, and the negative cautions that are used by teachers of technique in any art. But these lists and descriptions will not tell us what we want to know. Ideally, a rhetoric should show how the application of the devices and principles—and often their violation—produce in us the effects we admire and enjoy under the name of artistic experience.

I shall attempt in a moment to suggest an answer to that age-old question. But because of the peculiar attitude toward the arts in our century, I must first ask you to take a look at some of the rhetoric *about* the arts which is taken for granted by the critics and connoisseurs who consider themselves up to date.

Their prime assumption is that the arts are distinct from each other and should not be mixed. Opera may be tolerated for the sake of feebler souls, but music (like painting) should not be literary or programmatic, not meant to tell stories but to exhibit pure form. The notion of purity, singleness of purpose and effect, is and has been dominant since the 1890s. The writings of the Post-Impressionists, the Nabis, and the Fauves taught that painting is an end in itself. Art critics such as Roger Fry and Clive Bell expounded this dogma, which proved quickly congenial. It seemed to fit after Whistler, for instance, had entitled his works "arrangements," "harmonies," or "symphonies"—in blue and gray or some other colors. He himself explicitly gave it his intention to emulate the musician by making pure forms out of colors used like pure sounds. The desire, the purpose, was to exclude the world of ordinary experience. Nor was this rejection limited to the painters. Poets and musicians made the same point. True literature and true music, they said, had nothing to do with the common life of man. It was symbolic of a spiritual reality beyond, a world that could only be expressed through pure form. Though the arts were to be kept distinct, it seemed as if these artists and critics were hypnotized by music. Walter Pater, one of the oracles of the period, concluded that music being the purest of the arts, all the rest should aim at the same ethereal quality as far as they could, rarified and spiritualized by discarding facts and their depiction. Kandinsky gave the final statement of this view in his famous essay.

It was an effort to follow Plato's prescription for getting rid of earthbound attachments. It should sooner or later have made these artists give up art and turn into mathematicians, like Plato himself. For only in mathematics can one deal entirely—or almost entirely—in abstractions. But that isn't what happened. Painters continued to paint with thick, sticky stuff on real canvas; and musicians, to compose works requiring 110 instruments of wood and brass and men of flesh and blood to play them, while poets were eager for paper and print and favorable reviews in the daily journals. The purity of art was less in the art than in the rhetoric.

Still, great consequences did follow from the doctrine of pure art, which shows how important a rhetoric can be. One such consequence was what we now call non-objective painting. It carries out the principle that the pictorial art does not depict but creates. It organizes lines and colors and "animates" spatial entities. Such is the jargon. When occassionally a recognizable shape is offered, possibly a distortion or negation of reality, the viewer's mind must conscientiously reduce it to a purely pictorial effect. Painters generally try to help the public along this path by writing about their particular spatial entities in the catalogues of their one-man shows. Almost always, these are quasi-metaphysical comments about space, rhythm, structure, and other abstractions suggestive of science and technology.

The parallel movement in the art of music has led to the technique of serial or twelve-tone composition, where technique and ingenuity dominate, like the rules of a difficult game. Its appreciation is primarily visual; hearing the music does not adequately disclose its intricacy and does not arouse feeling—it is not expected to, any more than non-objective painting.

These encounters with arts which, relatively to former

practice, hold themselves incommunicado are now familiar. One would imagine that by contrast literature, which uses words, must necessarily have remained closer to common experience. But it too has withdrawn itself as far as it could. In the same decade of the nineties, poetry began its retreat from ordinary diction and syntax and became difficult, arcane, so as to remove any similarity with the ordinary. Next came the vocabulary and methods typified in *Ulysses* and *Finnegans Wake*, after which the "new novel" developed in France abandoned storytelling, characterization, and intelligibility. It has to be worked at like twelve-tone music, and it yields ambiguous impressions like those of certain painters and sculptors and even architects. The titles given to the works often deepen the uncertainty, a result generally considered all to the good.

These productions of our time clearly share a rhetoric in common. If its first rule is purity in the sense I have described, then the second is that the work of art is "autonomous." As. E. M. Forster said, it is a world of its own, obeying its own laws. What this means is that it mustn't be compared with anything outside it, such as the common world, or some other genre or other work of art, to say nothing of the beholder's previous feelings, expectations, or beliefs. Archibald MacLeish put it succinctly in his often quoted lines, "A poem should not mean / But be." Forster, also bewitched by sound, asserted that fiction was perhaps nearest to music in its formal beauty—a puzzling remark for a story-teller who mixed strong moral and social convictions with his narratives.

This new obsessive desire to empty the work of art of meaning and emotion, and at the same time to claim for it the appeal of a fresh-created world apart, can be accounted for on several grounds. It is, to begin with, a protest against the real world, which the artist finds ugly, overcrowded, vulgar, and what he calls materialistic. The judgment is a product not of esthetic theory but of social philosophy; it is a reformer's judgment, indeed it is the denunciation of a religious prophet, for whom this world is evil, while the world beyond, reflected solely in art, is pure and beautiful. No wonder art must no longer look like the world.

A second influence on the rhetoric of modern art is that of science. The autonomous work obeying laws of its own is a parallel to the universe that science postulates: nature is out there, apart from us, indifferent, and no quick understanding of it is possible: we must toil to find out how it works. Our pleasure comes from this arduous discovery, and this supposedly occurs also when we struggle over a work of modern art.

These suggestions may help to explain the rhetoric underlying modern art. But explaining it is less important for our present purpose than noticing the logical outcome of the whole tendency. In painting, music, and the rest, it is the gradual elimination of individual will and purpose—again in parallel with the scientific view of the cosmos—no will or pur-o pose there: it purely *happens*. Compare: in painting, the artist in his evolution ends by flinging or dripping paint on canvas. The sculptor exhibits under his own name what is called "found art," meaning a piece of jetsam from the beach, shaped by chance and the waves; or "junk art," which may be the discarded part of a utensil or piece of furniture. In poetry and music, the latest resort is "aleatory" art—composing by chance with the aid of dice or a computer; or—as in some modern scores—indicating by curved lines in various colors some general contours and contrasts, leaving the notes and all other particulars to the momentary mind of the performer. And one published novel, at least, contented itself with printing scattered extracts from a textbook on gynecology.

The abdication of the artistic will and purpose seems complete. Indeed, the late Harold Rosenberg, who writes of modernism with the utmost sympathy in his book *The Tradition of the New*, states the fact explicitly. The three steps in the evolution of the new have been: the elimination of meaning, the elimination of feeling, and the elimination of esthetic intention.

It is not an idle play on words to say that the rhetoric of the new has painted itself into a corner. This precarious position is recognized in the term *Non-Art*, which is the name of still another school. And yet this gradually expanding void—of meaning, feeling, and purpose—criticism has gone on. The end of art itself cannot stop critics from uttering. So we may ask: what have been the preferred rhetorical instruments of critics faced with less and less assignable intentions in the productions called art? Well, ever since the Symbolist Movement, symbols. What one is given in a work of art is a set of symbols; they have to be interpreted. In print or on canvas, nothing is what it seems; it is something else. At this very moment there are thousands of young men and women sitting in English classes and toiling to decode the symbols in Conrad's *Heart of Darkness* or Yeats's "Crazy Jane." Once started, symbol hunting is addictive, like a hard drug. Symbols are found in Hemingway's *The Old Man and the Sea*, even though it can be shown that the author had no symbolic intentions there at all. Or again, a symbol has to be found in Thomas Hardy's poem, "The Phantom Horsewoman"—is she Fate, or Death riding the pale horse, or what other gloomy abstraction? She is only the late Mrs. Hardy, whom Thomas remembers as the riding girl whom he courted forty years earlier.

To such skepticism as this about symbol-hunting, modern criticism replies: "Hemingway didn't *know* he was using symbols but they are there just the same. His unconscious was at work, codifying his impulses for him." Out of this dogma comes the theory that all artistic production, when genuine, is largely automatic; it works like a natural unction; the author is simply a good secretary. What is more, all stories, feelings, attitudes, designs, compositions have their source in a few archetypal myths, which are part of the collective unconscious and entwined with our instinctual drives. A trained critic can readily discern the myths beneath or within the outward appearance. Correct interpretation is confirmed by theme analysis, which shows how the maker of the work was obsessed by certain ideas he did not know he had and how the reader responds in the same reflex fashion. Fortunately, the critic is at hand to decipher the riddle and explain it to the ignorant pair.

Presumably, the principle of a few archetypal tales buried in the unconscious explains why the Arabian Nights stories resemble so closely the novels of Dostoevsky, while the related principle of ambiguity in design and expression accounts for the fact that the Parthenon and the Cathedral of Chartres are so easily confused. The fluted Doric columns in the one contain *in posse* the elongated figures of the Kings and Queens of Judah which adorn the north porch at Chartres. Indeed, if our minds and senses were adequately ambiguous, we would see that only one idea lies at the root of all works of art—fiction or painting, building or symphony—the urge to make a structure; not free, but of a culturally fated kind. Everything else is embroidery.

And so we find Structuralists and Post-Structuralists crowding like maggots over the great masterpieces of western art, arguing over which simple system of opposite rhetorical terms will fit the data, that is to say, the sum total of literature, painting, drama, music, and other artifacts. How the human passion for structure produces the work of art found on the beach, or the minimal art consisting of a plastic sheet wrapped around a tenement in ruins, is merely an incidental difficulty. What emerges from both the theory of unconscious, archetypal art and the existence of modern non-art is that art and non-art alike result from a mechanical determinism; they embody a process rather than record an activity. In other words, the scientific account of the works of nature has been made to explain the works of art: the rhetoric of the arts is a borrowing from across the way.

The foregoing assumptions, explanations, and critical terms that occupy our minds and fill current writings I have called a rhetoric *about* the arts, and I use the phrase in the unfavorable sense of a mode of speaking that is more fashionable than philosophical. For one thing, it is hardly consistent. According to it, the several arts must not mingle their ways, yet they all strive toward the way of music. Then, the work of art is autonomous, a world by itself, with laws of its own and symbolic of a reality beyond the workaday world, and yet it turns out to be a mere variation on old unconscious patterns, born out of simple human instincts. Again, artists and their rhetoricians ask us to contemplate pure form, but while never saying a word about what pure form is or what fun there is in it, the artists conduct what they call "experiments"—with color arrangements, with new materials, with electronic sounds, with made-up words, all of which are sensory experiences of the most material kind.
Moreover—so far from being autonomous—independent-modern work is allusive and can often be understood only through footnotes and scholarly commentary. The very assumption that art is a congeries of symbols and themes, archetypes and structures, has called forth an army of earnest decoders and turned part of the academic world into a growth industry. Nor must we forget the duplicity of the symbol business: while in one building the teaching is: a poem must not mean but be, the art historians across the campus will not let a painting be but make it mean all sorts of things, by showing how each item in it has a literal significance. Did you know that in Venetian painting of the Renaissance a quince in a bowl of fruit denoted marriage? Well, read Edgar Wind on Bellini's "Feast of the Gods" and then try to recover your sense of autonomy in art.

In saying these things, I am not making an effort to refute the current rhetorics about art. They refute themselves and each other. I am only giving illustrations of that generality. Their common error is misplaced abstraction. In trying to encompass the greater profusion of art, to bring order into its endless variety, the explanations leave the surface appearance and plunge into the depths, where we like to think things are simple and *cause* the surface variety. But in the presence of abstraction by reduction all differences disappear. With the abstraction *shelter*, a cave, a tent, a hut, and the Taj Mahal are identical. That is what we are left with when we seek in the unconscious, or structure, or pure form the answer to our quest.

Art, whether we like to admit it or not, is primarily surface; it is concrete stuff, not abstract, not concepts, not mathematics. The artist, whether he knows it or not, works with matter. It is absurd to say that music is immaterial. It is a perpetual molding of solid air beating on our skin as well as on our eardrums: standing too close to the sound of a church bell can kill a man. So music is no more ethereal and pure than the sculptured figures carved out of Mount Rushmore. Even literature in print, which might qualify as nonsensory, acts upon us sensorially, as it once did when it was a spoken art, because we have learned to see images and feel rhythms from the black marks on a white page.

The upshot of these reflections is that a useful rhetoric of the arts must give up remote abstraction and return to empirical elements. I say remote abstraction, for there is nothing wrong with abstraction in its common form of generality; there is no avoiding it if one is to supply a scheme, a set of ideas that may lead toward an understanding of art. And here, at the outset of sketching such a scheme, let me reaffirm what that great neglected American critic, John Jay Chapman, said on the subject: "We cannot hope to understand what art is." The reason is that art partakes of human experience. It is a curious man-made extension of life itself. And as we cannot, finally, understand life, so we cannot, finally, understand art.

But that very difficulty tells us where to concentrate our attention and what hypotheses to avoid. We have seen that art consists of pieces of matter arranged this way or that. History shows us how far these arrangements can differ and still afford the artistic experience. The rules that are said to govern composition in one period or one civilization are

directly flouted in another and the result is still art. In technique or medium or purpose, what one individual artist can
get away with brings another artist to disaster. It is all a
mystery. Again, the habits acquired by one generation for
receiving and savoring the arts of the day rarely strecth forward to accept the different arrangements and intentions of
the next generation. The artistic past, meanwhile, is a collection of the admired, the neglected, and the recently revived.
All this is but another proof that art is like life in requiring
continual adaptation. If the high abstract accounts of art
were true, this barrier would not exist.

A rhetoric of the arts, then, should not begin by ad-
dressing itself to the products of art, but to the nature of ex- ○
perience. It should begin with the mind and find out
whether any of its native tendencies foreshadow any
common features found in art. This inquiry incidentally
brings up the interesting fact that everybody—artists, critics,
and laymen—are eager to talk about art with a capital A, at
the same time as they profess the belief in distinct arts founded on divergent principles. If we talk about *the* artistic
experience, the arts must spring from some common source.

That source, I submit, is the mind, the conscious mind.
In what form does it experience reality? The answer has
been clear ever since William James published his *Principles
of Psychology* in 1890. Read chapter nine of that work if
you want to confirm or correct your ideas about art; then go
on to the other chapters on perception and conception.

The mind, experience, consciousness are three words for
one reality, which occurs in the form of a stream—that well-
publicized "stream of consciousness." The stream is a steady
but not an even flow. It has peaks of intensity, with a quiet-
er margin on each side. The peak of thought is clear and
strong for a moment but fades into a memory, while the next
pulse, which was dim a moment ago becomes the new strong
peak. Each pulse, which we call a thought, is thus surrounded by a fringe and both together can embrace any number of
ideas, objects, aspects, feelings, memories, relevant or irrelevant associations. The thought is an unpredictable complex,
not a simple mirror image of what we call separate objects in
the physical world. A third characteristic of the stream of
consciousness is that it seems driven toward some end; it follows what it finds interesting and turns away from the rest; it
jumps, takes short-cuts, and can draw on a vast network of
previous sensations, emotions, and conceptions to form its

present focus of attention. Please note *interest* and *attention.*

Right here, as I think, in this rough description of human thinking, are the first elements of a rhetoric of the arts. The shape of thought reproduces itself in the shape of works of art. In music and literature the inevitable pattern is: preparation (or exposition), development, climax, and conclusion. These are the original phases of oratory, of rhetoric, as well as the set forms of music. Poems, stories, essays follow the same program. In particular works it can of course be elaborated, and by tradition it is stylized; but no matter how complicated or conventional, the sense of moving toward some end and the presence of interrelated peaks and valleys is, in art, the governing *interest* that commands *attention.*

The single peak of attention and its fringe in the stream give us, in turn, the pattern of the plastic arts. They contrive a focus of interest—a central figure or space or motif—and place the surrounding elements so that they seem at first as helter-skelter as in the margins of a thought; yet on scrutiny they show a significant relatedness to the center. You may have noticed by the way that I do not bring in the familiar contrast between the arts of space and those of time. One reason is that the viewer of a picture can rarely see it all at once, but must look at it in detail like a panorama unrolling through time; and the reader or listener who knows a literary or musical work often thinks of it as offering simultaneous or spatial relations. Mozart said he planned his symphonies in one grand act as thought or vision. We should expect this double ability to move and to focus, from the nature of thinking, which streams yet attends. In some of the arts— theatre, motion picture, and the dance (especially when it involves a group)—the two patterns are combined: there is both the graphic and the oratorical, the organization of figures as on a screen and that of themes exposed, developed, and resolved.

These natural schemes are of course but a first outline of the rhetoric of the arts. The human mind has the power to complicate the stream, to abstract and classify, to choose and compare, and to devise short-cuts both to perception and conception by using signs and symbols. It can decide that a quince means marriage and that lines meeting at infinity on a flat surface represent objects in three dimensions. One of the mind's great feats come quite early in life: the eye sees objects upside down until the sense of touch spurs the mind to turn them right side up again.

All these wonders take place under the impact of things upon the sense, and whatever the mind does is done in the service of practical or esthetic interests. I mean that the way reality is "taken" either helps one to navigate in the world, or is pleasing as such, or both together. The arts, naturally, also show correspondence with these acquired traits. Take for example the pleasure of variety. We like to depart and re-turn—from and to a place or theme or feeling of whatever kind; we like to see apparent disorder untangle itself into simplicity; we respond to repetition close together and call it emphasis; likewise to repetition spaced out and call it echo or reminder or full close; we like smooth follow-through, called coherenece, and its opposite, which is clash and con-flict, called drama. We like above all unity and intensity, which together feel like our hold on the very pulse of life. We seem thereby to capture the stream and squeeze out of it all it has to give. Without going into further detail or illustration, I would suggest that this manhandling of the stream. this seiz-ing on the richest and most intensive experience, is precisely what art is originally for. Man makes scratches on matter or puts lumps of it together as a comprehensive memento of what he has lived.

A complete rhetoric of the arts would build on these premises and draw conclusions from the interplay between o our inner life as it is felt and the extant body of the arts. A first requirement would be to show how impossible it is for any work to keep out so-called extraneous elements. The mind that makes the work and the one that beholds it are alike filled with ideas, feelings, associations, and memories that link the present experience with the person's entire past, as well as with the common world of other things and people. We bring to any work of art a large fund of knowledge, with-out which it would be poor and shrunken. For the same reason, the several arts do not and cannot function in water-tight compartments. It is therefore proper to find the im-agination of love in a ballet, drama in a symphony, political satire in a painting, mysticism in a building. That is in fact what mankind has done from the beginning. You have only to read or listen to what has been said about art throughout history to see that—technical details apart—all criticism makes use of worldly ideas and common feelings to express praise or blame, delight or derision.

The unity of the arts is thus confirmed and their purity

denied. But it does not follow that the arts do not differ through their materials. A novel cannot be filmed verbatim without becoming an interminable bore. A poem cannot be paraphrased in prose. A play may inspire a musician, but he has to mangle it in order to make an opera; and he must effect a peculiar transmutation of elements if he wants to compose without words a suite or symphony on the dramatic subject. These necessities and limitations are so clear and so well known that it is surprising to hear them used again and again in solemn warning against the mixing of genres. Music and painting, says the purist, should not tell a story, because they can't. Well, if they can't there is no danger and the warning is superfluous. But if it is urged against painting, say, a Crucifixion with expressive figures at the foot of the cross, then the warning is twice foolish, first because the representation is not story-telling; and second, because paintings of this sort have claimed the talents of the greatest artists and given us some of the world's masterpieces.

The same holds true for every art. Literature is not just beautiful words, but doctrine and propaganda and journalism as well—witness Dante's *Divine Comedy*. Sculpture and architecture have embodied religious feeling, like painting, and music has served a great many workaday activities as well as expressed many supernal emotions. There is no use legislating at this late date against the artistic behavior of mankind.

I believe no one would be tempted to do so if a rhetoric of the arts established for each of them the equal validity of three kinds of program—the formal, the significant, and the introspective:

The formal program consists of the recognized genres and the set forms which have been developed out of the native action of the mind, in the way I tried to show.

The significant program comes from the cultural traditions or innovations of the time and place. A Crucifixion or a Requiem implies a Christian tradition and also the information that makes such works readily intelligible to the beholder. In a secular culture, the dance devotes itself to *Romeo and Juliet* or the Marxist revolution with equal ease; but just as the formal program involves conventions that have to be learned, so the significant program involves ideas or facts that have to be learned also.

The third or introspective program is what the artist finds stirring within him during the act of composition. It cannot be described or prescribed. It is at every moment his intention, conscious and semi-conscious. It is not a series of ideas or emotions, for he is probably quite cool and concerned with technical matters while he works, yet he is also under the influence of this visceral power of design. It is through it, of course, that he touches us most deeply. We are moved by all three programs—the form provides order and security and makes us admire; the meaning, by impressing itself, stirs and organizes a host of association; and the last, intimate, unique ୦ design overwhelms us by endowing the entire experience with the semblance of life.

At this point an adequate rhetoric would consider its task finished and yield its place to criticism, a much more detailed and voluminous business, in which the material differences among the arts obtain due recognition. But rhetoric should reserve the right to disallow critical practices that disregard or negate its own observations. It would, for example, call criticism to account when it assumes purity to be possible, or when it fails to note that the newest modern art, which ignores any or all of the three programs, is really asking the beholder to supply these out of his own imagination—an imagination fed and trained on earlier work.

An empirical rhetoric would also be concerned about one last difficulty of criticism—its terminology. The present state of the critical vocabularies is bad. The academic ones are pedantic and faddish, the journalistic ones are mindless and flossy. Both kinds are full of thought-clichés and conventional errors; and too often, when originality breaks in, it takes the form of unexamined metaphors. It is, to be sure, impossible to think or speak in words free of metaphorical origins, but in criticism the more literal the language, the better. For example, *rhythm* is often transferred from music or literature to painting, where it describes certain recurrences of line or alternations of color, or sometimes only matching intensities. It is a bad word for the purpose, since it remains indefinite and since the impression of true rhythm is not visual.

I do not mean to deny that things seen and things heard can resemble or suggest each other, but this impression should remain with the spectator; the critic's business is to differentiate in order to be clear. We know, for instance, what is meant by the language of music, the idiom of the baroque period; yet I think the critic should not use "language" and "idiom" when he is discussing music, which is inarticulate sound—any more than he should refer to the "music" of Milton's prose. To do so is only an appeal to what we already perceive; if we fail to perceive, our knowledge is in no way advanced; we merely record somebody's enthusiasm. Perhaps we should be warned by the example of Schelling, the German philosopher who launched the idea that architecture was forzen music, and ask ourselves after hearing the *Ninth Symphony* whether it sounded like melted architecture.

In short, critics must invent for each art a proper descriptive and evaluative vocabulary. It has largely been done for literature, though jargon like weeds always threatens it. The test of a critical term is its ability to lead us to a feature perceived, a sensation felt, an idea supported by evidence in one or more works of art. In making these demands on criticism, an empirical rhetoric is far from denying the elusive, the ineffable, the indescribable intimacies of intercourse with art. On the contrary, it is because there will always be something left over after description and judgment that criticism must be irreproachable and strict in dealing with what *can* be talked about. We cannot hope to understand what art is, but we shall come closer to the goal if we reduce nonsense and avoid *mere* rhetoric.

Columbia University

WILBUR SAMUEL HOWELL

PETER RAMUS, THOMAS SHERIDAN, AND KENNETH BURKE: THREE MAVERICKS IN THE HISTORY OF RHETORIC

I

Samuel A. Maverick, we are told. was a nineteenth-century Texas rancher who did not brand the calves in his herd of cattle as they roamed upon the unfenced ranges.[1] Thus his last name passed into the vocabulary of Texas and ultimately into that of North America as a term in the first instance for any unclaimed animal on open territory and in secondary instances for anyone not identified with the herd— for anyone, that is, whose opinions and habits differ from those of the establishment in matters of personal conduct, political beliefs, religious convictions, or educational practices. *Webster's Third International Dictionary of the English Language* brings all of these strands of meaning together by defining a maverick as a person who sets an independent course and often becomes as a result the favorite of intellectuals, nonconformists, and freethinkers. It is obvious from these definitions that "maverick" is not a term of abuse and that it may in some circles be a term of eulogy. Yet it is obvious, too, that it can function as a neutral term and in that capacity serve only to designate a person who does not subscribe to established conventions at some time or other in some given field.

In applying this term now to Peter Ramus, Thomas Sheridan, and Kenneth Burke, I have in mind only that these three men wrote on rhetoric and that their opinions on that subject differ from those which belong to the established European rhetorical tradition. I call these rhetoricians mavericks, in short, without pejorative intent. And what I propose to do in this lecture is to describe the established

rhetorical tradition and to show wherein these three rhetoricians departed from it. If my lecture shows sympathy for
the established tradition and a lack of enthusiasm for the
three rhetoricians under examination, I trust that the reasons
for my own value judgments will be clear and that I shall not
be considered prejudiced and unfair. I speak as a teacher who
taught rhetoric in American colleges and universities for
forty-seven years before his retirement in 1972, and my
present attitude towards that subject has been developed in
the presence of students in my classrooms as I have sought to
make my subject a significant contribution to their education. When a teacher tries to make his subject significant, he
is constantly aware of the possibility of failure. And he
comes to feel that he can succeed only by facing the important issues which lie within his subject and by trying to
communicate to his students a sense of the importance of
those issues. It is because the three rhetoricians whom I am
discussing today took away from rhetoric certain signifi-
cancies inevitably involved in it that my sympathies
developed against their teachings. But rhetoric has suffered
many setbacks from enemies and friends in its long history,
and I am quite prepared to discuss these setbacks without
animosity or anger. After all, whether I myself turn out to
have been an enemy or friend of rhetoric is still an open
question, and I hope that my present and future critics will
be as tolerant of what they perceive to be my faults and
shortcomings in that direction as I shall endeavor to be in
pointing out what I regard as the shortcomings of my three
mavericks.

II

The earliest one among them, Peter Ramus, lived between 1515 and 1572.[2] He probably attracted more attention to himself in his lifetime than did any European scholar
of that era. His reforms of dialectic and rhetoric were widely
popular for a century after his death, and those reforms may
be called the first great challenge that the established rhetorical tradition had faced in the two thousand years of its
existence. Thus he earns his place in my present lecture
without any difficulty at all.

Thomas Sheridan, the second of my mavericks, was a
playwright, actor, and theatre manager in Dublin during the
middle years of the eighteenth century. Perhaps his chief
claim to fame is that he was the father of Richard Brinsley

Sheridan, whose dramas are still favorites in the repertoires of the English-speaking theatrical world. But for us he has another claim to recognition. He turned away from his theatrical career in 1759 and dedicated the rest of his life to the advocacy of a standard pronounciation for the English language and to a sustained effort to institutionalize that standard by reviving what he called the long lost art of oratory.[3] His rhetorical ideas became very influential in England and America during the century that followed his death in 1788; and, although he fixed upon those ideas the stamp of the rhetorical tradition itself, they were in fact a poor fragment of that tradition. To omit him from my present subject would be to overlook one of the chief authors of the decline of rhetoric in our modern academic world.

The third of my mavericks is Kenneth Burke. Born in 1897 at Pittsburgh, Pennsylvania, and educated at Ohio State University, Kenneth Burke has enjoyed an honorable and distinguished career in his capacity as literary critic, music critic, poet, novelist, and teacher. Throughout his many published critical works the theme of rhetoric persists, and he has made that theme the foundation of his concept of literary theory. In fact, it would not be an exaggeration to say that he is today regarded in many literary and scholarly circles as Mr. Rhetoric himself. But his system of rhetoric departs in a fundamental way from the long-established rhetorical tradition of European learning,[4] and thus I feel constrained to include him in today's lecture and to put him in the class which to my reckoning also includes Thomas Sheridan and Peter Ramus.

III

In ancient Greece, rhetoric, dialectic, and poetics were regarded as the three basic theories of verbal composition. Grammar was of course allied to them as the study of the linguistic medium in which verbal structures are expressed would necessarily be the foundation of the study of all forms of discourse. And, if grammar is the foundation of literary study, formal logic in the ancient sense must be regarded as its capstone, logic being the discipline which finally protects the forms of discourse from inconsistency within themselves and from factual inaccuracy in relation to the outside realities which the forms of discourse deal with. But logic and grammar must be excluded from today's discussion, in order that the three other disciplines just enumerated may have as full a treatment as I can give them here; and I sincerely hope that, in deciding to omit two important members of the classical scheme, I shall not be adversely criticized.

Aristotle's *Topics* is the great formative influence upon ancient dialectic, although Plato's *Phaedrus* has many acute observations to make upon the subject of dialectical doctrine, and all of Plato's dialogues may justly be called applications of dialectical techniques to the examination and communication of philosophical subject matter. Let us briefly discuss the main lines of doctrine in Aristotle's *Topics*.

To Aristotle, dialectic has for its field what we would today call scholarly argument and exposition. Aristotle indicates what the definition of dialectic is when he calls it "a process of criticism wherein lies the path to the principles of all inquiries."[5] The aim of dialectic is to create discourses which would convince their audiences, and those audiences, as Aristotle takes for granted, are to be identified within a given community as the advanced students, the scholars, the critics, the educators, whose function is to decide learned questions and solve learned problems. The materials of dialectic are probable statements on both sides of the subject under discussion, these statements being analyzed to determine which ones are as close to the truth as the circumstances allow and which ones are to be discarded as erroneous. "For the study of the philosophical sciences," says Aristotle, "it [dialectic] is useful, because the ability to raise searching difficulties on both sides of a subject will make us detect more easily the truth and error about the several points that arise."[6] A truthful statement is one which accurately corresponds to its author's mental experience of reality, when that author's mental experience demonstrates its accurate correspondence to the realities under his observation. "Thus, if it is true to say that a thing is white," remarks Aristotle elsewhere in his writings, "it must necessarily be white; if the reverse proposition is true, it will of necessity not be white."[7] And probable statements of the most acceptable kind are those which best correspond to mental experience when that experience interprets as accurately as may be realities less certain of final definition than the reality of whiteness is. As for the procedures of dialectic, they are the major subjects of Aristotle's *Topics*, and they consist in the discovery or invention of all the probable statements to be made on both sides of a question and the arrangement of those probable statements in such a way as to bring out the ones closest to the truth under the circumstances. Probable statements of primary interest to dialectic are of four kinds: propositions of accident, property, genus, and definition.[8] These four kinds of propositions, and the methods of discovering the argumentative possibilities of each, make up the greater part of the first seven books of Aristotle's *Topics*, whereas Book VIII is devoted to arranging, putting, and answering dialectical questions.[9] The literary products which emerge from the application of dialectical method to subjects of philosophical inquiry are what we would call philosophical and scholarly writings: arguments, expositions, treatises, dissertations, discussions. These writings make use of logical statements alone. No emotional appeals, no attempts to establish the ethical credibility of the author, are present in them. Statements manifesting in their every accent that they are the closest approximation to certainty allowed by their subject matter are what these discourses should ideally contain and what the learned community should ideally expect if these discourses are to convince scholars and philosophers.

To Aristotle, rhetoric as a theory of verbal composition is closely allied to dialectic, but it nevertheless has distinctive characteristics of its own. Aristotle begins his *Rhetoric* by stating that either of these theories is "the counterpart" of the other,[10] and here at any rate is a strong affirmation of the systematic similarity between them. And yet the distinctive differences between them soon become evident as Aristotle proceeds to speak of rhetoric. Even if he does not indicate as much in so many words, it becomes clear that to him the field of rhetoric is popular argument as distinguished from scholarly argument of the field of dialectic. In defining rhetoric as "the faculty of observing in any given case the available means of persuasion,"[11] he suggests that the difference between popular argument and scholarly argument is allied to the difference between persuasion and conviction, the latter term being applied to logical appeals and the former to emotional and ethical appeals as well.[12] The aim of rhetoric as a theory of composition is thus in Aristotle's view to create discourses which would come as close to persuading an audience as the circumstances would allow, and the audience in this case, as Aristotle openly specifies, is "an audience of untrained thinkers."[13] Average citizens in popular governments have to bear the responsibility, at least in part, of deciding practical questions in the fields of public morality, public wrong-doing, and public political policy. As with dialectic, the materials of rhetoric are probable statements, usually on one side of a given controversy, probability being the closest approximation to what appears to have been, or what appears to be, or what appears to promise to be, the true state of affairs in the case at hand. Judgments as to what is most probable in popular argument are influenced by the emotions of the audience and moral character of the speaker, whereas similar judgments in dialectic tend to be based upon reason alone; and thus rhetoric has occasion to study emotions and moral character, as dialectic does not.[14] Aristotle specifically repudiates the corrupting idea that a probable statement is any superficially fair utterance whatever and that the speaker is under no obligation to discriminate between accurate and shaky probabilities or to elect to advance only those which, shaky or externally plausible as the case might be, are in tune only with the ignorance and prejudices of the mob. The law acting to prevent demagogic practices of this kind was as plain to Aristotle as it was to Plato:[15] that mankind has a natural disposition to prefer truth above error, and that, if a man embraces error, he does so only because he believes it to be the truth. Thus the natural bent of mankind in general directs a speaker or author to make his statements express those probabilities which recognizably lie on the side towards the clearer certainties. Aristotle's commitment to this law is obvious in what he asserts on three occasions in the first chapter of the *Rhetoric*. "Rhetoric is useful," he observes at one point, "because things that are true and things that are just have a natural tendency to prevail over their opposites, so that if the decisions of judges are not what they ought to be, the defeat must be due to the speakers themselves, and they must be blamed accordingly."[16] "Further," he says at another point, "we must be able to employ persuasion, just as strict reasoning can be employed, on opposite sides of a question, not in order that we may in practice employ it in both ways (for we must not make people believe what is wrong), but in order that we may see clearly what the facts are, and that, if another man argues unfairly, we on our part may be able to confute him."[17] And at still another point, after repeating that both dialectic and rhetoric teach authors to draw opposite conclusions without concern for the false or the true, Aristotle gives the following advice about the use of those conclusions: "Nevertheless, the underlying facts do not lend themselves equally well to the contrary views. No;

things that are true and things that are better are, by their nature, practically always easier to prove and easier to believe in."[18] In regard to the procedures of rhetoric, they, too, like those of dialectic, engage the author in the processes of invention and arrangement, and Aristotle's *Rhetoric* analyzes these processes for their capacity to produce the subject matter of political, forensic, and eulogistic speeches, even as these processes are analyzed in the *Topics* in relation to questions of accident, property, genus, and definition. In his discussion of oratorical arrangement, that is to say, arrangement as it applies to oratory and to all related kinds of nonfictional popular compositions, Aristotle defines the basic verbal ingredients of these discourses when he says that oratorical arrangement contains two elements, "Statements of the case" and "Argument," just as dialectical organization contains two elements, "Enunciation and Demonstration."[19] In addition to invention and arrangement, Aristotle's *Rhetoric* teaches that all popular discourses also involve the author in the procedures of style and delivery,[20] neither of which is mentioned in the *Topics* for the obvious reasons that style is less a matter of concern when scholars are being addressed than when the author speaks or writes for the people and that delivery, like style, is much more an imperative in speaking to the people than in talking to a small group of learned men and women. As for the literary products which emerge when rhetorical theory is applied to practical cases, they have been indirectly mentioned already in what I have been saying of rhetoric. But for the sake of having them explicitly in our record, I should like now to enumerate them in their primary and their derivative forms. Primarily they are described by Aristotle as political, forensic, and epideictic speeches.[21] But it requires no stretch of the imagination to see that these three forms of discourse give rise to related forms outside of the realm of oratory. For one example, the epideictic speech is akin to the popular biography. For another example, every speech has a standard part called narration, sometimes omitted, sometimes necessary;[22] and in this part the facts of the case under discussion are set forth in a manner suggestive of historical writing. For still another example, the statement of the case and its proof are not only required in oratory but in all sorts of popular arguments. Rhetorical eulogy, rhetorical narration, and rhetorical statement and proofs can therefore be declared to be seminal patterns not only in the composition of speeches but in the composition of biography, history, and other kinds of popular discourse in the field of nonfiction.

In fact, having in mind the varieties of the literary works which can be produced from dialectic and rhetoric, as Aristotle formulated these two disciplines, we may say without exaggeration that the theory behind all nonfictional literary composition is set forth, not finally to be sure, but in a most provocative pioneering preface, in Aristotle's *Topics* and *Rhetoric*. The subsequent history of dialectic and rhetoric in European education from Aristotle's time to the end of the seventeenth century of the Christian era could in fact be truly characterized as the history of these two Aristotelian works in various adaptations, reworkings, and sometimes brilliant expansions, as in the case of those produced by Cicero, Quintilian, and St. Augustine.

The third of Aristotle's basic theories of verbal composition requires for its analysis basic concepts quite different from those which dominate dialectic and rhetoric, as we see at once when we turn to Aristotle's *Poetics*.

This remarkable treatise locates the field of poetry by leading us systematically to understand that, whereas the learned and the popular arguments of dialectic and rhetoric deal with actual, poetry deals with imagined, realities.[23] We gain this understanding when Aristotle defines poetry by enumerating its various kinds, by selecting epic and tragedy as its major forms, and by characterizing tragedy as "the imitation of an action that is serious and also, as having magnitude, complete in itself; in language with pleasurable accessories, each kind brought in separately in the parts of the work; in a dramatic, not in a narrative form; with incidents arousing pity and fear, wherewith to accomplish its catharsis of such emotions."[24] We notice that this famous definition stresses catharsis, not conviction or persuasion, as the aim of poetry in one of its most influential species. We know from history and our own experience that the audience postulated in this definition is made up of both trained and untrained thinkers, usually gathered together in a theatre, instead of being distributed between academic seminars and popular assemblies. We see in Aristotle's definition that the materials of poetry are incidents, not probable arguments, and that these incidents are imitations of actual events, in a word, fictions, imagined realities, mimeses, which not only constitute the essence of poetry,[25] but which, like the arguments of dialectic and rhetoric, must be probable. In fact, the need for probability in a poetic composition is openly stressed by Aristotle when he later says that "the poet's function is to describe, not the thing that has happened, but a kind of thing that might happen, i.e. what is possible as being probable or necessary."[26] This insistence upon probability of incident in poetry, as distinguished from probability of argument in dialectic and rhetoric, leads into Aristotle's celebrated distinction between poetry and history—a distinction amounting at bottom to the recognition that the historian, like the orator and dialectician, pictures realities as faithfully as he is capable of doing, whereas the poet pictures imagined realities—things that might be, as opposed to things that are or have been. "The distinction between historian and poet," says Aristotle, "is not in the one writing prose and the other verse. . . ; it consists really in this, that the one describes the thing that has been, and the other a kind of thing that might be."[27] As for the procedures of poetry, they consist, not in the inventing, arranging, and styling of statements, but in the inventing, arranging, and styling of fictitious incidents, wherein plot, character, thought, diction, and melody are important. And it hardly needs mentioning that the literary kinds produced by the theory of poetry are not only the epics and the tragedies of the ancient and modern literary world, but all verbal compositions having reference in the first instance to what their authors imagine to have happened, that is to say, all narratives of fabled events, all feigned histories, all works of fiction. These, taken as a literary class, represent poetry in Aristotle's sense.

IV

The ancient triad which I have just been describing—the division of verbal composition into three distinct branches—was made the chief target of the reforms of Peter Ramus in the sixteenth century. Let us now look briefly at the general contours of Ramus's reforms.

First of all, Ramus separated dialectic from rhetoric upon a principle quite different from Aristotle's. As if believing himself to have been appointed to simplify the doctrines of that master,[28] Ramus ordained that dialectic was to teach invention and arrangement, and rhetoric, style and delivery, these four processes being conceived broadly enough to apply to any particular situation in which they could be used. Thus the essential constituents of the Aristotelian theory of nonfictional authorship were preserved in Ramus's reform, but these constituents were now distributed between dialectic and rhetoric with none of the redundancy and overlapping that Aristotle appeared to Ramus to have been guilty of. Here, at least, Ramus made a procedural gain.

Invention, as it would apply to the composition of any discourse whatever, was made by Ramus to consist of the examination of a phenomenon in each of ten different aspects or places: its causes; its effects; its subjects; its adjuncts; its opposites; its comparatives; its name; its divisions; its definition; and its witnesses.[29] These ten places appear to include the four propositions which Aristotle had established as the heads of his theory of dialectical invention; and these ten seem to extend beyond Aristotle's four, in respect to the inventional possibilities that Ramus's scheme allows. But Ramus's scheme, even so, does not extend as far as Aristotle's does, when we remember that invention to Ramus was a dialectical matter alone, whereas to Aristotle it was dialectical in respect to learned, but rhetorical in respect to popular discourse. In other words, invention for popular discourse was not of special concern to Ramus, except so far as his ten places could be used to some extent by an orator, while to Aristotle invention for popular discourse was treated as needing specific analysis.[30]

Secondly, Ramus made dialectical disposition or arrangement consist of teachings designed to help form the small, the intermediate, and the large units of discourse. Thus he spoke of the logical proposition as the joining together of logical terms; he spoke next of the syllogism as the joining together of propositions; and he spoke lastly of method, as the joining together of syllogisms and arguments.[31] In his treatment of method, Ramus outlined two possibilities, one for strict scholarly discourse and the other for more relaxed forms, like those of oratory and poetry.[32] He called the first of these possibilities the method of science, and it consisted in defining the subject under discussion, dividing it into its parts, subdividing those parts, and coming at last to elements which permitted no further division. Ramus's own *Dialectique* of 1555 offers a fine example of the application of the method of science to a learned subject. As for the second possibility in arrangement, Ramus called it the prudential method, and he outlined it so as to reveal its particular utility in arranging popular discourse. In fact, Aristotelian rhetoric, with its massive emphasis upon the composition of discourses addressed to the people, is really represented in Ramus's whole reform only so far as Ramus's treatment of the prudential method of arrangement would seem to suggest a concern for the needs of that kind of audience.

Thirdly, in making rhetoric address itself solely to style and delivery, Ramus not only took from rhetoric all of its ancient regard for substance and form in discourse, but he also discussed style by limiting it to the lore of the tropes and figures—metaphor, irony, synecdoche, resonance, rhythm, prosopopeia, apostrophe, and so on—and he discussed delivery by limiting it to voice and gesture.[33] Here again he must be acknowledged to have simplified in principle the ancient percepts governing these two parts of rhetoric. But only in principle. For we should remind ourselves that the true author of the rhetorical side of Ramus's system of verbal composition was his colleague and friend, Audomarus Talaeus, or Amer Talon, who endorsed Ramus's whole program of reform and under Ramus's guidance gave rhetoric its distinctive Ramistic cast. And that distinctive cast, whether attributed primarily or secondarily to Ramus, resulted in a very restricted, a very truncated, form of the rhetorical doctrine to which Aristotle had addressed himself so much more fully.

Fourthly, Ramus's reform of the theory of verbal composition does not make poetics a major subject, as Aristotle did, and indeed Ramus did not even make it a minor subject. But he can be said to have treated poetical theory directly when he spoke of dialectical invention and arrangement and of the tropes and the figures of speech; and he can be credited with using specific passages from poetry, and specific kinds of arrangement in actual poems, to illustrate the precepts of invention, arrangement, and style.[34] To poetics as a kind of verbal composition in Aristotle's sense, however, Ramus gave no heed, despite his apparent ambition to deal with the theory of verbal composition in relation to all of its products.[35]

In summary, then, Ramus's reforms may be said to have damaged rhetoric in particular. They deprived rhetoric of its concern for persuasion. They deprived rhetoric of its concern for the popular audience. They deprived rhetoric of its concern for content and form, as these vital aspects of discourse have to be considered each by itself when an author composes a work addressed to the people. And, by depriving rhetoric of its concern for content, Ramus's reforms barred rhetoric from a concern for the truthful utterance, the utterance, that is to say, which would represent the closest approach to truth under a given set of circumstances. The American cartoonist Webster once drew a picture of a tired business man in the act of saying, "Switzerland I don't like. Take away the mountains, and what do you have left?" Well, Ramus's reforms, which did no particular damage to dialectic, took away from rhetoric its mountains—its concern for making the truth move men and women towards justice and decency, in a world struggling always to prevent the triumph of human injustice and brutishness. Indeed, what kind of future was there for rhetoric after Talaeus, under Ramus's guidance, took away its connection with everything except the external ornaments and the graceful delivery of discourse? It is not too harsh to say that Talaeus and Ramus made rhetorical style stand in relation to popular composition as house painting stands in relation to architecture; and that, by requiring voice and gesture to be mastered apart from the substance and form of the discourses which delivery serves, Talaeus and Ramus reduced rhetorical delivery as an academic discipline to an exercise in triviality and meaninglessness. Style and delivery in literary compositions can only be mastered in the closest possible connection with the sobs and pain of human experience. But Ramus never seemed to grasp that principle as it applied to his precepts for rhetoric.

V

Our second maverick, Thomas Sheridan, may be said to have reduced Ramus's reform of rhetoric to the smallest compass in its range of possibilities. Sheridan made rhetoric consist of delivery alone, whereas Ramus, as we know, had allowed it also to claim style, and Aristotle, of course, had given it not only style and delivery but a vast stake in the procedures of invention and arrangement as well. How then did Sheridan arrive at his surprising simplification of what to the ancients and even to Ramus had been a more involved and complicated process? We have time here to answer this question only in a general way.[36]

We should note first of all that Sheridan, as actor and actor-manager of the Theatre Royal in Smock Alley, Dublin, from 1743 to 1754, dreamed of restoring the long lost art of oratory to a place of eminence in British education and that his dreams in this direction were founded, according to his own testimony, upon his acquaintance with the rhetorical writings of Cicero and Quintilian.[37]

We should note secondly that after 1754 Sheridan wrote a book called *British Education* and delivered a set of popular lectures later published under the title *A Course of Lectures on Elocution*, and that from these two works emerged a kind of rhetoric consisting only in doctrines associated with oratorical delivery.[38]

Thirdly, we should note that Sheridan called oratorical delivery elocution. Had he been following Cicero and Quintilian with care, he would have known that the word "elocution" was a translation of *elocutio*, the term for style in classical Latin rhetoric, and that Cicero and Quintilian had both called delivery *pronuntiatio*, that is, pronunciation.[39] But Sheridan, professing to restore the long lost art of oratory, as conceived by Cicero and Quintilian, was not sensitive to the nuances of the Latin vocabulary or even to its more obvious distinctions. To him delivery, ancient *pronuntiatio*, had to be called elocution. And, to be sure, that word, which is associated etymologically with eloquence, may well have been taken by Sheridan to signify forceful, moving discourse, and thus to be the most proper term for the long lost art of his dreams.

Fourthly, we should note that Sheridan, who was not the first to call delivery elocution,[40] became the first to form a cult around the use of the term. The cult grew into what we now call the elocutionary movement, and that movement caused oratorical delivery to be taught as a course in schools and colleges and to crowd out the teaching of the other three procedures of the European rhetorical tradition. In a word, rhetoric became oratorical delivery. The part became the whole, and public emphasis upon the part caused public awareness of the whole to fade.

Fifthly, we should note that personal circumstances connected with Sheridan's early career help to explain his own preoccupation with delivery. As an Irish boy he was sent by his parents to Westminster, the English public school, and there he probably found that his own way of pronouncing the English language caused among his peers an amusement that he did not relish. His later interest in fostering a standard pronunciation of English may well have been a reaction to that amusement. Moreover, his career in the Theatre Royal in Dublin forced him to give attention to training of young actors to speak their lines on the stage. Here the young actors would take words written for them by someone else and practice delivering those words until their delivery was so to speak perfect. This process, as we know, makes the procedures of invention, arrangement, and style into matters of no concern to the speaker. His job becomes delivery alone. And then, too, Sheridan as busy actor and actor-manager had no time for scholarly pursuits, and thus his reading in the classics in general, and in classical rhetoric in particular, must have been skimpy indeed. When he wrote *British Education* and embarked upon his crusade not only to revive the long lost art of oratory but to foster a standard for English pronunciation, he did so as a persuasive enthusiast who lacked the scholarly background for his enterprises. In sum, his early life had given him a special interest in what he called elocution, but that early life had not also given him a scholarly background in traditional rhetoric. Small wonder that he did not adhere to the rhetorical tradition with any nicety.

What I said of the plight of rhetoric after Ramus had made his reforms applies *a fortiori* to the plight of rhetoric under Sheridan and the elocutionists. Thus I shall not discuss that matter again. But I might illustrate the difference between Aristotelian rhetoric and elocutionary rhetoric by repeating a favorite contrast that I first noticed myself. Aristotle's *Rhetoric*, as we saw earlier, opens with the famous observation that "Rhetoric is the counterpart of Dialectic." An elocutionary textbook used at Princeton University in the late nineteenth century opens with the much less famous observation, "Always inhale through the nostrils."[41] Between these latter words and those of Aristotle falls the shadow, if I may borrow an image from T. S. Eliot's "The Hollow Men" to characterize what happened to the ancient rhetorical tradition after the elocutionists had captured places of academic authority and esteem. Indeed, the shadow in this case is so impenetrable that, as we stare into it from the modern side, we see nothing in its depths to remind us of the rhetoric that Aristotle's genius had created. All we can see in vague outline is Thomas Sheridan's rhetoric, and that particular development causes the historian of the great rhetorical tradition to exclaim, once more in the imagery of "The Hollow Men":

> This is the dead land
> This is the cactus land.

VI

Within the framework of this present lecture, Kenneth Burke earns the title of maverick on the strength of his having virtually obliterated from his otherwise impressive critical system the Aristotelian distinction between rhetoric and poetry. In fact, not only does Burke overlook that distinction, but he even goes so far as to bring within the scope of rhetoric the two literary kinds which Aristotle respectively described as the literature of popular statement and the literature of fiction. Let me now briefly explain this aspect of Burke's theory.

Before I explain it, however, I should like to observe that Burke seems to me in his critical thinking as a whole to preserve the traditional Aristotelian recognition of a species of verbal composition devoted pre-eminently to the learned audience. As we have seen, Aristotle assigned this form of composition to dialectic, and although Burke does not usually avail himself of the latter term in his discussion of literary theory, he plainly recognizes learned discourse as a separable segment of the literary spectrum. Thus his book *The Philosophy of Literary Form* contains a chapter entitled "Semantic and Poetic Meaning,"[42] and in that chapter he clearly distinguishes between written works expressed in the severely neutral vocabularly of science and written works expressed in the vocabulary of evaluative, moral, and emotional concepts. This distinction makes books with scientific content into a literary genre which clearly resembles Aristotle's conception of dialectical discourse. So far, so good, if our interest is to locate resemblances between Burke's idea of literary kinds and Aristotle's.

But trouble develops almost at once when we look for other resemblances of this sort, and it develops within the very chapter that we are now considering. It develops because Burke brings all works expressed in an evaluative, moral, and emotional vocabulary within the scope of rhetoric. True enough, the title of his chapter seems to promise an analysis of the differences between semantic and poetic meaning, that is, between science and poetry, with rhetoric perhaps somewhere in between. But in the very first sentence of the chapter Burke says, "This essay may be taken as a rhetorical defense of rhetoric," and from that point on he proceeds to discuss all works except those of a scientific character as examples of the rhetoric which he is defending, without once bothering to interest himself in critical distinctions between the uses of the evaluative and emotional vocabulary in respect to history writing, biography, and oratory, on the one hand, and the uses of that vocabulary in drama, epic poetry, and fiction on the other. Certainly the evaluative and emotional vocabulary is represented in oratory as well as in poetry, but this one similarity does not make an oration a poem, or a poem an oration. Yet the implication from Burke at this point is that a differentiation between these forms has no critical value whatever. As we have seen, Aristotle felt otherwise, and indeed if he had not, an important chapter in European literary criticism might never have been written.

The clearest statement of Burke's conviction that poetry is an aspect of rhetoric appears in his early book *Counter-Statement*. Admirable above all in respect to its thesis that the writer who uses the moral, evaluative, and emotional vocabulary aims not at private self-expression but at public impact, *Counter-Statement* arrives at the conclusion that "effective literature could be nothing else but rhetoric."[43] This conclusion *Counter-Statement* authorizes by declaring that rhetoric, "by lexicographer's definition, refers but to 'the use of language in such a way as to produce a desired impression upon the hearer or reader.' "[44] The lexicographer cited here turns out to have been the anonymous editor who revised for the eleventh edition of the *Encyclopaedia Britannica* R. C. Jebb's previous article on rhetoric in the ninth edition of that same work.[45] At any rate, *Counter-Statement* adheres to that lexicographer's definition by classifying under the heading, "Lexicon Rhetoricae," what Burke calls "the principles underlying the appeal of literature,"[46] and this "Lexicon" contains the terms and concepts necessary for the understanding and criticism of literary effort in all its forms, rhetorical and poetic.[47]

The Aristotelian theory of literary composition would of course amply justify Burke in arguing that all literature aims to produce an effect upon audiences. But, as we have seen, Aristotle richly demonstrates that orators, as well as historians and biographers, produce effects by means of statement and proof, whereas poets produce effects by means of incidents, plots, imagined events—in a word, by means of fictions. Thus it is in Aristotle's insistence upon the recognition of the difference between fiction and nonfiction that we find the distinctive characteristic of his system. Why Burke did not perceive the need for incorporating this same distinctive characteristic into his otherwise excellent system is indeed a mystery. But incorporate it he did not, and by that omission alone he qualifies as a maverick within the framework of my present lecture.

VII

As a teacher of rhetoric in American colleges and universities for almost half a century, I have never been able to present my subject in the terms proposed by Peter Ramus, Thomas Sheridan, or Kenneth Burke. My own interests as teacher have always included a love on my part for the literature of public address and for the literature of fiction and poetry as well, and thus I have been constrained to present rhetoric in its most carefully defined literary context. I could not bring myself to limit rhetoric to style and delivery, or to delivery alone, as Ramus and Sheridan had respectively done. Nor, despite Kenneth Burke's beguiling invitation, could I bring myself to think of rhetoric as if it were prepared on its own to unlock the mysteries of drama and fiction no less than those of oratory and public address. Such limitations would have required me either to emphasize the verbal and oral externals of discourse at the expense of substance and form, or to blind myself to distinctions between the making of persuasive statements and the devising of truly effective fictions. I did not want to impose these limitations upon myself. After all, the authors whom I most admired had not imposed these limitations upon themselves, and my commitment to those authors had involved me in a commitment to all the procedures which they had followed in doing their best work.

In closing, I do not wish to leave the impression that the European rhetorical tradition which Kenneth Burke, Thomas Sheridan, and Peter Ramus altered in their several ways was perfect as it originally stood. To my mind it was not perfect. But acceptable ways of reforming it are well beyond the scope of my present topic. Whatever rhetoric may turn out to be when it has finally adopted an acceptable modern stance, my hope is that it will still preserve the concern of Aristotle and Plato for truth-telling as a major ingredient of persuasive public discourse and that it will continue to recognize the Aristotelian distinction between rhetoric as the theory of the persuasive public statement and poetics as the theory of the kind of fiction which aims above all to present to humanity an enlightening and eloquent image of human life.

Princeton University

NOTES

[1]Mitford M. Mathews, ed., *A Dictionary of Americanisms on Historical Principles* (Chicago, Ill.: University of Chicago Press, 1951), s.v. maverick.

[2]For an analysis of Peter Ramus's dialectical and rhetorical theories, see my *Logic and Rhetoric in England, 1500-1700* (Princeton, N.J.: Princeton University Press, 1956), pp. 146-281.

[3]Thomas Sheridan's theory of rhetoric is examined and explained at some length in my *Eighteenth-Century British Logic and Rhetoric* (Princeton, N.J.: Princeton University Press, 1971), pp. 214-43.

[4]My criticisms of Kenneth Burke's rhetorical doctrines are set forth in my *Poetics, Rhetoric, and Logic: Studies in the Basic Disciplines of Criticism* (Ithaca and London: Cornell University Press, 1975), pp. 36-52, 234-55. See also the exchange between Burke and myself on the subject of rhetoric and poetics in his "The Party Line" and my "The Two-Party Line: A Reply to Kenneth Burke" in *The Quarterly Journal of Speech*, 62 (1976), 62-77.

[5]*Topica*, 101^{b}3. Translation by W. A. Pickard-Cambridge in *The Works of Aristotle Translated into English under the Editorship of W. D. Ross* (Oxford: Clarendon Press, 1908-52), Vol. I.

[6]Ibid., 101^{a}34-36.

[7]*De Interpretatione*, 18^{b}1-3. Translations by E. M. Edghill in Vol. I of the Ross edition of *The Works of Aristotle.*

[8]*Topica*, 101^{b}11-39.

[9]Chs. 1-10 of Book VIII of the *Topica* deal directly with arrangement.

[10]*Rhetorica*, 1354^{a}1. Translation by W. Rhys Roberts in Vol. XI of the Ross edition of *The Works of Aristotle.*

[11]Ibid., 1355^{b}25-26.

[12]For Aristotle's preliminary analysis of these appeals, which he

calls "the modes of persuasion," see *Rhetorica*, 1356[a]1-35. Later on he devotes considerable space to each one of them.

[13]*Rhetorica*, 1357[a]11-12. Just before making this statement, Aristotle had said, 1357[a]1-4: "The duty of rhetoric is to deal with such matters as we deliberate upon without arts or systems to guide us, in the hearing of persons who cannot take in at a glance a complicated argument, or follow a long chain of reasoning."

[14]For Aristotle's discussion of emotions, see Bk. II, Chs. 1-11; of moral character, Bk. II, Chs. 1, 12-17, *passim*.

[15]For Plato's views on this matter, note especially *Phaedrus*, pp. 246-48, 250, 273-74, 277. See Lane Cooper, *Plato: Phaedrus, Ion, Gorgias, and Symposium, with passages from The Republic and Laws Translated into English* (London, New York, Toronto : Oxford University Press, 1938), pp. 29-31, 33-34, 62-69, 68.

[16]*Rhetorica*, 1355[a]21-24.

[17]Ibid., 1355[a]28-34.

[18]Ibid., 1355[a]36-40.

[19]Ibid., 1414[a]30-35.

[20]For Aristotle's discussion of delivery and style in the *Rhetorica*, see Bk. III, Chs. 1-12.

[21]See *Rhetorica*, Bk. I, Chs. 3-15.

[22]See *Rhetorica*, Bk. III, Ch. 16.

[23]The true field of the work traditionally called Aristotle's *De Poetica* is brilliantly identified for the modern reader by L. J. Potts in the title of his epoch-making book, *Aristotle on the Art of Fiction: An English Translation of Aristotle's Poetics with an Introductory Essay and Explanatory Notes* (Cambridge, [Eng.]: University Press, 1953).

[24]*De Poetica*, 1449[b]23-28. Translation by Ingram Bywater in Vol. XI of the Ross edition of *The Works of Aristotle*.

[25]Ibid., 1447[a]13-16. At this point, Aristotle says: "Epic poetry and Tragedy, as also Comedy, [and] Dithyrambic poetry . . . are all . . . modes of imitation."

[26]Ibid., 1451[a]36-38.

[27]Ibid., 1451[a]38-1451[b]1-5.

[28]Ramus is reputed to have taken his M.A. degree by defending the thesis, *Quaecumque ab Aristotele dicta essent, commentitia esse*; and the thesis itself, according to earlier scholars, meant that everything accepted from Aristotle was falsehood. In actual fact, however, that thesis, if Ramus ever really defended it, is not to be construed as a

sweeping denunciation of Aristotelianism, but as a much milder reproach, perhaps meaning in effect that Aristotle's teachings were unrealistic and impractical. At any rate, Ramus's reforms of Aristotelian dialectic and rhetoric were directed neither to contradicting Aristotle nor to proving his doctrine false, but to rearranging it and to making it simpler and more practical for college students. For an enlightening discussion of the history and meaning of Ramus's thesis and of the uses assigned to it by earlier and by modern scholars, see Walter J. Ong, *Ramus, Method, and the Decay of Dialogue* (Cambrige, Massachusetts: Harvard University Press, 1958), 36-47. Cited as *Ramus Method*.

[29]See my *Logic and Rhetoric in England, 1500-1700*, p. 156.

[30]See the work just cited, pp. 154-55, for Ramus's own words in rejecting the idea of two logics, one for science and one for opinion.

[31]Ibid., pp. 158-64.

[32]Ibid., pp. 160-64.

[33]Ibid., pp. 165-72.

[34]In line with his belief that the principles of dialectic and rhetoric were as applicable to poetry as philosophical argument, oratory, and history, Ramus found the structure of Virgil's *Gorgics* to be an example of the method of science and the tropes and figures of rhetorical style to be features as much of poetry as of oratory. See *Logic and Rhetoric in England, 1500-1700*, pp. 163, 169; also 222, 226-27.

[35]Ramus's conception of poetry is made a specific subject of comment by Ong, *Ramus Method*, pp. 281-83.

[36]For an extended analysis of Sheridan's rhetorical theories and of the whole movement of which he was a part, see the work cited above, note 3. See also Wallace A. Bacon, "The Elocutionary Career of Thomas Sheridan (1719-88)," *Speech Monographs*, 31 (1964) 1-53.

[37]See my *Eighteenth-Century British Logic and Rhetoric*, pp. 216-21, 227-39.

[38]Ibid., pp. 222, 235. Sheridan's *British Education* was published at London in 1756 and given a second edition in the same place in 1769. His *A Course of Lectures on Elocution* came out at London in 1762.

[39]See Cicero, *De Inventione*, 1. 7. 9; Quintilian, *Insitutio Oratoria*, 3. 3. 1; 11. 3. 1.

[40]See *Eighteenth-Century British Logic and Rhetoric*, pp. 147-51, *passim*.

[41]Ibid., p. 714. See also George L. Raymond, *The Orator's Manual*, 9th ed. (New York, Boston, Chicago, 1879), p. 15.

[42]See Kenneth Burke, *The Philosophy of Literary Form*, 2nd ed.

(Baton Rouge: Louisiana State University Press, 1967), pp. 138-67.

[43]Kenneth Burke, *Counter-Statement* (New York: Harcourt, Brace and Company, 1931), p. 265.

[44]Ibid., p. 265.

[45]For a discussion of the origins of Burke's definition of rhetoric in *Counter-Statement*, see the works cited above, note 4.

[46]*Counter-Statement*, p. 156.

[47]Ibid., pp. 156-232.

KENNETH BURKE

MOTION, ACTION, AND THE HUMAN CONDITION

This is the basic polarity (like the traditional pair *res* and *verba*, things and the words for things).

It's at the root of such distinctions as mind-body, spirit-matter, superstructure-substructure, and Descartes' dualism, thought and extension.

I say "at the root of such distinctions" though no such terms quite match the motion-action pair.

Thus we can begin by logically secularizing the theological (Thomistic) view of "matter" as the "principle of individuation."

The human body, in its nature as a sheerly physiological organism, would thus be in the realm of matter, for which our term is "motion."

In that respect it would be like a fish or a tree or one of B. F. Skinner's operationally conditioned pigeons.

But the use of such resources as a tribal language would be in the realm of "action."

Action, as so defined, would involve modes of behavior made possible by the acquiring of a conventional, arbitrary symbol system, a definition that would apply to modes of symbolicity as different as primitive speech, styles of music, painting, sculpture, dance, highly developed mathematical nomenclatures, traffic signals, road maps, or mere dreams (insofar as a dream is interpretable as "symbolic" of the dreamer's "psyche," or whatever such term a psychologist might perfer to work with).

Thus this present use of language is an example of symbolic action, in which we variously participate by means of a "conventional, arbitrary symbol system"—this particular brand of English.

Since the overall topic of the conference at which the substance of this talk was orginally given was "Self and Culture," I take it that "Self" is meant to designate in some sense what has here been referred to as the "principle of individuation."

I take it that, even if the "Self" were thought to merge into the "Culture" as a whole, each member of the "Culture" would be thought of as having in some way a "Self" different from each and every other member.

It would be grounded in the realm of nonsymbolic motion and would mature into what one would call a "person" in the realm of symbolic action.

So far as is known at present, the only typically symbol-using animal existing on earth is the human organism.

The intuitive signaling systems in such social creatures as bees and ants would not be classed as examples of symbolic action.

They are not conventional, arbitrary symbol systems such as human speech, which is not inborn but has to be learned, depending upon where the child happens to be "thrown," an accident of birth that determines whether the child learns Chinese, or French, or whatever idiom may prevail in the given locality.

Symbol systems of that sort also differ from intuitive signaling systems in that they have a second-level (or "reflexive") aspect.

That is to say: they can talk about themselves.

Cicero could both orate and write a treatise on oratory. A dog can bark but he can't bark a tract on barking.

If all typically symbol-using animals (that is, humans) were suddenly obliterated, their realm of symbolic action would be correspondingly obliterated.

The earth would be but a realm of planetary, geologic, meteorological motion, including the motions of whatever nonhuman biologic organisms happened to survive.

The realm of nonsymbolic motion needs no realm of symbolic action; but there could be no symbolic action unless grounded in the realm of motion, the realm of motion having preceded the emergence of our symbol-using ancestors; and doubtless the time will come when motions go on after all our breed will have vanished.

With regard to the theory of evolution, obviously critical conditions for the emergence of culture arose at that stage in the prehistoric past when our anthropoid ancestors underwent a momentous mutation.

In their bodies (as physiological organisms in the realm of motion) there developed the ability to learn the kind of tribal idiom that is here meant by "symbolic action."

And thereby emerged what we might call a "mechanism" for the steps from nonsymbolic motion to symbolic action.

Descartes, in his speculations on a possible bridge between his polar realms of "thought" and "extension," proposed the possibility that a small gland in the brain, the pineal gland, might provide the medium.

But with regard to the materials for an intermediate step between the realms of "motion" and "action" we need not look for so recondite a locus.

The necessary materials are implicit in the physiological nature of sensation.

In his early essay on "Nature," Emerson described the process transcendentally, tender-mindedly thus:

> Words are signs of natural facts. The use of natural history is to give us aid in supernatural history; the use of the outer creation, to give us language for the beings and changes of the inward creation. Every word which is used to express a moral or intellectual fact, if traced

to its root, is found to be borrowed from some material appearance. *Right* means *straight*; *wrong* means *twisted*; *Spirit* primarily means *wind*; *transgression* the crossing of a *line*; *supercilious*, the *raising of the eyebrow*. We say the *heart* to express emotion, the *head* to denote thought; and *thought* and *emotion* are words borrowed from sensible things, and now appropriated to spiritual nature.

Jeremy Bentham would deal with considerations of this sort, perhaps not tough-mindedly but at least matter-of-factly thus:

All our psychological ideas are derived from physical ones—all mental from corporeal ones. In no other manner can they be spoken of . . . . In the case where to the object thus spoken of, existence is actually an object of one of the five senses, and in particular of the sense of touch or feeling. . . here there is no fiction—as this man, this beast, this bird. . . . The object spoken of may be a real entity.

On the other hand in the case in which the object is not a tangible one, the object, the existence of which is thus asserted, not being a real existing one, the object, if it must be termed, an entity—as on pain of universal and perpetual non-intercourse between man and man, it must be—it may, for distinction's sake, be termed a fictitious entity.

To every word that has an immaterial import there belongs, or at least did belong, a material one. In a word, our ideas coming, all of them, from our senses, . . . from what other source can our language come?

Thus, if we say that a given object leans at an *inclination* of thirty degrees, in Bentham's sense we should not be applying a fiction. But a fictitious expression enters when we say that a person has an "inclination" to do such-and-such.

Or a "corporeal" reference, such as "this object is so many feet *distant* from that object" would differ from a "fictitious" reference to the "great *distance*" between A's position and B's.

And "corporeal" ideas such as "hot" or "cold" as terms for physical sensations become "fictitiously" extended in words like "hothead" and "cold-blooded" as terms for personal traits.

Bentham's position was quite in line with the scholastic formula, "There is nothing in the intellect that was not previously in the senses (*nihil in intellectu quod non prius in sensu*)."

To which Leibniz had added, "except the intellect itself (*nisi intellectus ipse*)."

Thereupon, logologically shortcutting metaphysical issues, considering the matter purely from the standpoint of nomenclature (symbolic action), we could equate *intellectus ipse* with the elements of grammar and syntax that are intrinsic to any given language and are not directly reducible to the issue stressed in the quotes from Bentham and Emerson.

Though the mutation that makes speech possible is itself inherited in our nature as physical bodies (in the realm of motion), the formation of a nomenclature referring to sensory experiences is on the side of symbolic action.

All such developments constitute a medium that provides motives intrinsic to itself.

With the wider use of physicalist terms as necessary "fictions" for reference to supposed nonphysical entities or processes, the realm of specifically symbolic action is strongly involved, and is completed with the formally stylistic use of metaphor, or equivocation generally.

The nature of language is such that it could not possibly be confined to strictly literal, univocal usage.

If words did not admit of loose application, you couldn't apply the same terms to a variety of objects, processes, circumstances.

For in its details, every situation is unique.

In his book entitled *Poetic Diction: A Study in Meanings* (London, 1928), Owen Barfield would want to deny that the step from terms for sensation to their use in referring to nonsensory "entities" is metaphorical.

He would hold that the material objects (to which such terms had literally referred) themselves contain such a range of what Emerson would call "supernatural" connotations.

To meet the minimum conditions of what is meant

here by "symbolic action" all that is necessary is the inability of words to "stay put," as when even a proper name like "Caesar," referring to one particular person in history, gives birth to such words as "Kaiser" and "Czar."

The purely physiological aspect of the Self (its grounding in the realm of motion) is characterized by the centrality of the nervous system.

Its sensations are immediately its own, not thus felt by any other organism.

Like organisms presumably have similar pleasures and pains, but these are *immediately* experienced only within the centrality of each one particular organism's nervous system, as individuated at parturition.

The Self as a "person," member of a community (Culture) characterized by motives in the realm of symbolic action, is not thus differentiated.

In this respect the Self becomes a product of the Culture.

Whatever may be the genetic traits differentiating one individual from another, and whatever the distinct histories of individuals, the nature of symbolic action shapes the Self largely in modes of roles, of sociality.

Here figure the individual's relations to family, to groups, to ever widening and partially conflicting organizations such as church, business, political party, nation, "global" tentatives.

Here, in contrast with the *immediacies* of the body, we confront for our overall "reality" an indeterminately interwoven complexity of symbols, reports about local, national, and international affairs, about history, psychology, geology, astronomy, expectations true or false, promissory or forbidding, and so forth.

Though "reality," (the "world") as thus symbolically conceived, embraces a potential "universe of discourse" far beyond the realm of physiological sensation, the opportunities for such exercising (via resources in the realm of "symbolic action") depend wholly on the realm of physiological motion (the basic conditions that determine whether the individual organism lives or dies).

In sum, when to the principle of individuation (involving the underlying physiology of sheer motion) there is added an organism's ability to parallel the realm of sensations by learning to use *words* for them, the concept of Self must necessarily be defined in terms of a *polarity*.

In terms of nonsymbolic motion, the Self is a physiological organism, separated from all others of its kind at the moment of parturition.

In terms of symbolic action, it becomes a "person" by learning the language of its tribe, with corresponding identity and roles (beginning with the equivalent of a proper name and expanding variously in keeping with the currently available resources of symbolism and the institutional structures reciprocally made possible by them), the three corresponding Dramatistic axioms being:

There can be motion without action (as the sea can go on thrashing about whether or not there are animals that have a word for it).

There can be no action without motion (as we animals could not have words for anything except for the motions of our nervous systems and the vibrations that carry our words from one of us to another through the air or that make words visible on the page).

But (and this is the primary axiom that differentiates Dramatism from Behaviorism) symbolic action is *not* reducible to terms of sheer motion. (Symbolicity involves not just a difference of *degree*, but a motivational difference in *kind*.)

Yet this difference in kind amounts to a primary **DUPLICATION**.

This is due to the fact that the nomenclature of symbolic placement is borrowed from the materials of sensory motion.

And the terms are of such a nature that they are "fictions" or analogical extensions of their beginning in reference to physical processes and objects.

A Culture's symbolically conceived "world," or "universe of discourse," is thus built figuratively of terms originally grounded in reference to the nonsymbolic realm of motion.

Otherwise put: the realm of what is usually called "ideas" is constructed of symbolic material usually called sensory "images."

The Self, like its corresponding Culture, thus has two sources of reference for its symbolic identity: its nature as a physiological organism, and its nature as a symbol-using animal responsive to the potentialities of symbolicity that have a nature of their own not reducible to a sheerly physiological dimension.

Symbolicity itself being of a nature that can rise to higher levels of generalization until all is headed in some all-inclusive title, we can readily understand why psychologists like Jung are moved to talk of an overall oneness, an *Unus Mundus*.

Yet in the light of the critical Dramatistic distinction between the motives of a psychological organism as such and the motives of such a Self as *personalized* by participation in its particular Culture's modes of literal (univocal), equivocal, and analogical symbol-using, we can at least glimpse why Jung could be exercised by such a symbolically engendered "idea" or "ideal" of Ultimate Unity.

And by the same token we should see why the motion-action "polarity" is unabridgeable in the sense that, although, in every tribal idiom however rudimentary, there is a wholly reliable basic correspondence between a thing and its name; never the twain shall meet.

That might seem quite obvious, as regards the kind of "polarity" that prevails with the correspondence between a tree and the *word* tree.

But look how far afield from such obviousness you get when the distinction shifts from the realm of sheer motion (as with the physicality of a tree) to the corresponding word (which is in the realm of symbolic action) and you confront what Dramatism would view as inaccurate equivalents, such as "matter" and "spirit," "matter" and "mind," or even "brain" and "mind."

There could be no total unity between the realms except along the lines of orthodox religion's promise to the faithful that their bodies will be restored to them in heaven.

An unchartable complexity of behavings among the cells of the body may add up, for instance, to an overall "unitary" sense of well-being; but no sheer term for an ideal unity (such as Jung's expression, *Unus Mundus*) can match that purely physiological kind of "attitude."

Keats, dying, modified a passage in Shakespeare to state it thus: "Banish money—Banish sofas—Banish Wine—Banish Music; but right Jack Health, honest Jack Health, true Jack Health—Banish Health and banish all the world."

Though any attitude, even in purely theoretic matters, has a summarizing, unifying aspect, it must prevail only insofar as in some way it is grounded in purely physiological behavior (as per William James' charming and often quoted statement that we're sad because we cry).

In his chapter on "Attitudes" (*The Principles of Literary Criticism* [London, 1924]), I. A. Richards was presumably speculating on a behavioristic parallelism of this sort when he wrote:

> Every perception probably includes a response in the form of incipient action. We constantly overlook the extent to which all the while we are making preliminary adjustments, getting ready to act in one way or another. Reading Captain Slocum's account of the centipede which bit him on the head when alone in the middle of the Atlantic, the writer has been caused to leap right out of his chair by a leaf which fell upon his face from a tree.

Whatever the implications of an ATTITUDE, as a kind of incipient or future action, it must be by some means grounded in the set of the body now; and thus, though an *attitude* of kindness may be but the *preparation* for the doing of a kind *act* (a subsequent mode of behavior), it is already "behaving" physiologically in ways of its own (as a dog's implicit way of "conjugating the verb 'to eat' " is to begin by salivating, a bodily motion that in effect implies the future tense, "I will eat"; the present tense of the verb being bodily conjugated by eating; and "I have eaten" is also in its way a *now*, as the dog curls up for a comfortable, satisfied snooze).

But whatever the correspondence between purely symbolic attitudinizing and the kind of immediacy that poor Keats, with his dying body, confronted, his very efforts to endow his poetic attitudes with sensuous immediacy made him all the more cruelly aware of the respects in which the poet's modes of symbolic action were comparatively (to use his own word for his own poetry) "abstract."

His "Ode on a Grecian Urn" *symbolically* enacts the "transcending" of the body.

But that letter he wrote to Fanny Brawne while nearing death was concerned with a situation in which the sheer non-symbolic realm of motion (the plight of his diseased body) was taking over; for such in essence is the unbridgeable "polarity" between the social realm of "symbolic action" and motion's "principle of individuation" whereby the symptons of *his* disease were the *immediate* sensations of *himself* and none other.

All told, in our Selves sheerly as physiological organisms, our world is made of what Santayana would describe as but a single line drawn through an infinity of possible "essences."

But all of them are experienced *immediately*, as yours and no one else's, though you doubtless rightly assume that others of your kind experience similar immediate sensations.

Beyond that, in polar distinction, is the vast symbolic realm of tribal sociality, or orientation, as shaped by the influences that you encounter by reason of your being a symbol-using animal, whose "reality," at every stage, is determined by such terms.

In Santayana's *Realms of Being*, his *Realm of Matter* would correspond to what is here called the realm of nonsymbolic MOTION (for which his word is sometimes "flux," sometimes "action," though I must here employ a different usage).

His passionate *Realm of Spirit-* would be much what I mean by "symbolic action."

And his *Realm of Essence* would deal with "sensation" as the bridge between the realms of "matter" and "spirit," though his term "intuitions" here would ambivalently include both bodily sensations (such as color) and purely symbolic fictions (such as the character of Hamlet).

The Self as a "person," beyond the individual's identity as a strictly physiological organism, confronts with varying degree of comprehensiveness and profoundness the interrelationships among the manifold details of "reality" (whatever that "orientation" might be) as known and interpreted in terms of the symbolic lore current in the Culture of that time.

Necessarily, any individual's formal or informal version of such lore is selective, in keeping with the limitations and engrossments besetting that individual (as both person and physiological organism).

The interrelationships among such a conglomerate will be related consistently (this *therefore* that), antithetically (this *however* that), adventitiously (this *and* that).

When such an aggregate is felt to fall together "holistically," the gratification of such a purely symbolic symmetry can rise to an ecstacy of conviction that we call "mystical."

The fall from such a state (whereby the fullness, *pleroma*, of purely symbolic exercising gives way to a sense of its underlying emptiness as tested by a similarly structured physiological counterpart) is called "accidie," *acedia*, sloth, torpor, drought.

Or the sense of such a confluence among motives can also have the Allness of pandemonium, a Pandora's box let loose, a Walpurgis Night, a jangling conflict of all the pieces with one another, the very fullness of being felt as a drought.

In the state of contemporary Culture, I take it, the corresponding Self is likely to manifest "in principle" fragmentary aspects of all three such symbolically engendered "fulfillments."

The fragmentary delight is in putting anything together. The drought is usually met by purchasing some form of entertainment.

The variant of pandemoniac entanglement can even be attenuatively transformed into a bit of research on the problem itself.

Hart Crane is a notably pathetic example of a poet whose mode of mysticism terminated in a corresponding drought.

While he was writing portions of *The Bridge*, there were times when everything seemed to fall estatically into place, its many disjunctions inspirited by one transcendent principle of unity.

But the very strength of his hopes for the work as a wholly *organic* solution for his problems as a *personal Self* set the conditions for the drought that was necessarily implicit in his reliance upon symbolicity alone.

There may be drought, not as a comedown from the mystic exaltation of "holistic" symbolizing, but as a kind of sloth implicit in the sheer failure to take delight in the wonders of purely symbolistic enterprise.

For such a condition there are direct (nonsymbolic) resources available to the Self—and they are widely resorted to.

I refer to the many drugs that act directly upon the Self as a physiological organism (in the realm of motion), though there are attendant difficulties due to the fact that each such physical means of gratifying the organism also happens to tax the health of that organism; and even if it didn't, there is the problem that the very directness and efficiency of its appeal to the body robs the individual Self of the human gratifications resulting from engrossment with the manifold manifestations of purely symbolistic enterprise.

But surely, above all, in confronting the tangle of "global" problems that beset the current state of affairs, we should pay an appreciative tribute to the remarkable symbolic resources whereby "pandemonium" can become "attenuatively transformed."

All about us there are our various Selves, each to varying degrees tracking down the implications of his particular nomenclature.

For I take it that, just as each good poet speaks an idiom of his own, so it is with each symbol-using animal—and there is a kind of reciprocating relationship whereby the Self selects its key words, and they in turn become formative, to shape further developments of the Self, along with countless such uncharitable interactions, including reactions back upon the behavior of the Self's sheer physiology.

The reference to physiology enters here in connection with the concept of "psychogenic illness," which refers to a reverse relationship whereby, just as drugs can produce physical effects recorded as a corresponding "attitude" or "state of mind," so such attitudes or states of mind can function suggestively to induce corresponding physiological behavior (in the sense that, if you received some information you believed in, and the information was highly disturbing, it would affect your bodily behavior, your blood pressure, respiration, heartbeat and the like quite as though the situation were actually so, though the information happened to be in error).

In this sense there is the "polar" relationship whereby an individual's mode of symbolic action (his investment in a particular kind of literary style, for instance) might attain an organic replica in a kind of physical behavior that happened to be a kind of disease.

In cases of that sort there could be a mutually reinforcing relationship (a "feedback"?) between the author's symbolic prowess and corresponding processes of his body whereby the development of his skill at his particular mode of symbolic action would be making him sick and keeping him sick, as his symbolic exercising was reinforced by the effects of his physiological "misbehavior."

Our attitudes toward past or future (remembrances or expectations) are products of our symbolicity.

But their behavioral counterparts in the realm of physiological motion must be in the immediate present.

For the only way a body can possibly behave is from one present moment to the next.

In the realm of symbolicity, there are two totally different notions of sequence: the temporally prior (yesterday/today/tomorrow) and the logically (nontemporally) prior (as with the syllogism, first premise/second premise/conclusion).

Myth, being narrative, features the modes of temporal priority (as discussed in the section on "The First Three Chapters of Genesis" in my *Rhetoric of Religion* [Boston, 1961; reprinted Berkeley, 1970]).

The same work deals "logologically" with respects in which even *temporal* terms can be treated as in nontemporal relationships to one another (as per my "Cycle of Terms Implicit in the Idea of 'Order' ").

The strategic intermediate term here is IMPLICATIONS.

Thus the term "order" and "disorder" are nontemporally related in the sense that, being "polar," each implies the other, regardless of whether we go *from* the idea of "order" *to* the idea of "disorder," or vice versa.

But narrative (myth) can set up a temporal sequence whereby the story goes *irreversibly* "from" one "to" the other.

Insofar as IMPLICATIONS all fall harmoniously into place, any given exercise in symbolic action approaches the feel of mystic unity.

Insofar as they add up to a jangle (and though "polar" terms such as "order" and "disorder" imply each other without strife, they imply much conflict when reduced to terms of irreversible story), the IMPLICATIONS are under the sign of pandemonium.

Insofar as, of a sudden, all such symbolic enterprise seems vacuous in comparison with the immediacies of physiological sensation (in the realm of motion), we are on the slope of sloth, of drought, for which the alternative "remedies" are either physical "dissipation" (as with direct recourse to drugs) or further study (as thus fittingly when on the subject of sloth, Dante sums up for us the entire rationale of the *Purgatorio*, in this very canto where we are assured that, though rational [*d'animo*] love may err, "the natural" [*lo natural*] is always [*senza errore*].

Gershom Scholem's engrossing studies of the Kabbalists enable us to glimpse a further marvel with regard to the vibrancy of IMPLICATIONS among terms.

We see hermeneutic ways whereby, though the teacher would not so much as modify a single letter of the Torah, while honoring the text as the very signature of JHVH Himself, and considering the Law so basic to Creation that it was propounded *before* Creation (*there's* a "priority" for you), the disciple was taught modes of transformation that enabled him to see all such literalnesses double, in terms of esoteric IMPLICATIONS.

And thus some of us *goyim* can glimpse how St. Paul was doing exactly that, long before the Kabbalists, when scrupulously leaving the O. T. letter of the Law intact, he but introduced N. T. interpretations (as with the shift from a strictly *physiological* behavior of circumcision, which obviously had its symbolic aspects, he improvised a new symbolism, "circumcision of the heart").

Much of our engrossment with all such interpretations and reinterpretations (as exemplified, for instance, in the various schools of psychoanalysis) stems from the vibrancy of interrelated IMPLICATIONS that thus suggest themselves for the spinning.

And "case histories" are, as it were, the translation of such logically, doctrinally interrelated terms into the corresponding parables of narrative (the "mythic" parallel).

Thus the catalogues, or "inventories," of Whitman's poetry are unfoldings of terms that IMPLY one another, their associative interrelationship being revealed in a succession of tiny plots.

Since the principle of DUPLICATION begins in the polarity of our dual nature as symbol-using animals, the split across the two realms of nonsymbolic motion and symbolic action will necessarily manifest itself in endless variations on the theme of DUPLICATION.

For it is the combination of bodily sensation with symbolic counterparts and corresponding analogical extensions that "keeps body and soul together" until the last time.

And neither realm can be complete without the other, nor can they be identical.

Thus ultimately, when properly discounted along "logological" lines (whereby his "archetypes" are seen as *quasi-temporal* terms for terms *logically prior*), Plato's version of IMITATION, as a species of DUPLICATION, will be seen to go much deeper than Aristotle's.

Aristotle's is good common sense, inasmuch as there is a notable difference between real victimage (as with a Roman gladiatorial contest) and the mere IMITATION of suffering (as with the *pathos* of a Greek tragedy).

But Plato was digging into the IMPLICATIONS that once we turn from the realm of motion to the realm of symbolicity and try to envision everything in terms of that ideal symbolic universe, then all actual things in nature become in effect but *partial* exemplars of what they are *in essence*, as no single object can fit the exact description of the countless other and different objects classifiable under that same head.

Possibly the motion-action distinction, as conceptualized in this statement, implies that the line of demarcation between "conscious" and "unconscious" should be moved farther to the side of sheer motion.

That is, dreams would not be on the side of the "unconscious" insofar as dreams, like the most mature works of science, philosophy, literature, or the arts generally, admit of analysis as modes of symbolicity.

The "unconscious" would be relegated to such processes as digestion, metabolism, the healing of a wound, even if we study the physiology of such behavior.

DUPLICATION is so basic to the relation between motion and symbolicity, nothing of moment seems quite complete unless we have rounded things out by translating it into symbols of some sort, either scientific or aesthetic, practical or ritualistic.

Sex is not complete without love lyrics, porn, and tracts on sexology.

The nonsymbolic motions of springtime are completed in the symbolic action of a spring song.

But let's stop there, since further comments on that aspect of Duplication could readily lead into many comments along sociological and anthropological lines, in connection with what happens when the "mythman," adept at fitting ritualistic symbols to the season, can get things turned backwards (as indicated in the story of the missionary who wore a raincoat when it rained, hence, during a drought, was asked by the tribesmen to put on his raincoat, for the obvious reason that raincoat and rain went together). The Implications of DUPLICATION include a vast lore of ways in which the doublings get turned backwards, often with puzzling shifts in views on the nature of causality. I shall, however, add two items in an Appendix. The first will deal with an article by William Willeford, "Jung's Polaristic Thought in its Historical Setting." Comments on it help sum up the burden of this message. The second applies the termistic linkup to some poetic texts.

Recall the incident that I. A. Richards related in his Chapter on "Attitudes" (see above). He took his response to indicate that "Every perception probably includes a response in the form of incipient action."

This would imply a strongly behavioristic ingredient in the correlation between bodily motion and symbolic action. Yet I would take it also to imply a dualistic view that would be directly counter to Behaviorist reductionism—a psychology that is essentially monistic, in treating the distinction between verbal behavior and nonverbal behavior as but a difference in degree, not in kind.

Though there can be no action that is not grounded in the realm of motion, the realm of action cannot be reduced to the realm of motion—thus the duplication we have been considering is unbridgeably dualistic.

Andover, N.J.

PART FOUR

From Intention to Invention

As rhetorical investigations reveal, rhetoric has in recent years become a plastic discipline. Borrowing from such fields as psychology and neuropsychology, biology and anthropology, and philosophy, rhetoric has also drawn extensively from linquistics. Pragmatics, the study of speech acts in particular, has exerted an influence upon rhetorical studies. It explores the way in which sentences mean by focusing upon the importance of the context of the utterance. In "Speech Acts and Rhetoric," Martin Steinmann, Jr., whose New Rhetorics (1967) documented the revival of rhetoric, describes the nature and function of speech act theory. He treats speech act theory as a heuristic for discussing language as process or transaction, not as artifact. Frank J. D'Angelo in A Conceptual Theory of Rhetoric (1975) proposed a schema for discourse based upon linguistic and rhetorical priniciples. In "Up Against the Wall, Mother: The Rhetoric of Slogans, Catchphrases, and Graffiti," he illustrates aspects of that schema in the stylistic techniques and perlocutionary effects of these one-sentence messages. Richard L. Larson, in "The Rhetoric of the Written Voice," explains transactions that occur between the reader and writer. Using non-fiction prose passages, he describes transactions which happen when the language of a text affects the reader as he is discovering the ethos of the written voice and its intention. Just as linguistic theory has supplied tools for describing the transaction between writer/speaker and reader, it has also provided a basis for creating a heuristic for invention. Coupling tagmemics and physics, Richard E. Young, along with Alton L. Becker and Kenneth L. Pike in Rhetoric: Discovery and Change (1970), develops a nine-cell heuristic to generate ideas with the accuracy and precision of a mathematical formula. In "Methodizing Nature: The Tagmemic Discovery Procedure," Young demonstrates step-by-step this heuristic, not in theory, but in action.

MARTIN STEINMANN, JR.

SPEECH ACTS AND RHETORIC

Rhetoric is a notoriously amorphous or plastic discipline: perhaps the best answer to the question "What is rhetoric?" is "What isn't?" Though speech-act theory is not in itself a rhetorical theory of any kind, it can unify and define some of the traditional concerns of rhetoric—notably, those relating to effective expression and to figures of speech. What is speech-act theory, and how can it do this?

This theory—sketched by the late J. L. Austin in his William James lectures at Harvard in 1955 and elaborated by (among others) John R. Searle—postulates four kinds of speech acts:

Locutionary Acts

To perform a locutionary (or utterance) act is simply to utter, in speech or in writing, a sentence of some language—to utter S_1 or S_2, for example:

S_1: My uncle loves the blonde next door.

S_2: Does my uncle love the blonde next door?

Locutionary acts are governed by the grammatical (the phonological, the syntactic, and the semantic) rules of the language used. These rules specify, among other things, the meaning *potentials* of sentences—that is, their potentials for use in the performance of propositional acts and illocutionary acts.

Propositional Acts

To perform a propositional act is to perform a locutionary act so as to *realize* part of its meaning potential: namely, its potential for expressing a proposition—that is, its potential for *referring* to one or more things (my uncle and the blonde next door, say) and for *predicating* a property or a relation (the lover loved-one relation).

The key phrase here—it distinguishes a propositional act from a mere locutionary act—is so *as to realize its potential for referring and predicating.* In both S_1 and S_2, the referring phrases *My uncle* and *the blonde next door* give the sentence a potential for use in referring to two things, and the predicating phrase *loves* or *does love* gives it a potential for use in predicating a relation of them. But these referring and predicating potentials can be realized only under conditions specified by the rules governing propositional acts.

There is, for instance, a propositional-act rule that a referring phrase cannot realize its potential unless the thing it names or describes exists. If I have no uncle or if there is no blonde next door, I can perform the locutionary act of uttering S_1 or S_2, but I cannot perform the propositional act of uttering it to refer and to predicate. No referring is possible without something to refer to, and no predicating is possible without referring.

Illocutionary Acts

To perform an illocutionary act is to perform a locutionary act and a propositional act so as to *realize* the other part of the meaning potential of the locutionary act: namely, its potential for such a thing as *stating that* or *asking whether* the thing referred to (my uncle and the blonde next door, say) have the relation (the lover loved-one relation) predicated of them.

Again a key phrase—*so as to realize the potential of the locutionary act for such a thing as stating or asking*—is crucial, distinguishing an illocutionary act from both a locutionary act and a propositional act. The syntax of S_1 (subject + verb + direct object) gives it a certain illocutionary-act potential: for *stating that* the proposition expressed (that my uncle loves the blonde next door) is true. The syntax of S_2 (*does* + subject + verb + direct object) gives it a different potential: for *asking whether* that same proposition is true. But neither illocutionary-act potential can be realized except under conditions specified by the rules governing illocutionary acts.

There is, for example, an illocutionary-act rule that a sentence cannot realize its potential for *stating that* unless the speaker or writer (the person who performs the locutionary act) is committed to believing, and to having good reason to believe, *that* the proposition expressed is true. If I am not committed to believing and to having good reason to believe that my uncle loves the blonde next door, I can perform the locutionary act of uttering S_1 and the propositional act of referring to my uncle and the blonde next door and of predicating the lover loved-one relation of them; but I cannot perform the illocutionary act of stating that this proposition is true.

By another illocutionary-act rule, a sentence cannot realize its potential for *asking whether* unless the speaker or writer admits to not knowing, and to wanting to know, *whether* the proposition expressed is true. Even if everyone knows that I know that—or don't give a damn whether—my uncle loves the blonde next door, I can perform the locutionary act of uttering S_2 and the associated propositional act, but I cannot perform the illocutionary act of *asking whether* that proposition is true.

In other words, I may perform a locutionary act without simultaneously performing a propositional act and an illocutionary act as well (for example, as in practicing typewriting, testing a microphone, or teaching grammar), but usually a locutionary act is part of the other two acts.

To perform an act that is simultaneously a locutionary, a propositional, and an illocutionary act—let's call it a *locutionary-propositional-illocutionary act*—a speaker or writer must know grammatical rules, propositional-act rules, and illocutionary-act rules. And to understand such an act—to interpret it correctly, to get its meaning—a listener or reader must know them too: to a great extent, the listener/reader's act is the mirror image of the speaker/writer's. In speech-act theory, the listener/reader's act of understanding or misunderstanding a locutionary-propositional-illocutionary act is called the *illocutionary effect*.

Perlocutionary Acts

To perform a perlocutionary act is, by performing a locutionary-propositional-illocutionary act, to have upon a listener or reader an effect—called the *perlocutionary effect*—in addition to the illocutionary effect.

Unlike a locutionary-propositional-illocutionary act, a perlocutionary act is not rule governed. There are no rules or conventions or agreements among speakers and listeners or among writers and readers that tie a certain perlocutionary effect to a certain locutionary-propositional-illocutionary act. Indeed, a variety of perlocutionary effects, as many as there are listeners or readers, may result from the same locutionary-propositional-illocutionary act.

If, for instance, I perform the locutionary-propositional-illocutionary act of stating that my uncle loves the blonde next door, some listeners or readers may believe me; others disbelieve me. Believing me, some may think better of me for making this statement, others worse; or some may think better of my uncle or of the blonde next door; others, worse. Believing my statement, disbelieving it, thinking better of me, thinking worse, thinking better of my uncle or of the blonde next door, thinking worse—these are all perlocutionary effects, and, of course, different perlocutionary effects. Yet the locutionary-propositional-illocutionary act is the same. As this example suggests, this act is only one of a network of causes of a given perlocutionary effect, and the other causes are part of the listener or reader's nature or nuture.

So much for speech-act theory. How can it unify or define concerns of rhetoric relating to effective expression?

Making a principled distinction between illocutionary effects and perlocutionary effects distinguishes two kinds of effectiveness (call them *illocutionary effectiveness* and *perlocutionary effectiveness*), shows how they are related to one another, and defines two areas of rhetorical research. These two kinds of effectiveness correspond to the two problems of effective expression that all speakers and writers have.

One problem is to communicate a message to listeners or readers: to make a statement to them, for example, or to ask them a question or to make a request of them or to welcome them to a group, In traditional terms, this is the problem of speaking or writing clearly. Some speakers or writers are easier to understand than others. Clear speakers or writers choose and arrange their words so that listeners or readers will easily understand just what the message is. In speech-act terms, this is the problem of illocutionary effectiveness. To understand, or even to misunderstand, a locutionary-propositional-illocutionary act, listeners or readers have to go through a process of applying grammatical, propositional-act, and illocutionary-act rules to that act (that is, to the sentence or sentences uttered and to the circumstances surrounding their utterance). Experiencing an illocutionary effect—understanding or misunderstanding the act—is the end point of the process. The illocutionary effectiveness of the act is measured by the complexity of this process. The less complex the process, the greater the illocutionary effectiveness.

Little is known, except in an intuitive way, about what makes some locutionary-propositional-illocutionary acts more effective illocutionarily—less complex to process—than others. No doubt familiar words are easier to process than long ones; grammatically simple ones, easier than complex ones. Perhaps topic sentences, transitions, certain patterns of paragraph or overall organization, definitions, examples, analogies, and so on make acts easier to process. In any case, advice to speakers or writers to use such devices to achieve coherence or unity is based upon the assumption that they make acts more effective illocutionarily.

The other problem of effective expression that all speakers and writers have is to get listeners or readers—once they have understood or misunderstood the message, once they have experienced the illocutionary effect—to do something: to believe the statement or answer the question or grant the request or feel welcome. In traditional terms, this is the problem of speaking or writing persuasively; in speech-act terms, the problem of perlocutionary effectiveness. To get listeners or readers to do something, to influence them, is generally the purpose of performing a locutionary-propositional-illocutionary act. But though the illocutionary effect is a necessary condition of the desired perlocutionary effect (indeed, of any perlocutionary effect at all), it is obviously not a sufficient condition. Listeners or readers may understand a statement without believing it, a question without answering it, a request without granting it, a welcome without feeling welcome. Perlocutionary effectivenss is measured by the speaker/writer's success in having upon listeners/readers the desired or intended perlocutionary effect.

Even less is known about perlocutionary effectiveness than about illocutionary. And not surprisingly. For virtually any characteristic of listeners or readers may influence perlocutionary effects: their knowledge of the speaker or writer or of the subject; their intelligence, temperament, attitudes, affections, tastes; even the vicissitudes of their digestive tracts. Consider, for example, the traditional advice to speakers and writers to support statements with good reasons for believing them to be true (that is, with reasons for which the statements logically follow). Doubtless some listeners or readers are more likely to believe statements so supported than ones that are not. But with other listeners or readers, fallacious support—argumentation *ad hominem*, equivocation, *post hoc ergo propter hoc*, and the like—may be the royal road to perlocutionary effectiveness.

Let's turn now to the question of how speech-act theory can unify or define concerns of rhetoric relating to figures of speech—that is, to tropes such as metaphor, irony, rhetorical questions, polite requests, metonymy, synecdoche, oxymoron. Again speech-act theory is useful to rhetoric by making a principled distinction: here the distinction between locutionary acts on the one hand (simply uttering sentences) and on the other hand propositional acts and illocutionary acts (uttering sentences to refer and predict and to do such things as stating, asking, requesting, and welcoming). Thus, speech-act theory permits us to distinguish three things:

(1) *Intended meaning*—the meaning the speaker/writer *intends* his performance of a locutionary-propositional-illocutionary act to have; that is, (a) the thing or things to which he intends to refer, (b) the property he intends to predicate of it or the relation he intends to predicate of them, and (c) the illocutionary act he intends to perform.

(2) *Sentence meaning*—the meaning *potential* of the sentence uttered in the performance of the locutionary-propositional-illocutionary act; that is, (a) the referring *potential*, (b) the predicating *potential*, and (c) the illocutionary act *potential* of that sentence.

(3) *Meaning of the locutionary-propositional-illocutionary act*—the meaning potential the performance of the locutionary-propositional-illocutionary act *realizes*; that is, (a) the thing or things to which the speaker/writer *refers*, (b) the property he *predicates* of it or the relation he *predicates* of them, and (c) the illocutionary act he *performs*.

Speaking or writing *literally*, I suggest, occurs when (1), (2), and (3) are identical; and speaking or writing *figuratively* occurs when (1) is identical with (3) but (2) is different from both. In *literal* speech or writing, (2) predicts (3); in *figurative*, it does not. To put this distinction in another way, speaking or writing *literally* consists in saying what you mean by meaning what you say. The sentence you utter means what you intend to mean, and do mean, by uttering it. Speaking or writing *figuratively*, however, consists in saying what you mean by *not* meaning what you say. The sentence you utter does *not* mean what you intend to mean, and do mean, by uttering it.

Let me clarify this distinction by analyzing a few examples of figurative speech or writing.

Consider, first, a *rhetorical question*: "Had not Garfield, Hayes, and Harrison studied law in offices with a dark brown smell?" (Thomas Wolfe, *From Death to Morning*). The sentence Wolfe uttered has three potentials: for (a) referring to Garfield, Hayes, and Harrison and to certain offices, (b) predicating a certain relation of these men and those offices (the relation of *not*-having-studied-law-in), and (c) an illocutionary-act potential for asking whether these men bore that relation to those offices. Of these three potentials, however, Wolfe's locutionary-propositional-illocutionary act *realizes* only the first. It *realizes* a different predicating potential (for predicating the relation of *having*-studied-law-in) and a different illocutionary act potential (for stating that these men bore this relation to those offices). In other words, Wolfe's locutionary-propositional-illocutionary act *realizes* the potentials of a sentence different from the one he uttered: Garfield, Hayes, and Harrison had studied law in offices with a dark brown smell.

Now consider an example of *verbal irony*: ". . . it is not improbable that some scrupulous people might be apt to censure such a practice [viz., eating lads and maidens instead of deer] (although indeed very unjustly) as a little bordering upon cruelty. . . (Jonathan Swift, "A Modest Proposal"). Swift's locutionary-propositional-illocutionary act realizes the illocutionary-act potential of the sentence he uttered, for stating that something is the case. But it realizes the referring potential and the predicating potential of a different sentence: It is certain that all scrupulous people would censure such a practice (and indeed very justly) as extremely cruel. And examples of other figures or tropes can be similarly analyzed:

(1)   *Metonymy*: LEFT LANE MUST TURN LEFT (Traffic sign). The referring potential realized is clearly different from that of the sentence printed on the sign: CARS IN THE LEFT LANE MUST TURN LEFT.

(2)   *Synecdoche*: "A sail! A sail!" (*Othello*). The sentence whose potentials Shakespeare's locutionary-propositional-illocutionary act realizes is different from the one he uttered: "A ship! A

ship!"

(3) *Oxymoron*: "It was a soundless noise. . ." (D. H. Lawrence, "The Rocking-Horse Winner"). The predicating potential that Lawrence's locutionary-propositional-illocutionary act realizes belongs to a sentence different from the one he uttered: "It was a very soft noise."

As this last example suggests, some figurative speaking or writing not only does not realize the meaning potential of the sentence uttered; it could not. This is the case with all tropes such as oxymoron where the sentence uttered is semantically anomalous or self-contradictory. Lawrence's locutionary-propositional-illocutionary act, for instance, does not realize the meaning potential of the sentence uttered: "It was a soundless noise. . . ." How could it? No noise can have the property predicated here: soundlessness. If something is soundless, it is not a noise; if a noise, not soundless.

In such cases, moreover, the locutionary-propositional-illocutionary act performed is of indeterminate meaning; there is no determinate literal equivalent. Lawrence's act not only does not realize the meaning potential of the sentence he uttered, it does not realize the meaning potential of any other particular sentence either. And the sentence I suggest— It was a very soft noise—while not exactly arbitrary, could easily be replaced with another: It was a scarcely audible noise, almost like a whisper.

Obviously, being literal or figurative is not a property of sentences; it is a property of locutionary-propositional-illocutionary acts. There are no peculiarities of sentences that distinguish figurative speaking or writing from literal, only peculiarities of locutionary-propositional-illocutionary acts. But this is not the occasion for trying to say what these peculiarities are.

University of Illinois, Chicago Circle

FRANK J. D'ANGELO

UP AGAINST THE WALL, MOTHER!
THE RHETORIC OF SLOGANS, CATCHPHRASES,
AND GRAFFITI

UP AGAINST THE WALL, MOTHER! "Perhaps
nothing upset our enemies more than this slogan," contends
Mark Rudd, writing about the Columbia strike in 1968. "To
them it seemed to show the extent to which we had broken
with their norms, how far we had sunk to brutality, hatred,
and obscenity."[1]

The slogan "defines the terms. It puts the administration and the interests they represent on one side, leftist
students and the interests of humanity on the other. Those
undecided in the middle are forced to choose sides."[2]

These comments by Mark Rudd indicate in part the
extent to which slogans, catchphrases, and slogan graffiti
were used by protestors, radicals, and ordinary citizens, who
often felt themselves to be outside of the decision-making
processes of society, to express characteristic positions,
issues, feelings, and goals in the 60s and early 70s. Many of
these slogans, catchphrases, and graffiti derive from the disturbances at Columbia, San Francisco State, Berkeley, and
other universities, from the demonstrations at the Chicago
Democratic Convention in 1968, from the civil rights movement of the 60s, and from the Free Speech and war protest
movements of that period, but some have their origin in previous and subsequent political and social events.

Because slogans, catchphrases, and slogan graffiti are

essentially rhetorical in purpose, because they often deal with significant social and political issues, and because they sometimes force us to examine more carefully our most cherished attitudes and beliefs, I believe that they are worthy of our serious consideration. In this paper, therefore, I would like to explore the relationships that exist among slogans, catchphrases, and slogan graffiti and to consider their possible significance for the English classroom.

By the phrase *slogan graffiti*, I mean a class of graffiti similar to slogans and catchphrases in form, technique, and rhetorical purpose. Like slogans and catchphrases, slogan graffiti are characterized by conciseness of form, cleverness of phrasing, wit, inventiveness, and pointed observations. In many instances, slogan graffiti are identical to slogans and catchphrases, if we define graffiti in its broadest sense to mean any kind of writing or inscription on a wall or other surface. Thus a slogan or catchphrase becomes a graffito by virtue of its having been scribbled or scratched on some writing surface.

The word *slogan* comes from the Gaelic word *sluagh-ghairm*, meaning a war cry or a rallying cry of a Scottish clan. More recently the word has come to mean a motto or distinctive phrase associated with political parties, radical groups, or advertising agencies. The use of slogans is not confined to these groups alone, however. Almost every element of our society employs slogans: the federal government, labor unions, corporations, professional organizations, schools, churches, the armed services, various kinds of societies, cities, and states. In many ways, slogans resemble mottos. Like mottos, they are short and concise, and like mottos they may express some guiding principle, goal, ideal, aspiration, or exalted sentiment. They differ, however, in that they are often less sententious, more caustic, abusive, evocative, or emotional. Slogans are also closely related to catchwords, or catchphrases as they are sometimes called: concise words or phrases repeated so often that they become representative of some particular political or social point of view.

FORMS

The forms used by the graffitist are very similar to those used by the maker of slogans and catchphrases. Grammatically, these forms are quite simple, consisting of single words and short phrases ("Peace!" "Black power," "Up the establishment!") and concise subject-verb, subject-verb-complement, and verb-complement patterns ("ROTC must go!" "Impeach Johnson!"). The main functional type is the imperative ("Bring the boys home now!" "Ban the bomb!" "Legalize marijuana"). The declarative mode is used, but it is used sparingly.

The forms used by the maker of slogans and catch-phrases are so easily adaptable to the graffitist's purpose that in most instances all the graffitist has to do is substitute a word or a phrase or to extend a line slightly to make the needed changes. Thus a single slogan such as "Free Huey Newton" can generate an almost infinite number of imitations: "Free Angela Davis," "Free the Chicago Seven," "Free the Indianapolis 500," "Free Huey—and Dewey and Louie," "Free the Watergate 50, 500, 5000." By a slight alteration Patrick Henry's "Give me liberty or give me death" becomes "Give me liberty or give me meth." Once a form is appropriated by the graffitist, it is relatively simple for him to build on the appropriated form. General MacArthur's famous line, "Old soldiers never die; they just fade away," inspired a number of graffiti in the form of parodies: "Old soldiers never die, young ones do," "Old burglars never die; they just steal away," "Old blondes never fade; they just dye away," and "Old mailmen never die; they just lose their zip." Because of the similarity of form, it is easy to recognize the slogans and mottos embedded in the following graffiti: "Ban the bomb; save the world for conventional warfare," "In God we trust—all others strictly cash," "Serve your country; be a call girl," "Better sick than Bolshevik."

The imperative form of most political and protest slogans is readily appropriated by the graffitist for his own political, social, or satiric purposes as is evident in the following graffiti: "Make love, not babies" (slogan: "Make love, not war"), "Let's all get behind Nixon—and Push" (slogan: "Let's all support_____"), "Remember the alum, Moe" (slogan: "Remember the Alamo"), "Support our boys in the Pentagon" (slogan: "Support our boys in Vietnam"), "Legalize freedom" (slogan: "Legalize abortion," or gambling, or whatever), "Vote 'no' for President" (slogan: "Vote_____ for President"), "Repeal inhibition" (slogan: "Repeal prohibition").

The rhetorical techniques used by the graffitist are similar to those used by the maker of slogans and catchphrases. Among these, the most important are antithesis, repetition, alliteration, rhyme, and puns.

ANTITHESIS

Antithesis is the juxtaposition of opposing ideas, usually in parallel structure. The rhetorical effect of antithesis is that it forces an adversary to view the issues clearly, in terms of opposing principles. This forcing of issues into rigid antitheses was a technique used by both the radical left and the radical right during the Vietnamese War, as the following examples indicate: "America: Love it or leave it," "America: Change it or lose it," "Make love, not war," "Plant trees, not bombs." The war protestors did not have to search diligently to find suitable models in which to frame their sentiments. The political slogans of recent and bygone years made extensive use of antithesis, as in Patrick Henry's "Give me liberty or give me death," Stephen Decatur's "Our country, right or wrong," and John F. Kennedy's "Ask not what your country can do for you, ask what you can do for your country." Not all of the antithetical graffiti were cast in the form of an argument. Several were written in the form of a baseball or football score, and their main intent was satiric and ironic, as in the examples, "National Guard: 4; Kent State: 0" or "War: 2,485,321; Peace: 0." If the main weakness of antithesis is that it often reduces complex issues to a very simple form, its strength is that it does not admit of ambiguity.

REPETITION

Another commonly used rhetorical technique in slogans, catchphrases, and slogan graffiti is repetition. Repetition is usually associated with the highest excitement of feeling and emotional intensity, as in the slogans, "Close it down! Close it down!" "Burn, baby, burn." and "Overcome! Overcome!" It can also be used to ridicule and to needle political opponents. Repetition was employed with great effectiveness for just this purpose in the presidential rallies of 1968. Buttons and placards emblazoned with such slogans and slogan graffiti as "Hump the Hump" and "Do it like you did it in '60, Dick" appeared everywhere.

ALLITERATION

A third rhetorical technique frequently used in political slogans, protest slogans, catchphrases, and slogan graffiti is alliteration. Like word repetition or phrase repetition, alliteration emphasizes by concentrating the sense of an idea in sharp and clear outlines. Thus in the slogan "*B*an the *B*omb" and "*S*crew the *S*ystem," the meaning becomes more intense and emphatic as a result of the alliteration. Political slogans use alliteration with great skill. Very few deal with concrete issues, but instead invoke a kind of word magic which hypnotizes the voter into believing that he is dealing with something meaningful. Some slogans focus upon the man rather than upon the issues, as in the examples, "*L*ove that *L*yndon" and "*T*ried and *T*rue *T*ruman." Others deal with some abstract principle or goal, as in the slogan, "*P*eace and *P*rosperity" and "*K*orea, *C*ommunism, and *C*orruption!" Like the maker of slogans and catchphrases, the graffitist uses alliteration for emphasis ("*N*ixon for *n*othing"), but he also uses it for satiric purposes ("*K*ill a *c*ommie for *C*hrist").

RHYME

A fourth rhetorical technique employed in slogans, catchphrases, and slogan graffiti is rhyme. Rhyme makes a slogan easy to chant, and it condenses a powerful emotional appeal in its repetitive form. The streets resounded to the cries of anti-war slogans such as "Hell no, we won't go!" "Stop the war and feed the poor," and "Hey, hey, LBJ, how many kids did you kill today?" in the 60s. Sometimes the rhymes were humorous, as in the graffito "Columbia goes from jerk to jerk—Eisenhower to Grayson Kirk," but mostly they were used to rally people to a particular cause ("Better red than dead," "Gym Crow must go"). The slogan graffiti worked in similar fashion. Some were identical to protest slogans as in the graffito "1, 2, 3, 4—Tricky Dicky stop the war" and were used to directly emphasize anti-war sentiments. Others were used to abuse government officials that protestors believed were responsible for continuing the war ("Nixon in '72; don't stop in the middle of a screw").

PUNS

A fifth rhetorical technique used in slogans, catch-phrases, and slogan graffiti is the pun. The pun has both a serious aim and a ridiculous aim. For example, during the 1968 political rallies, puns were used to directly express anti-Humphrey sentiments because of his alignment with Johnson's policies. The play on the word *hump* in the slogans "Hump the Hump" and "Keep the country Hump-free" makes an acerbic, yet comic point. The word *hump* refers to a part of Humphrey's name, but it also has sexual connotations. The use of sexual connotations is also contained in the slogan graffito "Dick Nixon before he dicks you." The pun on the word *dick* alludes to the idea that Nixon is screwing the country. Puns were also used in protest slogans during the Columbia confrontation in 1968. The puns in the slogans "Stop Gym Crow" and "Gym Crow must go" make the satiric point that Columbia is engaging in ethnic discrimination against blacks while at the same time they focus on the immediate issue of the construction of the gym.

In addition to sharing characteristics of form and rhetorical technique, slogans, catchphrases, and slogan graffiti also share a similarity of rhetorical purpose.[3]

POLARIZATION

One purpose is to polarize, to divide people into diametrically opposed, antagonistic groups, emphasizing conflicting or contrasting positions and viewpoints. As Mark Rudd indicates, the slogans put the students on one side and the administration on the other, forcing those in the middle to choose sides. Because many students felt powerless to make changes within the university system or within society, they began to adopt some of the strategies of the civil rights movement of the 60s. Instead of seeking to work for slow, evolutionary changes, they began to demand immediate changes in the structure of a society that they felt was bound up with military, racist, and mercantile interests.

The protest slogans, catchphrases, and slogan graffiti they adopted often translated these controversial issues into words:

Hell no! We won't go!
ROTC must go!

Stop DOW now!
Give peace a chance!
End racism now!
Legalize marijuana!
Stop Columbia from taking over Harlem!

But often these slogans, like the demands, were too general, imprecise, unreasonable, or not clearly understandable to be translatable into action:

Power to the people!
Screw in the streets!
Do your own thing.
Trust your impulses.
Zap the world with love.
Turn on, tune in, drop out.
Be realistic, demand the impossible.
We want the world and we want it now!

The political slogans, like the protest slogans and graffiti, were also used to polarize. For example, some political commentators contend that the reason Goldwater lost the election in 1964 is that he willingly accepted the extremist labels pinned on him by moderates and liberals. One of the key lines in his acceptance speech, "Extremism in the defense of liberty is no vice . . . moderation in the pursuit of justice is no virtue," soon became a sloganizable issue in that campaign, an issue which became so inflammatory that it caused Nelson Rockefeller to label Goldwater's words as "dangerous, irresponsible, and frightening." Nixon himself and his vice-presidential running mate, Spiro Agnew, followed Goldwater's lead by seemingly looking for the right catchwords rather than the right policies. Thus "Law and Order" became one of the catchphrases in the election of 1968, and Agnew's vitriolic attacks on the press, on students, and on the academic establishment served to polarize the country even more.

INVOKING OF VIOLENCE

Another rhetorical purpose of protest slogans, political slogans, catchphrases, and graffiti is to invoke violence by the employment of epithets, obscene language, and invective. As Tom Hayden puts it, "Often the only words with emotional content are those that cannot be spoken or published in the 'legitimate' world: fuck, motherfucker, shit and other 'obscenities.' New words are needed to express feelings: right on, cool, outta sight, freaky. New language becomes a weapon of the Movement because it is mysterious, threatening to conventional power:"[4]

> Up against the wall, mother!
> Off the pigs!
> Freak the delegates!
> Screw the establishment!
> Dick Nixon!
> Hump the Hump!

The obscene language and the epithets were obviously used by the radicals for their shock value. It enabled them to attack a system which considers such words taboo, it brought the radicals to the attention of the media, it put into words what they had been thinking in private all along, it provided a kind of catharsis or release of hostile emotions, and it symbolized the fact that the traditional forms of authority had broken down.

Unfortunately, violence begets violence, and the response to the language and provocation of the demonstrators was unrestrained and shocking police violence at the Democratic National Convention in 1968, termed by some commentators "a police riot." Newsmen were reportedly clubbed and sprayed with Mace. An eighteen-year-old girl was reportedly thrown by the police toward the door of a paddy wagon which she hit with a thud. She fell, was picked up, and then thrown again head first into the wagon. When a demonstrator fell to the ground, three or four policemen would start beating him until he was bloody. The police, like the demonstrators, had their own chants and slogans. In a charge against the barricades in Lincoln Park, they chanted:

> Kill! Kill! Kill! Kill!
> Kill the mothers!
> Kill the bastards!
> Knock out their teeth!

Even though there was truth embedded in the rhetoric of the demonstrators, the obscenities and epithets embedded in the slogans proved to be a poor moral equivalent for rational discourse and civilized change.

SOLIDIFICATION

A third rhetorical purpose of protest slogans, political slogans, catchphrases, and graffiti is to unify, to solidify a group into a community of interests and endeavors. Protest slogans and graffiti such as "We shall overcome," "Right on," "Black power," and "All power to the people" not only gave the protestors a sense of solidarity, but also provided them with a sense of identity. This need for a sense of identity is echoed in the plaintive cry of one graffitist, "I am somebody! I am somebody!" These slogans, and the graffiti to which they gave rise, also helped to forge a bond between the protestors and potential allies in the community at large.

The political slogans work in a similar fashion. They give members of a particular party a sense of solidarity and identity. But unfortunately they convince some people to vote for political principles and policies of which they have little knowledge or understanding. For example, just exactly what do such slogans and catchphrases as "The Great Society," "Peace and Prosperity," "Home and Country," "Law and Order," "Save the West for Democracy," and "Bring us together again" really mean? Being against peace and prosperity or home and country or law and order is like being against the flag and motherhood. Rather than condensing the issues into some intelligible form, as some slogans clearly do, these slogans serve rather to obscure the real issues. They are intended to mean all things to all men.

But the graffitist sees through the glibness and superficiality of many slogans and catchphrases. Although his purpose is often similar to that of the protestor or sloganeer, he sometimes appropriates their material for his own purposes: to ridicule, to satirize, or to parody, as in the following examples:

Support relief for the oppressed majority.
Big Brother lives in the White House.
Ad Hoc Committee to draft George Hamilton.
War is good business; invest your son.
Take a Viet Cong to church with you on Sunday.
Fight air pollution. Get Spiro a gag.

The graffitist has put into comic or ironic perspective almost all of the sloganizable issues of the late 60s and early 70s:

racism, the draft, the Vietnamese war, the possibility of a nuclear confrontation, drugs, pollution, the economy, and our preoccupation with sex and violence. If, unlike the slogans and catchphrases they so faithfully mirror, graffiti seldom lead to action, they are valuable in attacking hypocrisy and sham and in satirizing individuals and institutions.

Whereas many slogans and catchphrases are so general and abstract as to be practically meaningless to the critical perception (perhaps this is why they are so appealing to the demagogue), graffiti are almost always concrete and specific, although some graffiti do rise to the status of universals (as in the case of the proverbial graffiti). But since the graffitist is often a satirist, he is not afraid to name names, as the following examples indicate:

William F. Buckley for God.
Gore Vidal for fairy queen.
Shriver for something.
Ted Kennedy is a dirty old man.
H. Rap deserves one.
George Wallace is a mulatto.
Ronald Reagan is one peach of a swell fascist.
Barry Goldwater wears pink underwear.
Spiro Agnew drives a Schlitz truck and wears combat boots.

Often, however, the graffitist is more humorous than satirical, as in the following slogan graffiti:

Use erogenous zone numbers.
Hire the morally handicapped.
Conserve water; shower with a friend.
Eat more beans; the country needs the gas.
Help the energy crisis—stop fueling around.
Save a tree; take Ewell Gibbons to lunch.
Support "National Motherhood Week"; make one today.
Help retard children; support our schools.

I think it should be evident from these examples that political slogans, protest slogans, catchphrases, and graffiti have much in common and that they deserve serious study. When they deal with specific and recognizable issues, they can be implicitly a force for social change. But if they are taken merely at their face value, they can easily become a substitute for analytical thinking and serious argument, thus preventing meaningful debate.

Slogans, catchphrases, and graffiti can have a variety of uses in the classroom. Because they are a source of contemporary social and political satire, they can be used to teach satire. Because they contain a great variety of forms, stylistic techniques, and purposes, they can be used to teach grammatical and rhetorical form, rhetorical technique, and rhetorical purpose. Finally, because they use the language of the man in the street, they can be used to teach usage, including slang, jargon, epithets, neologisms, dialect variations, and idioms. Whatever graffiti may have been in the 40s and 50s today they are literate, witty, and urbane and worthy of our serious attention.

Arizona State University

NOTES

[1] Mark Rudd, "Symbols of the Revolution," in *Up Against the Ivy Wall*, ed. Jerry L. Avorn and members of the staff of the *Columbia Daily Spectator* (New York: Atheneum, 1969), p. 291.

[2] Rudd, p. 292.

[3] The general discussion of rhetorical purpose and the categories of polarization, invoking of violence, and solidification are based on the following sources: John Waite Bowers and Donovan J. Ochs, *The Rhetoric of Agitation and Control* (Reading, Mass.: Addison-Wesley Publishing Co., Inc., 1971), pp. 16-38, 57-71; Irving J. Rein, "The Confrontation Strategy," *Rudy's Red Wagon* (Glenview, Ill.: Scott, Foresman and Co., 1972), pp. 33-45.

[4] Tom Hayden, *Trial* (New York: Holt, Rinehart and Winston, 1970), p. 39.

RICHARD L. LARSON

THE RHETORIC OF THE WRITTEN VOICE

In this essay I will be trying to comment on some elements in the rhetoric of style. I will not use the term *style* much, nor will my comments be about texts in imaginative literature, though I hope that these notes will be applicable to studies in imaginative literature as well as to the kind of non-fiction prose that I will be analyzing. I will not be talking about *style* in the customary rhetorical terms (through analysis of familiar patterns of syntax or through study of schemes and tropes), or in quantitative terms, or in the terms that Young and Becker use in defining style as an author's characteristic route through the choices presented to him/her during prewriting and writing ("Toward a Modern Theory of Rhetoric: A Tagmemic Contribution," in *New Rhetorics*, ed. Martin Steinmann, Jr. [New York: Scribner's Sons, 1967], p. 104). My comments do owe much to Richard Ohmann's essays, particularly to his "Prologomena to the Analysis of Literary Style," but I shall not be trying to apply his conceptual framework to my texts.

First, I need to identify and explain a few premises. I take it for granted that written discourse, even much literary discourse which is not easily identifiable as "addressed" writing in Kenneth Burke's sense of that term, participates in a transaction with its readers. One is, of course, harder put to think of writing than of speaking as part of a transaction with someone else, because the term *transaction* speaks of the receiver of the discourse having some impact on the discourse that is produced, and that may not appear to happen in written discourse except where the person receiving the discourse is an intermediary between the author and his ultimate audience—for example, an editor. Still, as recent research on reading is demonstrating to us, the feelings of the reader affect what the reader reads or discovers in the text, and, according to David Bleich, properly so: "with regard to symbolic works, *all* aspects of their existence, function, and effect depend on the processes by which they are assimilated by an observer. These processes are different in each individual, making the act of assimilation of special importance. To say that perceptual processes are different in each person is to say that reading is a wholly subjective process and that the nature of what is perceived is determined by the rules of the personality of the perceiver" (*Readings and Feelings: An Introduction to Subjective Criticism* [Urbana, Ill.: NCTE, 1975], p. 3). If the feelings of the one who receives discourse do indeed influence what he reads, then it is possible, I think, to speak usefully of a transaction between any reader and the writer of discourse, and my premise can be maintained at least for the purposes of this discussion.

Second, I take it that the transaction between reader and writer is influenced by the impressions formed by the reader of the writer, as the reader reads. These impressions add up, I am assuming, to a characterization of the perceived writer formulated by the reader. The reader discovers, without necessarily seeking the information or deliberately abstracting it into descriptive statements, what sort of person he or she is dealing with, and reacts accordingly to the ideas and representations of reality encountered in the text. The reader may form judgments of the worth of what is said, of its credibility or importance, and of his or her willingness to continue participating in a transaction with that writer.

Whence comes this characterization of the writer, on which the reader bases in part the role he or she will play in this communications transaction? Partly, of course, from what the writer says directly about himself or herself, and from what the writer allows to be inferred about his or her knowledge, way of organizing or approaching discourse, and fairness in dealing with divergent ways of viewing that subject. We refer to these matters when we speak of the writer's *ethos* and discuss the *ethical proof* that a writer brings to bear on his subject and argument. In this essay I want to argue briefly that, in addition to being influenced by what the writer says and how he or she approaches the subject, we are influenced as readers by how the writer *sounds*, by what my title refers to as the "written voice" in a text we read.

I am suggesting that our experience of a written text—the transactions in which we participate with a writer when we read—has elements of a dramatic encounter; it includes a response by the reader's imagination—his or her auditory imagination—to the sounds heard during this imagined encounter with the text. I am suggesting that a part of our response as readers is to the way we *hear* a text in our imagination and that every written utterance we encounter has its own imagined sound to which we as readers respond. I am further suggesting that a good part of the *ethos* of the writer—I am tempted to refer to the *speaker* of the piece— that we infer from reading comes from the way the piece sounds to our auditory imagination. What we hear leads us to make judgments about our affinity with, our sympathy for, or our distance from the writer and about the kind of appeal or claim that the writer is making on us. If we are prepared to recognize this imagined auditory appeal, we will have to evaluate the importance of that appeal as we consider the rhetorical design and functioning of any piece of discourse.

In citing the auditory appeal of written texts and in saying that each text we encounter probably has its own distinctive auditory appeal, I doubt that I am making assertions that will contradict the experience of most listeners or readers. I expect that most of you may have remarked to yourself, as I did some years ago in teaching a class in freshman English about some major essays by well-known twentieth-century writers, that a major reason for the differences in our experience of writers is not just in the subjects they treat, the premises they work from, the positions they take, the perspectives from which they view their subjects, the lines of reasoning they adopt, the conclusions they come to, and so on, but is also in the differences in how they sound. If one examines a group of writers such as Orwell, Mailer, Baldwin, Steinem, Didion, or Sontag, he will respond to them differently because they produce different experiences in the auditory imagination. And one will develop preferences among them, not to mention willingness to keep company with some and reluctance to read others, because some of those auditory experiences are pleasing and attractive, or provocative, and some are unpleasing and unrewarding. A writer's words, that is, do much more than refer (as symbols) to reality and establish relationships among ideas and events. They express feelings and reveal attitudes. For the writer/speaker, indeed, they create a self.

The question I raise in this paper, then, is to what can we

attribute the differences in the *sound experience* (the term is often applied to poetry, I think) of texts we encounter. I believe that identifiable elements in the language used by writers contribute a good deal to our auditory experience, interacting no doubt with the substance of what we hear and how we feel about that substance, but independently describable, too. I suggest that these elements in the language of various writers are open to empirical description, and I am reasonably sure that sophisticated studies in grammar, phonetics, prosody, and semantics could assist the rhetorician in identifying the sources of different kinds of auditory appeals. I am not prepared yet to attempt systematically these kinds of studies in language—though they would be one area in which the colloboration of linguistics, semantics, and rhetoric might, I think, be especially fruitful—but I do want to suggest here the beginnings of some common-sense empirical investigations of prose texts that might put us on our way toward some sensitive investigations.

What I am calling for, and would like to try to initiate very modestly, is a heuristic for the study of vocal/auditory effects in the rhetoric of written discourse—a study of effects that go beyond the transmission of ideas and points of view into the psychology of response to rhythms, intonations, emphases, and distinctive locutions. The goal would be an organized way of talking about the production of sound and analyzing the effects of sound in discourse—an organized way of inquiry that would illuminate the work not only of the scholar and theorist in rhetoric, but also the work of the *rhetor* (i.e., the practicing writer who wants to address a message to a reader).

There have been some attempts at a heuristic of the sort I am discussing, though the writers I am about to cite might not recognize my characterization of their work. The first scholar who comes to mind is Leslie Whipp of the University of Nebraska, whose descriptive studies of professional and student writers have demonstrated that the systematic examination of syntax and semantics in a text can yield important understanding of how an author works. Whipp's work is not widely published, and the best example I can cite of his studies is in an unexpected place, an essay in *Elementary English* entitled "Conflicting Claims: Parental Expectations and Professional Expertise," in which Whipp applies his analytical techniques to an example of children's writing.*

*I have reprinted that essay and another less well known, called "Morning Haze," which argues a similar thesis, in my collection *Children and Writing in the Ele-*

But Whipp is not talking so much about the written voice as he is talking, in great detail, about a variety of features in the language of a piece of writing. And his emphasis is not so much on understanding and interpreting the auditory experience of a text as it is on discovering the differences between relatively mature and relatively less mature writing—on giving the young writer a standard for judging his or her own work by showing what are the attributes of mature writing. Thus, although Whipp's procedures are suggestive, they don't offer the heuristic I'm calling for in this essay.

A second writer, more familiar to most of us, whose work has been moving much more squarely toward the goal I am seeking here, is Walker Gibson. Gibson helped to direct the study of composing in the NDEA/EPDA institutes of the sixties toward the writer's control of voice, by a kinescope he did for the old Commission on English called, as I recall, "The Speaking Voice and the Teaching of Writing." But neither in that short essay nor in subsequent articles did Gibson do much more than call attention to some of the phenomena I am talking about as apt emphases in the teaching of writing. I am not aware that he has yet attempted to explore the implications of his ideas for rhetorical theory and for study of the workings of rhetorical texts generally. The closest Gibson has come to offering the kind of heuristic I am calling for is in the Appendix to his book *Tough, Sweet, and Stuffy*, published some years ago by Indiana University Press, but not so well known as it should be. In that book Gibson tries to classify some American prose into one or another of the three classes indicated in his title, and he provides an Appendix, called "The Style Machine," in which he develops some tests of toughness, sweetness, and stuffiness in the writing about him. Gibson's style machine has helped me personally, and I commend it to anyone who is interested in the problems I am discussing here. But Gibson in that book is at the beginning of his recent concerns with public language; he is trying to assess the kinds of languages that members of the public encounter from novelists, advertisers, bureaucrats, journalists and so on, and his main concern seems to be to help readers gauge the extent to which what they are reading qualifies as tough talk, sweet talk, or stuffy talk. Such

mentary School: Theories and Techniques (New York: Oxford University Press, 1975). Edward P. J. Corbett mentions an earlier essay of Whipp's in *Classical Rhetoric for the Modern Student.* See *College English*, 25 (October 1963), 18-22, "A Slide-Rule Composition Course," by Margaret A. Ashida and Léslie T. Whipp.

guidance is valuable, but in my judgment the relatively sharp focus in Gibson's book keeps it from being the sort of heuristic needed for inquiring into sounds of skilled writers who do not obviously qualify as tough talkers, sweet talkers, or stuffy talkers. We still need, I think, a heuristic that will help us get at the varied and complex phenomena of language that cause us to hear what we hear when we read, thus causing us to experience a work in a special way in our auditory imaginations—with important consequences for our role in the rhetorical transaction.

In the rest of this paper, I want to cite just a few examples of the kinds of phenomena I am talking about. Obviously I cannot give an exhaustive enumeration of these phenomena. The passages simply illustrate and highlight a few features that, together, help establish the authors' voices in the pieces before us. The passages are by reasonably well-known writers, but are not from works usually identified as literary (though, as David Bleich cites Norman Holland on p. 21 of *Readings and Feelings*, it is the reader who determines whether a given work is literature). Nor are they from the Norman Mailers and the Tom Wolfes of our time—people whose voices are so conspicuous as not to tax any heuristic we might be experimenting with. Yet they do appear to be rhetorical in the sense of being "addressed"; and therefore, though I have time to cite only a few of the most obvious elements in each passage, they may suggest the kinds of data I hope this heuristic can accommodate and explain.

I

Meanwhile I am assuming that the tendency of mechanical progress *is* to make life safe and soft. This may be disputed, because at any given moment the effect of some recent mechanical invention may appear to be the opposite. Take for instance the transition from horses to motor vehicles. At a first glance one might say, considering the enormous toll of road deaths, that the motor-car does not exactly tend to make life safer. Moreover it probably needs as much toughness to be a first-rate dirt-track rider as to be a broncho-buster or to ride in the Grand National. Nevertheless the *tendency* of all machinery is to become safer and easier to handle. The danger of accidents would disappear if we chose to tackle our road-planning problem seriously, as we shall do sooner or later; and meanwhile the motor-car has evolved to a point at which anyone who is not blind or paralytic can drive it after a few lessons. Even now it needs far less nerve and skill to drive a car ordinarily well than to ride a horse ordinarily well; in twenty years time it may need no nerve or skill at all. Therefore, one must say that, taking society as a whole, the result of the transition from horses to cars has been an increase in human softness. Presently somebody comes along with another invention, the aeroplane for instance, which does not at first sight appear to make life safer. The first men who went up in aeroplanes were superlatively brave, and even to-day it must need an exceptionally good nerve to be a pilot. But the same tendency as before is at work. The aeroplane, like the motor-car, will be made foolproof; a million engineers are working, almost unconsciously, in that direction. Finally— this is the objective, though it may never quite be reached— you will get an aeroplane whose pilot needs no more skill or courage than a baby needs in its perambulator. And all mechanical progress is and must be in this direction. A machine evolves by becoming more efficient, that is, more foolproof; hence the objective of mechancial progress is a foolproof world—which may or may not mean a world inhabited by fools. Mr. Wells would probably retort that the world can never become foolproof, because, however high a standard of efficiency you have reached, there is always some greater difficulty ahead. For example (this is Mr. Well's favourite idea—he has used it in goodness knows how many perorations), when you have got this planet of ours perfectly into trim, you start upon the enormous task of reaching and colonising another. But this is merely to push the objective further into the future; the objective itself remains the same. Colonise another planet, and the game of mechanical progress begins anew; for the foolproof world you have substituted for the foolproof solar system—the foolproof universe. In tying yourself to the ideal of mechanical efficiency, you tie yourself to the ideal of softness. But softness is repulsive; and thus all progress is seen to be a frantic struggle toward an objective which you hope and pray will never be reached. Now and again, but not often, you meet somebody who grasps that what is usually called progress also entails what is usually called degeneracy, and who is nevertheless in favour of progress. Hence the fact that in Mr. Shaw's Utopia a statue was erected to Falstaff, as the first man who ever made a speech in favour of cowardice.

—George Orwell, *The Road to Wigan Pier*

The voice that comes through this passage by Orwell is that of one who is both assertive and playful. Most, though not all, of the sentences are categorically declarative—the work of one who is unqualifiedly confident in his pronouncements and criticisms of his society. The speaker relishes forceful comparisons and emphatic adverbs (as Orwell often does): "anyone who is not blind or paralytic can drive it [the motor-car] after a few lessons," and "The first men who went up in aeroplanes were superlatively brave." He evidently enjoys bringing his argument to a close by following up a vision of the ultimate ("Colonise another planet . . . the foolproof universe") with a paradox ("all progress is seen to be a frantic struggle towards an objective which you hope and pray will never be reached"), and then adding the further paradoxical reference to a statue erected to one who speaks in favor of cowardice.

But this playful assertiveness is qualified by the structure of the passage; the speaker is not just gamesome. Regularly he cites what seems to be the case, then corrects the misapprehension; he contrasts his listener's gullible inferences with the facts as he clearly sees them, until he is ready to unfold his vision of an endless train of mechanization. The occasional subjunctives help make the contrasts between what might appear to be the case and what is true. At the very moment of enjoying the wit in which he puts his visions of the future, the speaker is identified as one both perceptive and earnest in his reasoning. Hardly any analysis of the passage is needed in order for the reader to hear this self-characterization.

II

Every weekday morning at eleven o'clock, just about the time the sun burns the last haze off the Santa Barbara Hills, fifteen or twenty men gather in what was once the dining room of a shirt manufacturer's mansion overlooking the Pacific Ocean and begin another session of what they like to call "clarifying the basic issues." The place is the Center for the Study of Democratic Institutions, the current mutation of the Fund for the Republic, and since 1959, when the Fund paid $250,000 for the marble villa and forty-one acres of eucalyptus, a favored retreat for people whom the Center's president, Robert M. Hutchins, deems controversial, stimulating, and, perhaps above all, cooperative, or *our kind*. "If they just want to work on their own stuff," Hutchins has said, "then they ought not to come here. Unless they are willing to come in and work with the group as a group, then this place is not for them."

Those invited to spend time at the Center get an office (there are no living quarters at the Center) and a salary, the size of which is reportedly based on the University of California pay scale. The selection process is usually described as "mysterious," but it always involves "people we know." Paul Hoffman, who was at one time president of the Ford Foundation and then director of the Fund for the Republic, is now the Center's honorary chairman, and his son is there quite a bit, and Robert Hutchins' son-in-law.

—Joan Didion, *Slouching Towards Bethlehem*

Unlike the voice in the passage by Orwell, this voice is calculatedly unempathetic. Seemingly we hear a person just recording details, without inference or comment. Points are made through the juxtaposition of details ("shirt manufacturer's mansion" and " 'clarifying the basic issues' "), through understated colloquialism ("quite a bit"), through metaphoric exaggeration ("mutation"), and through the detachment hinted at in such phrases as "what they like to call," "reportedly based," and "usually described as." The speaker lets us know that she is committed to none of the language that follows these phrases and is indeed doing nothing more than reporting. The effect is reinforced by the writer's extended use of quotation marks, which suggests that the words enclosed should be sounded, perhaps, with a hint of skepticism in the auditory imagination. The reader/listener is warned to be vigilant, though the speaker says nothing here that is directly critical of the Center.

III

Bud was not a heartless killer. He did his best not to kill, if I am to believe his story. He was weak and vain—like most of us. He had done a bit of thieving first, not anything however to compare with the operations of our illustrious industrial magnets, our bankers, politicians and colonial exploiters. No, Bud was just an ordinary crook, an honest crook, so to speak, with an exaggerated sense of loyalty and honor. Toward the fair sex he was fatuously romantic and chivalrous, far more so than a pugilist or sex-starved member of the clergy. There were two things he could not countenance—cruelty to children and disrespect for woman. He was adamant there.

He would never shoot a man down except in self-defense, he said, and I believe him. There was a bit of the dandy about him, and of the swashbuckling braggart too, traits which we find among the higher-ups as well. He was a consummate liar, but then what is a diplomat, a politician, a lawyer? The worst thing about him, and I am trying to look at him dispassionately, is that he no longer had any faith in his fellow man. That had been knocked out of him by those who talk about having faith and never show the evidences of it. He had done at least five stretches and was probably wanted by the authorities when our paths met.

He had paid for his crimes in full, that is my belief. If he should commit fresh ones I would blame it on the police, on the lawmakers, on the educators, on the clergy, on all those who believe in punishment, who refuse to help a man when he is down or try to understand him when in impotent range he turns against the world. It doesn't matter to me what crimes are chalked up against Clausen; our crimes,

> all of us who are on the outside, who got off scot-free, are
> greater. If we did not actually force him to become a crimi-
> nal we most certainly helped him to remain one. And in
> speaking of Bud Clausen I am speaking for the great major-
> ity of men and women who suffered the same fate; I am
> speaking for all those to come, who will follow in his foot
> steps and who have no redress until we on the outside be-
> come more enlightened and more humane.
> —Henry Miller, *The Air-Conditioned Nightmare*

This message, more than the others, depends for its effect on variety in the length of sentences and on rhythm. The insistent comparisons are part of the substance of what is said and are obvious aids in the establishment of a voice and an attitude. Less obvious is the speaker's early preference for short sentences and longer sentences made up of short phrases, with consequently heavy internal punctuation. Many of the sentences are made up of series or of appositives and other qualifiers (sometimes both). The effect is that of a speaker making a deliberate effort to be fair toward his subject and toward his reader and at the same time trying to control his discomfort with those who make up ordinary society—the hypocrites whom he cannot at times refrain from listing.

As the passage progresses, the rhythms of the sentences change. At the end of the second paragraph are a couple of emphatic sentences (the next to the last heavily ironic) without internal punctuation, and the second sentence in the second paragraph, though it starts as a conditional with a number of items in series, ends with a relative clause that gains emphasis from its very lack of qualification or punctuation—a lack which forces the reader to hear the clause without stopping and particularly to notice the intensity with which it is uttered. The final sentence emphasizes the intensity of the speaker's convictions with two relative clauses —one short, the other much longer—underlining the plight of the speaker's subjects and the speaker's call for people to become "more enlightened and more humane." The warmth and urgency of the voice here contrast with the satiric irony, even the sportiveness, that accompanies the speaker's more detached analysis in the early part of the passage.

Writers' voices change within works (as the passage from Miller shows) and they change from work to work, and so the features that establish the voice in a given passage cannot be reliably extended to characterize the whole of a work, let alone the output of an author, though I sense that different works by the authors cited might well show some of the same features of voice as the passages cited. A heuristic would need to be able to recognize and explain changes in the voices we hear and the feelings we experience. I have a hunch that we could arrive at a heuristic with this capability.

This heuristic would have to be quite sensitive, as I think the passages just cited will show. It could not be content to deal with mannerisms of language, with dominant metaphorical fields, favored rhetorical schemes, insistent rhythmic patterns, or variations in level of usage—though it would have to take account of all these. The heuristic would also have to take note of what I think Richard Ohmann has referred to as a writer's "epistemic choices" and of the writer's habitual ways of seeing and comparing, the ways in which his mind moves over his material (I am convinced that the reflection in language of these habits of mind does characterize a person we hear). It would have to take account of the connections a writer makes among diverse parts of experience in the process of creating new rhetorical wholes.

It may seem here that I have gone beyond the features of a text that establish a voice into the entire region of stylistic analysis. It may be that I have. But that broadening of focus is justifiable, I think, because the study of style in rhetoric has not up to now—so far as I am aware of its development—been adequately concerned with the reader's auditory experience of a text. Rhetoric has not dealt sufficiently with the dramatic encounter between reader and text that, because what the reader hears shapes his or her perception of the text, is properly called a *transaction*. I think that the study of rhetoric needs to give more attention to this auditory experience and to the resulting transaction. Giving that kind of attention will help to account for the reactions we intuitively have, I believe, to the different authors we read.

Herbert H. Lehman College, CUNY

RICHARD E. YOUNG

METHODIZING NATURE:
THE TAGMEMIC DISCOVERY PROCEDURE

John Holt once brought a cello to class and watched a child try to discover the function of its various parts:

> It doesn't take a child long [he says] . . . to grasp the basic idea of the cello, the relationship of the bow, the string, and the left hand. But while he has been figuring this out, he has been ceaselessly active . . . . His way of attacking the cello problem is to produce the maximum amount of data possible, to do as many things as he can, to use his hands and the bow in as many ways as possible. Then, as he goes along, he begins to notice regularities and patterns. He begins to ask questions—that is, to make deliberate experiments. But it is vital to note that until he has a great deal of data, he has no idea what questions to ask, or what questions there are to be asked. [1]

Holt's student is not doing anything very unusual; we have all engaged in similar activity and have frequently observed it in others. I quote the passage to call attention to the kind of activity I wish to discuss and to emphasize that it is something we all do normally and spontaneously.

The child is engaged in solving what is sometimes referred to as an "ill-defined" problem, that is, a problem whose dimensions are not clearly specified and for which there may be more than one reasonable answer. By contrast, well-defined problems, such as arithmetic problems or problems of logical inference, have single correct answers. Although we have rules for solving well-defined problems, sets of operations which infallibly lead us to correct answers in a finite number of steps, we have no rules for solving ill-defined problems. Finding reasonable answers involves careful exploration of the problematic data and imaginative guessing. Most of the problems we must solve in our day-to-day lives are ill-defined problems.

In his search for a solution, the child has followed a classic pattern. He has moved from the perception of the problem, through a careful exploration of the data, to hunches, and finally to playing his hunches and evaluating the results. John Dewey called the activity the *process of inquiry*.[2]

Between the time he perceives the problem and the time he gets a hunch (or more elegantly, a hypothesis), the child manipulates the problematic data, seeking to learn as much as possible as rapidly as possible. Anyone who has raised a child knows what manipulation means. In the very young child it means using all his sensory abilities in an effort to understanding: touching the unfamiliar object, shaking it, smelling it, taking it apart, putting it in his mouth, and so on. As I. A. Richards remarks, "we are things particularly responsive to other things."[3] Older children and adults learn to be more decorous, although not more eager or energetic problem solvers.

What do more mature minds do when confronted with ill-defined problems? Obviously we do not abandon physical manipulation as a means of understanding, but we do come to rely more heavily on the intellectual equivalent. Rather than things, we manipulate symbols, an activity which immensely increases the subtlety and efficiency of exploration. Intellectual manipulation involves turning something over in the mind—comparing, classifying, contrasting, segmenting, reordering, shifting focuses of attention, and so on. To paraphrase a line by William Stafford, we do tricks in order to know.[4]

But I am concerned here not only with what we *do* when we engage in intellectual exploration, I am also concerned with what we *can do* to increase our control over the activity—to make it more deliberate, efficient, and complete. The two concerns are, of course, closely related. Learning to do something better implies that we already do it. One thing we can do to increase our control is to methodize nature by developing an explicit plan, a heuristic procedure, for exploring the problematic data. Such a procedure enables us to explore the data more deliberately and efficiently because it specifies in advance what manipulations we are to perform. A really powerful plan would be useful with many kinds of problems (e.g., literary, social, historical, psychological), rather than with a single problem such as the one Holt posed for his students or a single kind of problem.

Tagmemic invention consists of a series of heuristic procedures for increasing the effectiveness of the process of inquiry; it provides procedures for analyzing and formulating problems, for exploring problematic data, and for testing hypotheses. But our concern here is with the second of these procedures only—that is, with the procedure for exploring problematic data. It was derived from a method originally developed for discovering the semantic, phonological, and grammatical systems of languages which have no alphabet, written grammar, or dictionary. The lines of inquiry specified in this method reflect the assumption that, as Kenneth Pike states, "certain universal invariants underlie all human experience as characteristics of rationality itself."[5] If this assumption is true, then a discovery procedure based on these invariants might well strengthen our ability to engage in effective inquiry. Those of us working on tagmemic invention have sought to modify the linguistic method in order to extend its range of application beyond linguistic problems, to make it useful for exploring any kind of problematic data. We have also sought to put it in a form readily teachable to non-linguists.

As presently conceived, this heuristic procedure has two parts: an ordered set of heuristic probes, or lines of inquiry, and a set of underlying assumptions which provide the rationale for the probes. Because the assumptions have been discussed elsewhere, most succinctly in Pike's "Beyond the Sentence,"[6] I will not discuss them here. The three-by-three matrix (Figure 1) is a convenient way of displaying the lines of inquiry and their relationships.[7] Each cell of the matrix describes a perspective and poses a question implied by the perspective and designed to elicit a particular kind of information. The procedure explicitly takes account of the various cognitive domains to which a unit of experience can be related and which together give the event its meaning. It forces the investigator to shift domains systematically and often leads to unexpected insights. The probes complement each other, and taken together they constitute, we believe, an operational definition of thinking well.

FIGURE 1*

	Contrast	Variation	Distribution
PARTICLE	1) View the unit as an isolated, static entity. What are its contrastive features, i.e., the features that differentiate it from similar things and serve to identify it?	4) View the unit as a specific variant form of the concept, i.e., as one among a group of instances that illustrate the concept. What is the *range* of physical variation of the concept, i.e., how can instances vary without becoming something else?	7) View the unit as part of a larger context. How is it appropriately or typically classified? What is its typical position in a temporal sequence? In space, i.e., in a scene or geographical array. In a system of classes?
WAVE	2) View the unit as a dynamic object or event. What physical features distinguish it from similar objects or events? In particular, what is its nucleus?	5) View the unit as a dynamic process. How is it changing?	8) View the unit as a part of a larger, dynamic context. How does it interact with and merge into its environment? Are its borders clear-cut or indeterminate?
FIELD	3) View the unit as an abstract, multidimensional system. How are the components organized in relation to one another? More specifically, how are they related by class, in class systems, in temporal sequence, and in space?	6) View the unit as a multidimensional physical system. How do particular instances of the system vary?	9) View the unit as an abstract system within a larger system. What is its position in the larger system? What systematic features and components make it a part of the larger system?

*From Richard E. Young, Alton L. Becker, and Kenneth L. Pike, *Rhetoric: Discovery and Change* (New York: Harcourt, Brace and World, 1970), p. 127.

The three-by-three matrix is a concise statement of the procedure, but it suggests that its application is more mechanical than it in fact is; effective use requires both conscious, systematic activity and intuitive activity as well. To borrow a phrase from Robert Frost, it requires moving easy in harness.[8]

The following inquiry, by an engineering student in a senior-level rhetoric seminar, illustrates the use of the procedure.[9] He begins with a problem:

> "The Heavy Bear Who Goes with Me," a poem by Delmore Schwartz, metaphorically connects an individual's personality and subconscious with certain animal characteristics. The bear metaphor, however, is rather difficult to understand . . . . This paper is an inquiry into the question, what does the bear represent?

He then moves systematically, cell-by-cell, through the matrix:

> *How does this unit, viewed as a particle, contrast with similar units?*
>
> This unit is different from other metaphors because it is about . . . a bear. A bear has certain distinguishing characteristics: bulk, a large appetite and special craving for sweets, an indifferent, steady temperament but one which can be aroused to great heights of anger, a need for long periods of sleep, and a quiet power.
> The heavy bear is different, though, than other bears. He desires "a manifold of honey to smear his face." This is a clue that the heavy bear does not represent a simple emotion or desire. Apparently he has many hungers. The heavy bear can also think or dream. Through much of the description he is seen as stupid. But he can long for sweetness and tremble at the inevitability of the future. The bear is aware of his desires and fears.

Notice that this first line of inquiry, like all the others, could be extended. The student pairs the unit with one significantly similar and then notes how they differ, a process rather like making an analogy and then pointing out the negative analogy. His ability to continue doing this is constrained only by his knowledge, imagination, time, and a sense of what is useful. Notice also that in this account he has pared

away all the psychological messiness and complexity characteristic of inquiry—and so important to it. This is not a tran-
script of what actually went on in his mind but something
like a summary or an economical paraphrase.

How does this unit, viewed as a particle, vary?

The heavy bear's behavior or state varies considerably in the poem. First, he is lumbering here and there,
a hungry, beating brute. He is a picture of hostility and
physical activity. But he is also pictured as a whimpering
baby. He howls in his sleep for sugar, as a baby for his
bottle. The heavy bear trembles at the uncertainty of the
future. Thirdly, the bear is pictured as neither a brute nor
a babe, but as a creature which follows his master about.
The bear is not simple in his behavior. He varies to extremes.

*Where is this unit, viewed as a particle, located in tempor-
al, spatial, and class distribution?*

The heavy bear has "followed me since the black
womb held." It represents not a new emotion or desire,
but one which has been with the man since his birth. The
heavy bear is natural, an instinct or desire present at birth.
Nowhere does the poem say that the bear has grown with
experience or time or learning.

There are a "hundred million of his kind. The
scrimmage of appetite everywhere." The heavy bear is
not unique to this man. All of us have heavy bears. And
our heavy bears are in constant combat with each other.
The bear "boxes his brother in the hate-filled city."

What is the relation of the heavy bear to his companion? The heavy bear seems to be in a vague location,
outside yet inside the man. The bear goes "with" the
man, follows him, and drags him. He sleeps and walks independently of his companion. Yet the heavy bear is
described as "too near, my private, yet unknown." Note
that "too near" and "my private" are separated by
commas. The bear is not too near something that is
private; he is that something!

Summary of the particle perspective

Several important conclusions can be made with
this data. This is a complex metaphor in which the bear's
behavior varies. The bear does have a manifold effect on a
person. He is found in everyone, and he is present from

birth. Though he is sometimes apart from one's personality, he can also be indistinguishable from a person's deepest and unknown motives. I want to advance this hypothesis: the heavy bear represents animal instincts, desires, and drives which are present in all of us. These animal characteristics need defining. Hopefully, the subsequent data will make these characteristics clear.

Here he steps back from the exploration and guesses about the meaning of the metaphor; later he will reject the guess. Inquiry is essentially trial and error activity; the function of a heuristic procedure is to reduce the number of trials and errors necessary for reaching a reasonable solution.

How does the unit, viewed as a wave, differ from other similar processes?

Viewed as a dynamic event, this metaphor is a cycle, rather than a process with beginning and end. At both the beginning and end of the poem, the heavy bear is a hungry beast, seeking to satisfy his appetite. He appears as a beating, kicking, boxing brute. And he leaves, dragging his victim into a scrimmage of appetite. A third person is not compatible with the bear. He boxes his brother, and touches the loved one grossly. At the end, the bear is "going with" his companion again. This cyclic process suggests that the bear doesn't change over long periods of time. The beginning follows the end. The same boxing and gross touching will happen again. The companion cannot change the bear's behavior.

What are the different dynamic processes of the unit, viewed as a wave?

There are several processes going on simultaneously. The heavy bear's aggressiveness changes with time. At first, he is a brute, beating and boxing as he seeks food. Suddenly, in the next stanza, his attitude changes to one of cowardice. The ephemeral quality of life terrifies him. Next, the heavy bear is passive, following and shadowing his companion. Finally, he becomes aggressive again, carrying off his victim. The moods and influence of the bear change.

There is another wave propagating with time. The physical attachment of the bear with his companion changes. In the beginning the heaving bear lumbers here and there, not paying much attention to his companion. In the next stanza the bear is sleeping next to his companion, but isn't conscious of the companion's presence. The bear follows the man around until the roles are switched and he drags his victim off.

A third process involves other characters. Initially, only the bear and man are present. Soon, the bear boxes his brother. When a loved one appears, he touches her grossly. The bear does not just interact with man, but with other people as well.

How is the unit, viewed as a wave, part of a larger context?

The bear metaphor is part of the poem. Notice that the poem is organized into three stanzas. Each stanza can be separated from the next depending upon the activities of the bear. In the first stanza, he lumbers here and there. In the second, he is sleeping. In the third, the bear is following and then leading the man. There are three distinct actions taking place.

Consider the bear in relation to his companion. In the first two stanzas, there is very little interaction between the bear and man. Yet in the last stanza, the bear takes on a new relationship. He is an inescapable animal, now, who moves where the man moves. Eventually, he drags the man away. The bear has much more influence on the man at the end of the poem than in the beginning. His relationship with the man becomes more intimate and complex. Note, too, that the stanzas become longer as the metaphor grows more complex.

Summary of the wave perspective

The wave perspective adds new data to what I termed "animal characteristics." The bear's presence and behavior is fairly constant over long periods of time. In short periods, though, there are variations in the bear's influence. At times his presence goes virtually unnoticed, while at other times he directs the behavior of his companion. He can be aggressive and hating. He can be cowardly and afraid. He can affect people, as well as the mental state of his companion.

The reader might object that the student is overlooking important features of the poem or other possibly useful information, that he is failing to perceive essential relationships, and so on. But in original inquiry one is, finally, on his own, using whatever resources he has as intelligently as he can. Furthermore, there is no single correct way to carry out the process. The test of effective inquiry is pragmatic: does he get where he wants to go?

If the unit is viewed as a field, how do the components contrast with other units?

The bear is a complex system of many values and impulses. I want to explore this statement, noting the instances where the bear is paired against another value or emotion. For instance, the bear is described as "A stupid clown of the spirit's motive." Here, the bear is paired against the motives of the man. He distorts truth and obstructs communication. The bear "perplexes and affronts with his own darkness, the secret life of belly and bone." He gets in the way of man's deepest desires and needs. Though a word would make his heart clear, the man's love is perverted by the bear. Is the bear lust, or just a fear of exposing an intimate part of the man? The bear "trembles to think that his quivering meat, Must finally wince to nothing at all." Why is he afraid of the inevitability of the future? It should be evident that the bear reacts differently to different stimuli: honesty, love, sincerity, communication, the future.

How does the unit, viewed as a field, vary?

The image of the bear varies in the field of metaphors; that is, the bear is metaphorically described in many ways in the poem. He is a crazy factotum, who seems to mess up many matters. Physically aggressive and hating, the bear climbs, kicks, and boxes. In the second stanza he is described as a show-off in his dress suit and bulging pants. Does the bear represent ego and pride? Or is lust arousing him sexually? He is also a caricature, a swollen shadow, and a stupid clown. This series of metaphors implies that he is not deliberately plotting to distort the man's feelings. Rather the bear is stupidly and instinctively following the man. There are many possible emotions and desires metaphorically linked with the bear.

Viewed as a field, how does the unit fit into a larger system?

The heavy bear is a group of emotions within a larger system we call personality. It occupies the "central ton of every place."

Summary of the field perspective

The bear is not just animal instincts. He represents other emotions not associated with animals: pride and hatred, for example. The heavy bear occupies a central position in every individual's personality.

At this point he makes a more sophisticated guess about the meaning of the metaphor:

> I would advance this hypothesis: the bear metaphor represents a complex system of emotions and desires. Lust, hatred, aggression, stupidity, and pride are in this system. For lack of a better term, I will group all these emotions and impulses into a system called selfishness—a concern with self above all else. Selfishness varies with time. Sometimes we express it and other times not. It is at the very center of our being. We can separate it at times, but not permanently. . . .

Is this a reasonable hypothesis? Does it solve the problem, and does it solve it better than alternative hypotheses? Although, to say the least, literary criticism has not been overly concerned with such questions, they must be asked by the responsible inquirer. For a hypothesis, no matter how sound it seems to its discoverer, is only a tentative solution; it carries with it no guarantee that it will in fact solve the problem and solve it well. If the effort to verify the hypothesis reveals weaknesses, inquiry begins again. But the issue of testing takes us beyond the scope of this paper, though not beyond the scope of tagmemic invention. I want instead to consider for a moment the relation of the work I have been discussing to a recent development in the discipline of rhetoric.

Conventional approaches to composition, with their heavy emphasis on the products of composing, especially on style and usage, offer the writer little help with the composing process. He is left to explore enigmatic experiences in much the same way the child explored the cello—by unaided trial and error, gradually becoming aware of promising lines of inquiry and eventually achieving the insight which will become the nucleus of his discourse. That at least is what all of us want our students to do, what we hope they can do. But if hope springs eternal, so do student complaints that they have nothing to write about, that they can't get a good idea, and so on.

Partly in response to this problem, many rhetoricians

have become increasingly interested in the process by which one discovers and develops concepts, systems, and generalizations. Rohman and Wlecke, for example, argue that traditional approaches to the writing process are . . . inadequate if they fail to take account of the radically perspectival nature of writing. Typically such approaches stress only the virtues of hindsight—the 'rhetoric of the finished word'—without giving attention to the primary necessity of insight—the stage of discovery in shaping experience into perspective."[10] The art of invention seems to be re-emerging as a rhetorical discipline; competing with the topics of classical rhetoric, however, are a number of new methods, among which is tagmemic invention.[11]

Those of us who helped develop it believe we have a promising hypothesis, comparable to classical invention but more economical and systematic and with a wider range of application. Classroom experience and formal testing tend to support our belief.[12] We have been playing the hunch; indeed, we must do so if we are to be responsible inquirers. As Einstein pointed out, "truth is what stands the test of experience."[13]

Carnegie-Mellon University

NOTES

[1]John Holt, *How Children Learn* (New York: Pittman, 1967), p. 50.

[2]The process is discussed in John Dewey, *Logic: The Theory of Inquiry* (New York: Holt, 1938) and *How We Think* (New York: Heath, 1933).

[3]I. A. Richards, *The Philosophy of Rhetoric* (New York: Oxford University Press, 1936), p. 29.

[4]See "With My Crowbar Key" in William Stafford's *Travelling Through the Dark* (New York: Harper and Row, 1962), p. 17. The original is:

> I do tricks in order to know:
> careless I dance,
> then turn to see

the mark to turn God left for me.

[5]Kenneth Pike, "Beyond the Sentence," *College Composition and Communication*,15 (October, 1964), 129.

[6]Ibid., pp. 129-30.

[7]For a more extensive discussion of the matrix, see Richard E. Young, Alton L. Becker, and Kenneth L. Pike, *Rhetoric: Discovery and Change* (New York: Harcourt, Brace and World, 1970), pp. 119-36.

[8]I have been unable to resurrect the source of the quotation.

[9]For a description of the course and for further discussion of tagmemic invention see Richard E. Young and Frank M. Koen, *The Tagmemic Discovery Procedure: An Evaluation of Its Uses in the Teaching of Rhetoric* (Ann Arbor, Mich.: University of Michigan, NEH Grant No. E0-5238-71-116, 1973).   The report is available through ERIC:ED 084517.

[10]U. S. Department of Health, Education and Welfare, Cooperative Research Program of the Office of Education, *Pre-writing: The Construction and Application of Models of Concept Formation in Writing*, by D. G. Rohman and A. O. Wlecke, Cooperative Research Project No. 2174 (Washington, D.C.: Government Printing Office, 1964), p. 20.

[11]For a discussion of this renascence, see Richard E. Young, "Invention: A Topographical Survey," in *Teaching Composition: Ten Bibliographical Essays*, ed. Gary Tate (Fort Worth: Texas Christian University Press, 1976).

[12]For discussions of formal testing of tagmemic procedures, see Young and Koen, *The Tagmemic Discovery Procedure,* and Camillus Lee Odell's "Measuring the Effect of Instruction in Pre-writing," *Research in the Teaching of English*, 8 (Fall, 1974), 228-40.

[13]From Albert Einstein, "The Laws of Science and the Laws of Ethics," in *Out of My Later Years* (New York: Philosophical Library, 1950), pp. 114-15.

PART FIVE

Squiggles on a Moebius Strip

Rhetorical criticism joins literary criticism to rhetoric and provides a holistic framework for discovering the meaning of texts. When used, this critical method prevents the fragmentation inherent in traditional literary criticism because in this system specific features of a text must be accounted for, thus insuring that logos, pathos, and ethos as well as structure and style be considered before completing an analysis of a text and arriving at its meaning. Because individual squiggles can confuse a reader and prevent the understanding of a particular text, this fruitful approach produces an adhesive which sticks squiggles together, allowing the reader simultaneously to hold all parts of a text in a continuum like a Moebius strip. W. Ross Winterowd outlines in "The Three R's: Reading, Reading, and Rhetoric" the reciprocal relationships between reading theory and literary criticism. Beginning with the contributions of reading theory (psycholinguistics), he surveys four critical methods (mimetic, expressive, pragmatic, objective), and then offers a framework for a holistic criticism. Gerald J. Prince in "Questions, Answers, and Narrative Legibility: A Structuralist Heuristic" elucidates the marriage of rhetorical function to structuralist criticism. In his concern for the reader and the ways through which a reader constructs a text, he sets forth the conditions for textual communicability and clarifies the means for deciphering a text. Directing the reader's attention to pictorial images created by the printed word, Kay Parkhurst Easson in "'Description as Cosmos': Blake's Settings in Milton" maps out Blake's descriptive practice and maintains that his method of visualization is "primarily a rhetorical tool, stimulating a reader to precise visual identification of the artifact being described." In "Beauty's Spouse's Odd Elysium: Barth's Funhouse" Thomas O. Sloane continues to explore the relationships which bind reader to text and argues that the reader actively participates with an author as co-creator.   He details ways a reader achieves identification with the author by engaging in dialectic.   In these explorations of rhetoric in the reading process, the importance of the reader emerges as central to the deciphering of a text.

W. ROSS WINTEROWD

THE THREE R's:
READING, READING, AND RHETORIC

Any theory of literary criticism states or at the very least (and more usually) implies a theory of reading. It should be illuminating, then, to examine prominent movements in criticism from the standpoint of what we have learned, in roughly the last ten years, about the phenomenon of reading. Freed from the limitations of structuralist-behaviorist theory, psycholinguistics of the "mentalistic" transformational-generative school has made a quantum leap in explaining what happens when a visual system mediates between strange black squiggles and a receptor mind in the process of deriving meanings. Insofar as a theory of criticism contradicts what we know to be the case in reading, that theory must be faulty; on the other hand, reading theory can verify some of criticism's hermeneutic, exegetical techniques and pro-cedures. In general, it turns out to be the case that reading theory almost always illuminates critical theory, and often critical theory illuminates reading theory. (In order to cut down on awkward verbiage, I will henceforth use *criticism* to mean *critical theory* and *psycholinguistics* to denote *reading theory.*)

Before I undertake to map out the correspondence be-tween criticism and psycholinguistics and before I elaborate the second premise of this discussion (that criticial theory is usually nothing more than fragmented rhetorical theory), I would like to pause long enough to illustrate what I mean concerning the relationship between criticism and psycholinquistics.

It is virtually a dogma of modern criticism that all literature is ironic, must be ironic to qualify as literature. And part of the irony arises from texture, which is, in effect, the intractability that arises from the conflict of matter with manner, the tension between what is being said and the way in which that content is expressed. As Robert Penn Warren (only one among a great number that could be cited) puts it: "Can we make any generalizations about the nature of the poetic structure? First, it involves resistances, at various levels. There is the tension between the rhythm of the poem and the rhythm of speech . . . between the formality of the rhythm and the informality of the language; between the particular and the general, the concrete and the abstract; between the elements of even the simplest metaphor. . . the poet is like the jiujitsu expert; he wins by utilizing the resistance of his opponent—the materials of the poem. In other words, a poem, to be good, must earn itself. It is a motion toward a point of rest, but if it is not resisted motion, it is motion of no consequence."[1] In effect, a poem has *texture*, which arises from the various resistances inherent in the nature of the art.

Psycholinguistics is extremely useful in clarifying the irony of poetic structure.

It is axiomatic that the reader employs three cue systems in the process of deriving meaning; in the jargon, these are the *grapho-phonic*, *syntactic*, and *semantic systems*.[2] Each of the cue systems demands brief explanation.

To be sure, there is a correspondence between the graphic system of the poem as written and the phonic system of the reader's spoken dialect. So much goes without saying. It is obvious, however, that there is not a letter-by-letter correspondence, for a word such as *phthistic* contains only five phonemes: roughly /tizik/. Not so obvious, but hardly astounding, is the fact that proficient readers derive meanings from graphemes, not phonemes. That is, meaning is derived from the configuration on the page without the mediation of sound. This is a well-established principle of psycholinguistics.[3] Even though there is a grapho-phonic correspondence between the written and the spoken versions of a text, in nonesthetic reading that correspondence is ignored, and the reader proceeds directly from the graphemic system to meaning. And here I will stress the difference between what I call *nonesthetic* and *esthetic* reading, a point that I will clarify in a moment.

The function of the syntactic cue system is obvious. There is all the difference in the world between *Man bites dog* and *Dog bites man*. Furthermore, the syntactic system determines the parts of speech that can fill various slots in a sentence. In the sequence DOG BITES ____, the empty slot can be filled only by a nominal or an adverbial. Thus much is obvious. Equally obvious is the principle of accessibility, that is, the relative difficulty or ease with which meaning can be derived from a sentence. Both

(1) The child tossed up the ball which its father put down

and

(2) The child tossed the ball which its father put down up

are perfectly grammatical, but (1) is clearly more accessible than (2). It goes without saying that the less accessible version of any sentence is more *visible* than the more accessible version. Grammatical distortions, as in Cummings, are maximally *visible*, call attention to themselves as structures. In nonesthetic reading, the optimal condition is invisibility of syntax.

Meaning in a sentence is not, of course, a mere 1+ 1 +1 sum of its parts, a principle that is easily illustrated by the fact that no one is really uncertain about the meaning of the following: Last month we flew to New York in a____. (I think there are only two words that will fill the slot, *plane* and *jet*, and they are virtually semantic equivalents.) But, in fact, the semantic system of nonpoetic and poetic writings differ in radical and significant ways. Perhaps the best discussion of this difference is by Philip Wheelwright.[4] In literal language, symbols are discrete, univocal, invariant; in expressive language, symbols have iconic significance, are characterized by plurisignation, are given soft focus, are semantic variables which shift their meaning (to some extent) in context. In literal language, the significance of utterances as speech acts is normally definite; utterances are commands, requests, promises, and so on. But in expressive language, *assertorial tone* is softened.[5]

In sum, for maximum efficiency in nonesthetic reading, the grapho-phonic system must be invisible, sentences must be maximally accessible syntactically, and semantics must be *logical* rather than *translogical*, to use Wheelwright's terms.

Much poetry—perhaps most—seems particularly designed to make reading (in the sense of the efficient processing of black squiggles on a page to derive meaning) difficult, if not impossible. Consider what happens in the reading of this stanza from a relatively easy poem:

> There is a Garden in her face,
> Where Rose and White Lillies grow;
> A heav'nly paradice is that place,
> Wherein all pleasant fruits doe flow.
> There Cherries grow which none may buy
> Till Cherry ripe themselves doe cry.

The insistance of rhythm and rhyme makes the grapho-phonic system highly visible; the reader inevitably finds it more or less difficult to keep the phonics of the poem from coming between himself or herself and the meaning, which, as we have said, should emerge without the mediation of sound. Reading a metered and rhymed poem, then, is in a real sense a primitive activity, taking one back in time to the halting period of childhood, when reading was indeed the tortuous process of making enigmatic black squiggles correspond to meaningful sounds. (In the jargon, the reading model GRAPHEME→ PHONEME→ MEANING is called mediated word identification.)[6]

As to syntax and accessibility, the structure here is relatively straightforward, but clearly the following is more easily read than its original version: "There cherries grow which none may buy until they themselves do cry Cherry ripe." If syntax calls attention to itself, it does not function with maximum efficiency in the unmediated acquisition of meaning through use of the cue system. In other words, once again, the cue system becomes an object, not an instrument.

The translogicality of the semantic system in the stanza is pervasive, and I will comment on it briefly. *Garden* and *cherries* are both metaphoric and iconic. It is almost impossible to assign an exact meaning to *pleasant fruits*. And so on.

144

Here, then, is a great irony: the expressive language of poetry is not efficient language. A Coleridgean metaphor comes to mind: the language of poetry is like a pane of glass textured by frost which partially blocks the vision and which calls attention to itself as an object worth contemplating. This irony of texture is precisely—though not completely—explicable in terms of how the cue system works in the psycholinguistic process called reading.

The purpose of the foregoing was to give immediate demonstration of a principle: that it is productive to consider criticism from the viewpoint of psycholinguistics. Now I would like to become more general in my survey and to introduce the notion of rhetorical criticism.

In the first chapter of *The Mirror and the Lamp*, M. H. Abrams gives a concise and brilliant outline of critical viewpoints, which, as everyone recalls, fall into four categories: mimetic, expressive, pragmatic, and objective. Mimetic theory, viewing the poem as a mirror of reality, stresses the ratio between the poem and *reality* or *truth*. Expressive theory, viewing the poem as an expression of the poet, stresses the ratio between the poem and the poet. Pragmatic theory, viewing the poem as it affects the reader, stresses the ratio between the poem and the reader. And objective theory, viewing the poem as a unique artifact with its own ontological status, solipsistically implies a ratio between the poem and itself. Singleminded focus and close attention to the text bring the poem into being and create its value.

Schematically, then, we have the *mimetic ratio*: poem-reality, the *expressive ratio*: poem-poet; the *pragmatic ratio*: poem-reader; and the *objective ratio*: poem-poem. It must be said emphatically that seldom does an individual critic or school remain *pure*. Nonetheless, the four categories are a roughly accurate way of placing critics and schools; more important, the categories are a productive heuristic, as will be seen.

Out of context, statements that purely represent all of the viewpoints are easy to come by:

Mimetic

Tragedy, then, is an imitation of an action that is serious, complete, and of a certain magnitude.—Aristotle

Expressive

Poetry, in a general sense, may be defined to be "the

expression of the imagination"; and poetry is connate with the origin of man. Man is an instrument over which a series of external and internal impressions are driven, like the alternations of an ever-changing wind over an Aeolian lyre, which move it by their motion to ever-changing melody. But there is a principle within the human being, and perhaps within all sentient beings, which acts otherwise than in the lyre, and produces not melody alone, but harmony, by an internal adjustment of the sounds or motions thus excited to the impressions which excite them.—Shelley

Pragmatic

As virtue is the most excellent resting place for all worldly learning to make his end of, so poetry, being the most familiar to teach it, and most princely to move towards it, in the most excellent work is the most excellent work-man.—Sidney

Objective

Most of the distempers of criticism come about from yielding to the temptation to take certain remarks which we make *about* the poem—statements about what it says or about what truth it gives or about the formulations it illustrates—for the essential core of the poem itself.
—Cleanth Brooks

Granted that these out-of-context statements quite unfairly represent the extremes of the four viewpoints, nonetheless there is a tendency for critics and criticism to emphasize one or the other and thus to become reductive. To demonstrate this reductiveness—and to make an essay toward a different kind of criticism—I would like now to turn back to psycho-linguistics and to introduce the concept of discourse that is traditional in rhetoric. In other words, I want to survey critical theory in the light of psycholinguistics and rhetoric. In order to do this, I will construct two bare-bones schemata, one of rhetoric and one of the psycholinguistic phenomenon of reading.

Ignoring memory and delivery, we can say that the traditional body of rhetoric consists of three departments: invention, arrangement, and style. In turn, invention con-sists of three elements: *logos* (or reasonableness), *ethos* (or the character of the speaker), and *pathos* (or the nature of the audience). This age-old schema is not to be written off lightly, and perhaps its usefulness is no better illustrated than by demonstrating how it, in its totality, fits with the fragmented view of discourse presented by critical theory.

Critical Viewpoint	Ratio	Correspondence to Rhetoric
Mimetic	poem-reality	←*logos* ⎤
Expressive	poem-poet	←*ethos* ⎬—invention
Pragmatic	poem-reader	←*pathos*⎦
Objective	poem-poem	←arrangement, style

This chart is, of course, simple enough, but it is also dramatic. It demonstrates the holistic, synthetic nature of rhetoric and the fragmented nature of literary criticism. Hereafter we will discuss the implications of the chart more thoroughly.

The axioms of psycholinguistic theory are a productive heuristic for thinking about critical theory. First, one hardly needs proof that by far the most important factor in the phenomenon of reading is the perceiving mind with all its limitations, its emotional sets, its reservoir of past experience. In fact, it is empirically demonstrable that the amount of information a skilled reader derives from a text is amazingly small. In general, "There is a limited-capacity short-term memory that creates a bottleneck in the transmission of visual information to the comprehension processes of the brain; therefore, it is essential that the brain provide more information from its side of the eyeballs than the eyes pick up from the page."[7] Psycholinguists talk about the magic number 7 plus or minus two: short-term memory is capable of holding only between five and nine bits of information. A *bit* is a piece of information that reduces uncertainty by one-half. For instance, if I am holding a card from an ordinary deck and ask you to name the suit, you will need two bits of information to do so. First bit: "Is the card black?" (I answer, "No." You are now certain that the card is red.) Second bit: "Is the card a heart?" (I answer, "No." You are now certain that the card is a diamond.)

Second, we obviously derive meanings that are somehow independent of the words that originally carried them. If I were to ask you to tell me what I have said so far, I would think you mad—and be convinced you are an idiot savant—if you quoted what I have so far written word-for-word. Obviously, whole texts—poems, articles, novels—have deep and surface structures, just as sentences do.

Third, reading is a process of *scanning, predicting, testing,* and *confirming.*[8] It is simply demonstrable that close reading during initial contact with the text reduces one's ability to derive meaning. During the first contact, the closer the reading, the less the meaning derived. (I am not arguing against ultimate close reading.) Or another perspective: ". . . the perception of serial displays has three stages: *scanning,* to form a schema; *ordering* of the schematic elements; and *impleting* or filling in of the schematized but ordered items."[9] And if you have now picked up my cues and have begun to think about the New Criticism as a theory of impletion, you are on the right track.

All of the foregoing has, in fact, been prefatory to the main thrust of this paper. The preface having been gracefully danced through, we can now begin to saw wood.

Mimetic theory implies that the meaning *in here* in the poem somehow corresponds to a truth or a reality *out there* in the universe beyond the poem. The mimetic critic typically asks, "Is the poem true? Is it verisimilar?" In these questions is implied a system of values. If the answer is yes, the poem is *good.* In other words, as the schema that was developed some pages back would indicate, mimetic theory is concerned with what rhetoricians call *logos.* Here is Yvor Winters: "The theory of literature which I defend in these essays is absolutist. I believe that a work of literature, in so far as it is valuable, approximates a real apprehension and communication of a particular kind of objective truth. . . . The poem is good in so far as it makes a defensible rational statement about a given human experience (the experience need not be real but must be in some sense possible) and at the same time communicates the emotion which ought to be motivated by the rational understanding of that experience."[10]

In regard to *logos,* it turns out that poetics and psycholinguistics are of great help to rhetoric. We are dealing essentially with the question, "What is the meaning of meaning?" In the essay "Myth, Fiction, and Displacement" from *Fables of Identity*, Northrop Frye argues that as we are reading fiction, we are directly concerned with continuity, but after we have read, we lose sight of and interest in sequaciousness. Our knowledge is of what is generally called *theme*, and theme consists of *subject, allegory* (Hamlet personifies indecision, for instance), and *mythos*, which is the work "as a simultaneous unity, when the entire shape of it is clear in our minds." It is *dianoia.* (One might say that *dianoia* is the deep structure, and Frye does argue that the same *mythos* can have various surface realizations.) Frye says, ". . . because myths are stories, what they 'mean' is inside them, in the implications of their incidents. No rendering of any myth into conceptual language can serve as a full equivalent of its meaning. . . . its life is always the poetic life of a story, not the homiletic life of some illustrated truism." Naturalism and realism are just indirect mythologizing, to which Frye applies the term *displacement*. "Literary shape cannot come from life; it comes only from literary tradition, and so ultimately from myth."[11]

The mystique of contextualism, as in Eliseo Vivas and Murray Krieger, deals interestingly and productively with meaning in a way not too far removed from Northrop Frye. In summary, the contextualists argue something like this: In the world *out there* are unformed, inchoate ideas floating in and forming the stream of experience. These can become the materials of poetry—the *substance*. The poet shapes these materials through the form of the poem, gives them *insistence* and hence more than merely inchoate being. Through the insistence of the poem, these materials gain *existence* and become cultural artifacts.[12] The poem itself *means* as what Krieger calls a *reductive metaphor*. As he explains, "The repetitive patterns of a work, which gives stillness to the movement by freezing freedom, must be read by the critic into his hypothesis of the work's form, as he makes it a reductive metaphor—an emblem, a constitutive symbol—for all the moving life and liveliness of the work. The metaphor, while excluding so much of the middle in its reductive, extremist purity, is in its emblematic fullness at the same time all-inclusive."[13]

So far, so good. Both Frye and Krieger are telling us in their own ways that meaning has an independence of the text, and this only makes sense: you and I can meaningfully talk about the meaning of *Hamlet*, but we certainly could not recite the text, beyond a few of the soliloquies which have become set pieces. But in their discussions of meaning,

Frye and Krieger, like most critics, keep their eyes too firmly focused on the poem-reality ratio which characterizes mimetic statements. (I am not necessarily saying that Frye and Krieger are mimetic critics.) For Frye, the ultimate reality is myth, while for Krieger, interestingly enough, the ultimate reality is the poem.

As a rhetorical-psycholinguistic corrective to critical discussions of meaning, I propose the following:

> . . . all perception might be regarded as a process of decision-making based on significant differences detected in the environment. The actual nature of the significant differences is not determined by the physical effects themselves, but by the perceiver's rules for distinguishing those events that he wishes to treat as functionally equivalent from those that he wishes to treat as different. Events to be treated as equivalent will be allocated to the same cognitive category, which is specified by the rules that are represented in its feature lists. In other words, the perceiver brings a highly structured knowledge of the world into every perceptual situation. Rather than saying that he discovers order and regularities that are properties of the environment, it is more appropriate to say that the perceiver imposes his own organization upon the information that reaches his receptor systems. The organization of his knowledge of the world lies in the structure of his cognitive categories and the manner in which they are related—in the way the perceiver *partitions* his knowledge of the world.[14]

An account of meaning, then, that does not take the perceiving mind into consideration is only a partial account. In this respect, we are more satisfied with Frye's conception of the rockbottom mythic nature of literary knowledge than we are with structuralist or contextualist theories of meaning as a function of the text exclusively.

In surveying mimetic criticism as a source for an account of *logos*, we have now argued, on the basis of pscyholinguistics and rhetoric, that the mimetic ratio of poem-reality must be expanded to include *pathos*, and our ratio becomes poem-reality-reader. Obviously this expanded ratio is highly rhetorical in nature, for the concept of audience has entered.

In its various manifestations, objective criticism, particularly New Criticism, is deeply anti-expressivist. Wimsatt and Beardsley's classic essay "The Intentional Fallacy" comes to mind here, and it is so widely known that it need not be quoted. Expressive criticism, however, is undergoing a renaissance in a variety of quarters, some of which I would like to survey briefly. In their work, J. L. Austin and John Searle have begun to work out a grammar of expressivism, in effect arguing that without intention, any language is meaningless.[15] I am reluctant to explore even the peripheries of speech act theory here, but perhaps some brief illustrations will nail the concept down sufficiently. If you think about a sentence such as "Could you raise the window?" you will realize that, even though it is interrogative in form, it is ambiguous until you can supply an intention. The sentence is either a yes/no question or a request. In other words, your supplying an intention is not a fallacy at all, but a necessity.

Walter Ong argues movingly that "all words projected from a speaker remain, as has been seen, somehow interior to him, being an invitation to another person, another interior, to share the speaker's interior, an invitation to enter in, not to regard from the outside."[16] And, of course, Wayne Booth's fascinating *A Rhetoric of Irony* is largely an argument in behalf of the intentional fallacy.

In dealing with mimetic theory, we argue that the ratio had to be expanded from poem-reality to poem-reality-reader, else the criticism would fall short of its pretensions to explain and evaluate works of literature. Expressive criticism, from the Romantics onward (indeed, from Plotinus onward), has stressed the poem-poet ratio. Can we not productively combine mimetic and expressive theory to arrive at a poem-reality-reader-poet ratio? If we do this, we are coming even nearer to what might be called rhetorical criticism, for we have introduced the concept of *ethos*. In fact, however, our own intuition as well as tradition tells us that rhetorical criticism and literary criticism are different sorts of activities. The nature of the difference becomes clear when we take the pragmatic and the objective viewpoints toward texts.

Blatantly Marxist, gay, or feminist criticism is often representative of pragmatism at its most raucous and least interesting, but to claim that there is not a pragmatics of literature is to deny that literature has an effect. Once again, Northrop Frye can help us. In his terms, the imaginative world of literature is virtually the short-stopping of action, of strictly pragmatic results: "So we begin to see where the imagination belongs in the scheme of human affairs. It's the power of constructing possible models of human experience. In the world of imagination, anything goes that's imaginatively possible, but nothing really happens. If it did happen, it would move out of the world of imagination and into the world of action."[17] Thus the use of literature is to construct a vision of the possible, not to effect the actual.

One of the great shortcomings of modern psycholinguistic theory in reading is its pragmatic nature, viewing reading as the processing of information to bring about understanding, which is defined as the reduction of uncertainty: "Reading is an act of communication in which information is transferred from a transmitter to a receiver, whether the reader is a scholar deciphering a medieval text or a child identifying a single letter on a blackboard. Because of this basic nature of reading, there are insights to be gained from the study of theories of communication and information; there are concepts that are particularly useful for the construction of a theory of reading, and a terminology that can be employed to increase the clarity of its expression."[18] This language, which represents the thrust of reading theory and the mental sets of the theorists, can be significantly influenced by a corrective from literary criticism. What the critics realize and describe again and again is an experience that I call *esthetic immersion*. What I mean by esthetic immersion has been stated again and again by critic after critic, for anyone who reads imaginative literature passionately has had the experience. This experience of reading has never, I think, been more beautifully described than by Sartre, and I will quote him in lieu of compiling a chrestomathy or of compounding words: ". . . the characteristic of aesthetic consciousness is to be a belief by means of commitment, by oath, a belief sustained by fidelity to one's self and to the author, a perpetually renewed choice to believe. I can awaken at every moment, and I know it; but I do not want to; reading is a free dream. . . .reading is an exercise in generosity, and what the writer requires of the reader is not the application of an abstract freedom but the gift of his whole person, with his passions, his prepossessions, his sympathies, his sexual temperment, and his scale of values."[19] In other words, esthetic reading is a passionate exchange in freedom between an author and a reader. Freedom being mankind's greatest good, the value of reading lies in the exchange of freedom.

Whether or not we are moved by Sartre's dithyramb, we must admit that in some sense esthetic reading is less purposeful than nonesthetic reading. The pragmatics of esthetic reading involve immersion; the pragmatics of non-esthetic reading stress the acquisition of information *for some use*.

Meaning is, of course, independent of reference, but purpose in nonesthetic reading is closely tied to reference; that is, we do frequently read to gain mastery over Reality. Teleologically, then, esthetic reading is radically different from nonesthetic reading, and, as we all know, the experiences themselves differ. The pragmatics of esthetic reading are anti-pragmatic.

The anti-pragmatic nature of esthetic reading has been dealt with most extensively by objective critics. You will re-call that at the beginning of this discussion we developed a long digression concerning the cue system in reading and the nature of poetic texture. The concept of texture is, of course, one of the major ideas in objective criticism. In general the objectivists explore the ontological status of the poem. Of particular significance are structure and style.

In nonesthetic reading, structure and style achieve, as I have pointed out, a certain invisibility that they do not have in esthetic reading. The objective critic—in his attempt at purity—views the poem as an esthetic structure, but the interpretation of *structure* here must be broad enough to allow for the totality of the imaginative construct, from the prosody of a sonnet to what Percy Lubbock called (as I para-phrase him) "the shadow and phantasmal form of the novel."

As far as they go, the great objectivists—Brooks, Warren, Tate, Ransom—are perfectly right. Structure, texture, irony, tension, ambiguity—these do constitute a good deal of what we point to when we differentiate poetry from rhetoric. The objectivists, however, as psycholinguists might point out to them, have a strange notion of that highly personal idiosyncratic receptor, the brain, which cannot

153

lobotomize itself at will and exclude its intuition that someone did have a motive for writing this poem, that this novel
does bear on the facts of American history, that that play is
uncannily near to the viewer's actual experience.

In other words, criticism must be rhetorical criticism in
that it takes account of *logos, pathos, ethos,* structure, and
style. In fact, critical logomachies are largely the result of
the failure to place the study of literature within a holistic
framework such as that provided by rhetoric.

In this paper, there are many problems that I have not
dealt with—the persona of the narrator, for instance. What I
have tried to suggest is simple enough. Literary criticism
deals with reading, either implicitly or explicitly, and reading
is the process of deriving meaning from written discourse. It
should be the case, then, that literary criticism would shed
light on reading theory and vice versa. I hope that I have
demonstrated as much. Furthermore, I have argued that
rhetoric—transformed at crucial points—is a vital corrective
for the fragmentation of literary criticism. It seems to me
that literary studies are vital to rhetoric, but even more so,
rhetoric is vital to literature, for the field has a robustness
that can be a healthy corrective for the effeteness of some—
perhaps most—literary studies.

University of Southern California

NOTES

[1] Robert Penn Warren, "Pure and Impure Poetry," in *Critical Theory Since Plato*, ed. Hazard Adams (New York: Harcourt Brace Jovanovich, 1971), p. 991.

[2] Kenneth S. Goodman, "Psycholinguistic Universals in the Reading Process," in *Psycholinguistics and Reading*, ed. Frank Smith (New York: Holt, Rinehart and Winston, 1973), p. 25.

[3] See, for instance, Frank Smith, "Decoding: The Great Fallacy," in *Psycholinguistics and Reading*, pp. 70-83.

[4] Philip Wheelwright, "The Logical and the Translogical," in

Critical Theory Since Plato, pp. 1103-12. (This is Chapter 4 of *The Burning Fountain: A Study in the Language of Symbolism*.)

[5]Wheelwright does not use the term *speech acts*, but he is clearly talking about the principle that Austin and Searle, among others, have explored in detail.

[6]Frank Smith, *Understanding Reading* (New York: Holt, Rinehart and Winston, 1971), pp. 159-84.

[7]Ibid., p. 69.

[8]Goodman, pp. 23-24.

[9]Paul A. Kolers, "Three Stages of Reading," in *Psycholinguistics and Reading*, p. 32.

[10]Yvor Winters, *In Defense of Reason* (Denver: Alan Swallow, 1947), p. 11.

[11]Northrop Frye, "Myth, Fiction, and Displacement," in *Fables of Identity* (New York: Harcourt, Brace and World, Inc., 1963), pp. 21-38 passim.

[12]Eliseo Vivas, "The Objective of the Poem," in *Critical Theory Since Plato*, pp. 1069-77.

[13]Murray Krieger, "Mediation, Language, and Vision in the Reading of Literature," in *Critical Theory Since Plato*, p. 1244.

[14]Smith, p. 187.

[15]J. L. Austin, *How to Do Things with Words* (Cambridge, Mass.: Harvard University Press, 1962); John R. Searle, *Speech Acts: An Essay in the Philosophy of Language* (Cambridge, Eng.: Cambridge University Press, 1970).

[16]Walter J. Ong, S.J., "A Dialectic of Aural and Objective Correlatives," in *Critical Theory Since Plato*, p. 1162.

[17]Northrop Frye, *The Educated Imagination* (Bloomington: Indiana University Press, 1964), p. 22.

[18]Smith, p. 12.

[19]Jean-Paul Sartre, "Why Write?" in *Critical Theory Since Plato*, p. 1063.

GERALD J. PRINCE

QUESTIONS, ANSWERS,
AND NARRATIVE LEGIBILITY:
A STRUCTURALIST HEURISTIC

In recent years, the study of literature in general and narrative in particular has been shifting from a concern with the author or with the text to a concern with the reader. Instead of establishing the meaning of a given text in terms of an author's intentions or a set of textual patterns, for example, students of literature have focused more and more frequently on the ways in which readers, armed with interpretive expectations and conventions, structure a text and give it meaning. Ideal readers, virtual readers, implied readers, informed readers, competent readers, experienced readers, superreaders, arch-readers, average readers and plain old readers now abound in literary criticism; and we seem to have entered an age in which the writer, the writing, and the written are less important than the read, the reading, and the reader.[1]

But what is a reader and what is reading? Very generally speaking, reading may be defined as an activity presupposing a text (a set of visually presented linguistic symbols from which meaning can be extracted), a reader (an agent capable of extracting meaning from that set), and an interaction between the text and the reader such that the latter is able to answer correctly at least some questions about the meaning of the former. Indeed, reading a text may be said to be grossly equivalent to processing textual data gradually by asking questions of the text and answering them on the basis of it.[2]

Note that, according to this definition, reading a text and a reading of a text need obviously not be equivalent: the latter may consist in (and very often does consist in) a selection, development, and reordering of the answers reached during the former. Similarly, reading a text and responding to it need not amount to the same thing at all even though one may influence the other. Given a subtext like

(1) John was Jim's brother

I may fantasize all sorts of things about John and Jim—that they were both tall, dark, and handsome, that they both liked to play cards, that they both excelled in sports—and may respond to them accordingly. However, that fantasizing (and response) is not part of my reading (1) even though it may occur while I am reading (2) and even though it may give rise to some of the questions I ask about the rest of the text and to some of the answers I formulate.[3]

Moreover, it is clear that not every set of visually presented linguistic symbols can be read: some such sets—a series of letters randomly scattered on a page, for instance—may not constitute a text. No meaning can be extracted from them. They do not make any sense or, at best, they merely trace some of the limits between sense and nonsense. Likewise, it is clear that it is not enough to recognize visually presented symbols as linguistic in order to be a reader. Identifying a series of symbols as specific graphemes is not the same as extracting meaning from them; and I would not say, except as a joke, that I read German (or Rumanian, or Russian) very well but that I did not understand it. Finally, reading a text implies that the questions asked are not relevant to textual meaning. Some questions are not relevant because they have nothing to do with the extraction of meaning: to ask how many consonants there are on the first page of *The Sun Also Rises* will not prove helpful for reading that page, for understanding it; and other questions are not relevant because they cannot possibly be answered on the basis of the text, as the following riddle illustrates:

(2) The third deck of the ship is six hundred feet long

and two hundred feet wide. How old is the captain?

Of course, reading a text in no way implies that all the relevant questions are asked and all the possible answers found. Indeed, it frequently implies the opposite. The set of relevant questions (and answers) is often a very large one, and as I read (in order to keep on reading!), I have to select certain questions rather than others. Of course too, learning how to read is—among other things—learning how to ask more and more relevant questions. The ingenious reader is not only one who can find new answers to well-known questions, but also one who can think of new questions.

The relevant questions that may be asked while reading a text are very varied in kind, and their number, in the case of some texts at least, may be infinite. These questions pertain to the denotational meaning of the sequences of symbols presented, their connotational meaning, their symbolic meaning, their functional meaning, their significance in terms of other literary or non-literary worlds, and, very generally speaking, the connections that can be made among the answers arrived at. For example, given the following passage from Perrault's *Le Petit Chaperon rouge*:

(3) "Little Red Riding Hood left immediately to go to her grandmother, who lived in another village. Passing through a wood, she met Brother Wolf who felt very much like eating her; but he did not dare because of some woodcutters who were in the forest. He asked her where she was going. The poor child, who did not know that it was dangerous to stop and listen to a wolf, told him: 'I am going to see my grandmother and bring her a griddle-cake, with a little pot of butter that my mother is sending her.' "

I may ask such questions as:

(4) Where did Little Red Riding Hood go?
(5) What for?
(6) Why didn't Brother Wolf eat her?
(7) Will he get another chance?

(8) Will he succeed?
(9) Will the child's ignorance cost her dearly?
(10) What is a griddle-cake?
(11) Does it have any special connotations?
(12) What is the connotation of the name "Brother Wolf"?
(13) What about "Little Red Riding Hood"?
(14) Is Brother Wolf's desire to be understood as sexual?
(15) Will the child's grandmother protect her?
(16) What is the grandmother's name?

and so on and so forth. Naturally, even if all of my questions have a certain relevance as I am reading, I may not find any answers to them: (16), for instance, will always remain unanswered.

In view of the above, it is not easy to determine what reading maximally would be: we can only say with certainty that, for reasons which I have already indicated in passing, it does not always consist in asking all the relevant questions and coming up with all the right answers.[4] Nor does it always make very much sense to speak of the total reading (as finished product rather than ongoing process) of a given text, since the set of relevant questions and answers pertaining to the meaning of the text may be an infinite one. On the other hand, it is not easy to determine what reading minimally would be, either: we can only say that it entails the understanding of the linguistic meaning at the level of the sentence and at least some understanding of that meaning at the level of discourse; or, to put it in other terms, it entails the capacity to paraphrase and summarize the denotational content of the text (and of its constituent parts).

Note that, in the case of narrative texts, some questions are more narratively relevant than others: they specifically pertain to features characteristic of narratives rather than non-narratives. Questions about the plot, for example, questions about the chronology of the events presented, questions about what has happened and what will happen are narratively relevant whereas questions about the connotative meaning or symbolic significance of a given event are not (or, at least, not necessarily). Indeed, reading a text narratively (reading it "for the story") means asking above all questions that have narrative relevance—questions generally referring to the proairetic dimension and finding answers to them. If attempting to read a narrative maximally involves questions and answers about meaningful aspects, reading it minimally merely involves questions and answers about "what happens." Given *Little Red Riding Hood*, for instance, and even though I may have gathered a lot of interesting data about the similarities between the mother and the grandmother, the symbolism of the wolf, and the heroine's Electra complex, I will not have read it narratively if I have not processed that the wolf eats the grandmother, gets into her bed, then eats the granddaughter too. On the other hand, I will have read it narratively merely by focusing on the chronological sequence of events and understanding it.

Certain (sub)texts allow only one correct answer to some of the questions asked. A text like

(17)   John was twenty-five

for instance allows only one correct answer to

(18)   How old was John?

A text like

(19)   John had no siblings

allows only one correct answer to

(20)   How many siblings did John have?

And a text like

(21)   John was very tall

allows only one correct answer to

(22)   Was John very short?

Should anybody reading (17), (19), and (21) answer (18),

(20), and 22 with

     (23)   John was seventy-eight
     (24)   John had three brothers and three sisters
     (25)   Yes, he was very short

respectively, we would most probably not conclude that he was reading (17), (19), and (21) in a highly idiosyncratic manner but, rather, that he was misreading them or not reading them at all. Thus to a certain extent at least and as I have already said or implied several times, the text I read acts as a constraint on my reading.

    Note that the text may allow only one correct answer to a given question without spelling this answer out. Given

     (26)   Harry was five years older than Joan and Joan was twenty-five

or

     (27)   All professors are crazy and Mary was a professor

for instance, it is obvious that Harry is thirty and Mary crazy. Note also that, sometimes, the text not only provides answers to various questions but explicitly asks questions that a reader himself might have asked anyway. In *A la recherche du temps perdu*, for example, an exquisite pleasure invades Marcel's senses when he tastes a *petite madeleine* soaked in tea and several questions are raised in relation to this extraordinary event: "Whence could it have come to me, this all powerful joy? I was conscious that it was connected with the taste of tea and cake, but that it infinitely transcended those savours, could not, indeed, be of the same nature as theirs. Whence did it come? What did it signify? How could I seize upon and define it?"; in *Les Thibault*, the narrator finds young Jacques' power over Daniel de Fontanin remarkable and writes: "Why didn't this big thoughtful boy rebel against the urchin's influence? Didn't his education and the freedom he enjoyed give him an indisputable *droit d'aînesse* over Jacques?"; and in *Le Père Goriot*, Poiret's physical appearance seems to require explanation: "What kind of work could have thus shriveled him up? What kind of passion had darkened his bulbous face?" Indeed, there is at least one modern novel, Robert Pinget's *L'Inquisitoire*, which largely consists of such explicit questions and answers to them.

If the text constrains my reading by the unequivocal answers it brings to some of my questions, it also constrains it in various other ways. Thus it may answer my questions— or the questions it itself asks—more or less quickly. In

> (28) John was getting impatient. He had been trying to reach Jim for over an hour now

> (29) Why was John getting impatient?

is answered immediately; but in the case of *A la recherche du temps perdu*, a reader reading the novel from the first page to the last has to wait for a very long time until his (and Marcel's!) questions about the *petite madeleine* are answered. In fact, as Roland Barthes pointed out, many narratives can be viewed as a certain kind of space stretching between a question and its answer, and their unfolding is partly characterized by the kinds of delays they bring to the answering of the question.[5] In a classical detective story, for instance, the most important early question often centers around the identity of the muderer, and the correct answer usually comes only after several other suggested answers have been rejected as unsatisfactory.

Furthermore, the text may force me to update more or less frequently the information I gather as I read, by introducing data which make some of the answers I have reached (and some of the questions I have asked) obsolete. Consider the following, for example:

> (30) John had many friends, but then he committed a crime and lost them all
>
> (31) John very much wanted to go to the party; then he changed his mind
>
> (32) Jim was twenty-three and he was desperately in love with Mary, but she wouldn't even look at him. Three years passed, three years of endless

humiliation and saddness. One day, as Jim was walking down the street, he saw Mary sitting dejectedly on the curb.

Questions

    (33)   Did John have many friends?
    (34)   Did John want to go to the party?

and

    (35)   How old was Jim?

would get different answers at different points in my reading (30), (31), and (32) respectively. Of course, the updating of information is particularly important while reading narrative texts since their chronological dimension often implies very many changes in the situations and characters presented.

Note that, sometimes, a text provides an unequivocal answer which it later modifies (more than once) because it had been the wrong answer. Suppose, for instance, that the information was supplied by a narrator who lied then decided to tell the truth or by one who thought that he understood a situtation then found out that he did not. I may be told that John is twenty-three, then he actually is twenty-seven, then that he is only sixteen but looks old for his age; or that Mary loved Joan, then she really hated her but disguised her hatred very well. In such cases, I may feel that I have been misled, especially if I think that the modification indicates the narrator's bad faith rather than his ignorance. There are, of course, other reading circumstances in which I may feel cheated: instead of giving me wrong information, the narrator may simply omit information that is essential; or he may give me too much information and lead me on a tangent; or again, he may allow me to reach certain conclusions only to tell me later that these conclusions, though most plausible, are not correct.

On the other hand, a text may prove to be particularly helpful rather than deceptive. It may remind us of information it had given us previously if this information is necessary to the understanding of some new event or situation: think of such sentences as *The reader will recall that. . ., It is important to remember that. . .,* or *As we pointed out much earlier. . . .* It may explain how newly provided data, seemingly conflicting with what data we have already processed, is actually not at all inconsistent with it. When, in *A la recherche du temps perdu*, Swann, who has been portrayed as most delicate, modest, and discreet, acts in a vulgar manner, the narrator quickly notes that there is no inconsistency there: after all, "who has not seen very unpretentious royal princesses adopt spontaneously the language of old bores?"; and, in *Journal d'un curé de campagne*, when the protagonist, who is inept in dealing with people, suddenly gets the upper hand in his confrontation with the Countess, there is no inconsistency either: the text makes it clear that God is on his side. The text can also summarize for us a long series of events, or give us the gist of a complex argument, or indicate the relative significance of various actions, or reveal the symbolic implications of different situations. In fact, a text can comment appropriately on any aspect of its constituent parts and partially do the reader's work for him.

* * *

Although a text may answer many of my questions explicitly, unequivocally, and correctly, there may frequently be points in my reading where, in order to find an answer, I have to rely not only on my linguistic knowledge and the information provided by the text, but also on my mastery of logical operations, my familiarity with interpretive conventions, and my knowledge of the world. I have already indicated how, in the case of (26) or (27) for example, the text may provide an answer to a given question without spelling it out. Very often, however, I need much more than textual data and arithmetic or syllogistic operations to arrive at an answer. Consider the following:

(36) John was seven foot two
(37) Jim was throwing a big party, and Mary went to the liquor store to buy some Scotch.

Given (36), I am able to answer

(38) Was John very tall?

in the affirmative because I believe that anybody over six foot five is very tall and because I know that my belief is not uncommon. As for (37), it provides explicit answers to such questions as

    (39)   Who was throwing a big party?
    (40)   Where did Mary go?

and

    (41)   What was she going to buy?

But, in order to answer

    (42)   Why did Mary go buy some Scotch?

with something like

    (43)   She went to buy some scotch for Jim's party

I not only have to assume that Jim's party and Mary's action are somehow connected, but I also have to know that one often drinks liquor at parties. Reading is not, therefore, merely equivalent to the processing, through questions and answers, of semantic data explicitly furnished by the text or logically implied by it.

Indeed, if it is obvious that reading depends on the text being read, it is also obvious that it depends on the reader reading that text. In the first place, and even though the questions I ask while reading are—to a certain extent, at least—constrained by the text since they must be somewhat relevant to it, it is important to remember that these questions are very numerous and that I am the one who, in the final analysis, decides which questions to ask and which not to ask. Given a narrative text, for instance, I may tend to ask questions pertaining above all to the way in which some of the activities recounted combine into larger activities; or I may decide to focus on symbolic elements; or I may do both; or I may ask still other questions. Depending on the questions asked, I will reach certain answers which may lead me to modify some of the information I have already gathered and which may govern, in some measure, some of the questions I will pose as I go on reading. In other words, depending on the questions asked, my reading will vary more or less considerably.

Moreover, if a text frequently allows only one correct answer to some of the questions asked, it also frequently allows more than one answer to some other questions. In fact, it may allow an indefinite number of valid answers to a given question. After all, a text may be constituted in great part by words and sentences having many semantic possibilities, only a few of which it specifies as irrelevant (through metalinguistic commentary, for instance, or contextual constraints); it may lead to a larger number of inferences which are neither mutually exclusive nor mutually dependent; it may allow different kinds of connections to be made among its constituent parts; it may be summarizable in several ways; it may lend itself to several symbolic interpretations; and so on and so forth. If we asked how the first fifty pages of *Finnegan's Wake* could be summarized, for example, we could come up with a very large number of perfectly suitable answers. Of course, the answers would determine, to some extent, what further questions and answers would arise and would thus affect reading. In short, a text may lend itself to being read in many ways which are more or less different from one another, and a reader may read that text in any of these ways.

As I have stated or implied earlier, any reader obviously contributes significantly to his reading of any text since, in order to read, he cannot merely rely on his linguistic knowledge and the textual information provided. On the one hand, and very generally speaking, he must be capable of perceiving visually presented symbols; he must have the capacity to store information, retrieve it, and modify it as necessary; he must possess the competence to make inferences and deductions; and, naturally, he must have the ability to ask questions and find answers to them. On the other hand, and just as importantly, he must bring to his reading various kinds of knowledge, interpretive strategies, assumptions, and presuppositions. Thus the reader must have a certain knowledge of the world (of certain worlds) in order to answer certain questions (or even raise them). Further-

more, the reader must be acquainted with several codes or
sub-codes in terms of which the text is more or less de-
cipherable and interpretable.   Given a narrative text, for
instance, he will obviously use a linguistic code which will
allow him to understand the linguistic meaning of the words
and sentences making up that text; but he may also use a
symbolic code allowing him to map that linguistic meaning
onto other signifying systems (sociological, existential,
psychoanalytic, and so on); and he may use a hermeneutic
code, in terms of which he can read portions of the text as
enigmas and other portions as solutions to these enigmas; a
proairetic code, thanks to which he can combine various
narrated actions into larger actions; a code of characters,
according to which he can organize the text around heroes,
false heroes, villains, helpers, or donors; a literary code, allowing him to recognize that the text belongs to a certain narrative genre and can be read in terms of conventions of that
genre; and so forth. Finally, the reader will make certain
fundamental assumptions about the set of symbols he is deciphering. For one thing, he will assume that they are interpretable, that they do indeed make some sense; for another,
he may assume that they cohere, or can be made to cohere,
into various trans-sentential patterns, even though they may
seem strangely disparate at first. Thus if the text brings a lot
to the reader, the reader brings a lot to the text.[6]

Of course, a given reader may be very tired or not at
all, very young or very old, in an excellent mood or a bad
one; he may have a very good or a very deficient memory, a
very great or a very limited capacity for decentration, a considerable or moderate attention span; he may know very
little or an awful lot; he may be reading the text for the first,
second, or tenth time; he may want to read for fun or out of
a sense of duty; he may show particular interest in the language, the plot, the characters, or the symbolism; he may
hold one set of beliefs or another. In other words, his physiological, psychological, and sociological conditioning may vary
greatly and so may his reading: his knowledge, his capacities,
his interests, and his aims determine to a certain extent the
conventions, assumptions, and presuppositions he takes to
underlie the text, the kinds of connections he is particularly,
interested in making, the questions he chooses to ask and the

answers he finds for them. In fact, the same reader may read the same text very differently on different occasions.

*   *   *

We often characterize a (narrative) text in terms of its readability: we say that it is highly readable, or barely readable, or practically unreadable, and we usually mean that it is more or less easy to decipher and make sense of and that it is more or less interesting and pleasing when read. It is clear that, just as reading a text is a function of the text and the reader, so is readability; more particularly, just as reading varies with the individual reader, so does readability. After all, one reader may find it more difficult than another to extract meaning from a particular novel because his knowledge of various codes and interpretive conventions is more limited. Similarly, one reader may find it more boring than another to read a certain story because he is less psychologically motivated to do it. It is therefore practically impossible to measure the readability of a text in absolute terms, and it is exceedingly difficult to measure it for a given reader in a given situation. However, it is perhaps not as complicated or hopeless to try and assess at least in part what I will call the legibility of any text: the legibility of x can be equated with how easy it is to make sense out of x; and that easiness can be computed in terms of the number of operations it takes to make sense, their complexity (how many elements constitute one of them), their diversity, and their very possibility, given x. In other words, to determine how legible a given text is, we would have to determine how many questions one must ask in order to arrive at an answer, how complicated they have to be, how different they are one from the other, how they are answered or could be answered, and even whether they can be answered at all. We would thus not be concerned with whether a given reader shares the assumptions of a given text, whether he knows the conventions and codes necessary to decipher that text, whether he is experienced, or whether he is in the right frame of mind, but rather with such problems as the number of conventions and codes which would be necessary for any reader to make sense out of that text. Of course, should we attempt to define the narrative legibility of a narrative text, we would be particularly concerned with how well the text lends itself to narratively relevant operations (ones directly related to such features as plot, chronology of events, hermeneutic units, and so on and so forth).

Consider the following, for instance:

(44) "Apportez-moi une bière," said the man
(45) "Bring me a beer," said the man
(46) It was 110 degrees in the shade. "Boy! It sure is cold today!" said John sarcastically
(47) It was 110 degrees in the shade. "Boy! It sure is hot today!" said John cordially.

According to the above discussion, (44) is less legible than (45) since the knowledge of two linguistic codes is needed in order to understand it; and (46) is less legible than (47) since more operations are required in order to establish what John meant. Similarly, we could say that a story like

(48) John met Joan; then, as a result, John was unhappy; before John met Joan, John had been happy

is less narratively legible than one like

(49) John had been happy; then John met Joan; then, as a result, John was unhappy

since the chronological order of its events is more difficult to arrive at; and we could say that a novel like *La Bataille de Pharsale* is less narratively legible than *Eugénie Grandet* because it does not lend itself as readily to interpretation along proairetic and hermeneutic lines, or that *Gravity's Rainbow* is less narratively legible than *Ragtime* for similar reasons.

In discussing the degree of legibility of texts, many textual elements must be taken into account; so many, in fact, that I will not attempt to deal with all of them (nor could I succeed if I attempted to!). Thus I will not examine the influence of material criteria on legibility, although it is well known that such features of a text as the size of the symbols constituting it, their shape, or their spacing definite-

ly play a role in making it more or less legible. Nor will I
discuss problems of style, although, once again, it is well
known that such elements as sentence length and sentence
structure affect more or less considerably our capacity (and
inclination) to read a text. Rather, I will concentrate on
various traits with seem to me particuarly pertinent to narrative texts, though often not exclusively so.[7]

* * *

The more work (per number of constituents)[8] a text
requires in order to be understood, the less legible it tends to
be. All other things being equal, an ambiguous text would
then be less legible than a non-ambiguous one since the processing of the information it carries would certainly prove
more complicated. Similarly, a text requiring much updating
of information, a text where little of what is given remains
given, is less legible than one in which the given is more
stable. Imagine, for example, a novel in which the name of
the protagonist would change very frequently (and without
warning); or in which the same setting would be described
very differently at several different points; or in which one
could never be sure whether an event had occurred or not because the text would constantly send contradictory signals.
In general, if the text conforms to what it has already said (if
it is consistent with itself), it is more legible than if it does
not. Note that the same is true of a text conforming to a
reality familiar to the reader: this is why a novel abounding
in clichés, in stock characters and situations, is often found
to be more legible than one describing an unconventional
world. Note too that this "principle of consistency" applies
not only to the universe presented by the text, but also to
the way this universe is presented: a text alternating between
narrative discourse and lyric poetry, for instance, is more
difficult to process than one adopting narrative discourse
from beginning to end; and a text written in several different
languages is more difficult to interpret than one using a single
language. In general, the more homogeneous a text is, the
more legible it is.

If legibility tends to decrease when the textual information is not clear (ambiguous texts) or when it is not consistent (heterogeneous or contradictory texts), it also tends
to decrease when the textual information is not sufficient or

sufficiently explicit (elliptical texts, vague texts) and when it proves to be incorrect or irrelevant (deceptive texts). All other things being equal, a novel where information crucial to the understanding of a particular situation or event is not presented will be less legible than one in which all of the information needed is provided. One of the reasons why some modern narratives (and even less modern ones) are difficult to read even though they adopt such conventional forms as those of the pornographic tale or detective story is that they keep immoderately silent: the difficulties encountered in understanding exactly what is going on in Raymond Queneau's *Pierrot mon ami* partly comes from the fact that it is a detective story which never names the detective, the crime committed, or the criminal; the disturbing quality of some of Bataille's fictions—*Histoire de l'oeil, Madame Edwarda, Le Mort*—results to some extent from the many holes in the tissue of events and situations presented; and we know how much trouble *Amance* has occasioned simply because Stendhal did not bother to mention that his protagonist was sexually impotent. Similarly, should a text supply what information is necessary but do it through implication and suggestion rather than explicit and direct statements, its legibility will be affected: to reconstruct what is zeroed, to recover what is deleted, to arrive at meaning by inference require more operations to be performed. Given (46), for instance, and in order to understand what John meant, I have to go through a series of questions and answers like

(50) What was the temperature? 110 degrees
(51) Is that very hot? Yes
(52) What does John say? That it is very cold
(53) But doesn't he know that it is very hot? Of course
(54) What does he mean then? He is being funny and really means that it is very hot.

Ironic texts, allusive texts, suggestive texts may be considered elliptical and are less legible than their opposites.

Finally, the legibility of a text depends on how deceptive that text is. As indicated earlier, textual deception can take many forms. Two events in a narrative may be presented as temporally contiguous, for instance, even though they are not: something else happened in between which, for any number of reasons, the text did not see fit to mention at the time. Or else, a narrator may imply that a certain piece of information is particularly important to the understanding of a given situation, yet that piece of information proves to be totally irrelevant. Or again, the narrator could make statements which are supposed to be helpful and confirm or institute a degree of coherence among various events, but his statements do not make any sense: consider, for example, a narrator writing

> (55)   As we pointed out earlier, John was very much in love with Mary

when nothing of the sort was ever pointed out. Generally, the narrator may provide all sorts of information which has to be discarded or reinterpreted when it becomes clear that he is far from reliable: he is a liar, he is stupid, he is insensitive, he is not really conscious of what is going on. In short, a deceptive text, by encouraging false assumptions and conclusions, by leading to the wrong questions and the wrong answers, can only make for more difficult reading.

Obviously, there are many other factors which contribute to textual ambiguity, heterogeneity, insufficiency, or deception (and thus to a diminution of legibility) and which are relatively easy to isolate and describe. Should events in a narrative be textually but not temporally contiguous, for instance, or should the order of their appearance in the text not correspond to the order of their occurrence in time, more operations would be required to establish the chronology along which the narrative is deployed. It is no accident that children's stories, fairy tales, folktales, and parables follow chronological order very closely; or that modern narratives—in their refusal to constitute mere objects for consumption and digestion—often favor significant disturbances in the chronology of the events they present. Like chronological disorder, spatial instability can affect legibility: events that are contiguous in the space of the text but not in that of the narrated, frequent switches of the action in space (especially when they are not explicitly indicated), can mislead and necessitate frequent readjustment and readaption. Consider, for instance,

>   (56)   At ten o'clock, John finally kissed Mary. Peter sighed, and Janet smiled

and imagine that the setting for the kiss proves to be different from the setting for the sigh and the smile. Of course, disturbances in the spatial and temporal scheme of the narrative can transcend the level of the narrated: whenever there is no clear distinction made between the here-and-now of the narration and there-and-then of the narrated, for example, whenever we do not know whether we are on one level or the other, legibility will be seriously perturbed.

A multiplicity of points of view can have the same consequences, especially when the different points of view adopted represent different degrees of authority and reliability or, what is perhaps more disconcerting, when it is difficult or impossible to relate with certainty a given passage to a specific point of view. Similarly, even if spatio-temporal contiguity and textual contiguity correspond and if the same point of view is maintained throughout, a narrative which generates in parallel fashion several actions around several different centers (by presenting several protagonists each with his own distinct story, for instance) will be less legible than a narrative exploring one action around one center. Finally—and this is in part a corollary of my statements about spatial, temporal, or plot perturbations—whenever a text invites a question more or less explicitly but delays providing the information necessary for answering it, the processing of textual data becomes more arduous. Thus should a narrative introduce a character without quickly giving his name (or vice versa) or should it open a sequence of actions but postpone closing it, its legibility is decreased.

Sometimes, serious disturbances occur in the proairetic armature of a narrative. The main activities recounted (getting up in the morning, shaving, getting ready for a fight, etc.) may be presented only through a mere enumeration of their component parts ("he stretched his arms, wiggled his toes, opened and closed his mouth three or four times, put his left hand over his face," etc.) and may not be immediately recognizable for what they are; or else, the activities recounted may be so heterogeneous that it is very difficult to combine them into larger activities and make them cohere into meaningful sequences. Sometimes, too, the disturbances occur along hermeneutic lines; there are, for instance, many references to an enigma, but what it consists in is never made clear; or there is an enigma and there is a solution, but they are one and the same; or even, there is an answer, but we never find out what the question is.

But perhaps the most striking perturbations (and the most exploited by modern texts in general and modern narratives in particular) are the ones that take place in what we may call the referential system of the text. I have already mentioned in passing the difficulties occasioned by narratives which use many different names to designate the same character but do not make clear that they all apply to him. The reverse phenemenon can raise even more problems: imagine a narrative in which two, three, or ten different characters all bear the same name. A character's name functions like a summary of his attributes; its stability partly guarantees the stability of the world presented and allows us to organize large segments of that world around it; should it be put in doubt or disappear, the stability of the narrative universe as a whole would be threatened.

Naturally, such referential problems may extend beyond characters and their names, with different nouns referring to the same object and the same noun to different objects, even though (or because) coherence and unambiguousness would thus be imperiled. If, for instance, I read

(57)   John came out of the restaurant

a few lines after a restaurant has been mentioned, I may well believe that the same restaurant is being referred to, yet I may be wrong. Similarly, certain pronominal uses may be the source of various ambiguities or incoherences. Consider, for example, such simultaneist novels as Sartre's *Le Sursis*, in which identical pronouns appearing in contiguous sentences or even in the same sentence refer to different objects.

Note that, just as there are many textual factors which

may decrease legibility, there are, conversely, many factors which may increase it by making the text homogeneous, unambiguous, and easy to interpret. Thus, as I indicated earlier, commentary may be textually prominent and may function as an important guide to reading. It could be directly provided by a narrator explaining the motivations of a character, disentangling a very entangled situation, assessing the moral value of an act, defining the meaning of a given locution, determining the symbolic dimensions of an event, or eliminating various ambiguities; or it could occur in the course of a meditation by a particularly lucid character, or during a dialogue, or in an exchange of letters; and so on and so forth.[9] Various organizational elements can also help insure a certain degree of legibility: anaphoric and epiphoric references add homogeneity and make for smooth transitions; and strong distinctions among characters, spatio-temporal settings, and actions point to an uncomplicated model for processing and storing information. Furthermore, and generally speaking, textual redundancy—at the architectural and contentual level, in the deep structure or the surface structure—is the most important ingredient of textual coherence. It may consist in patterned repetition of phonological and graphological features (as in rhyming and alliteration) or of semantic features (as in synonymy, near synonymy, antonymy, and paraphrase); it may manifest itself through frequent definitions of the terms used or periodic summaries of the material presented; it may result from the sustained use of certain rhetorical figures; and so on. Of course, redundancy may have a more strictly narrative nature. Sometimes, the subplot in a given novel parallels the plot of that novel; with the technique of *mise en abyme*, it can even reproduce it entirely on a small scale. Sometimes, several plot units are repeated (the hero performs one difficult task, then another one, then another one; he violates various interdictions; he liquidates a series of lacks) or several characters perform identical or similar actions. Or else, the name of a place underlies its symbolic significance, the name of a character captures his essential qualities, the settings for his actions emphasize his deepest feelings, and so forth. Finally, if the distance between the questions raised or suggested by a text and the answers provided by the text is relatively small, legibility will tend to be relatively high. Should a character be mentioned, for instance, he is immediately introduced; should an order be given, it is quickly carried out; should a sequence of actions be opened, it is rapidly closed; should a mystery be posed, it is rapidly solved. In short, and once again, any element in a text which facilitates the processing and storing of information contributes to the legibility of that text.

Note also that a text can be highly legible yet not very readable, and vice versa. When discussing the notion of readability, I stated that a text is usually considered readable not merely because it is easy to decode and make sense of, but also because it is interesting and pleasing. Now, a text may be so legible that it becomes unreadable. Too much homogeneity, too much redundancy, too much explicitness may result in a lack of interest and a lack of pleasure. A text consisting of one sentence repeated a thousand times can be very boring; and a narrative where there is very little action and very little change, where most of what is given remains given, where there are few surprises, few mysteries, and few problematic passages can become tedious very quickly.[10] Conversely, a text which abounds in ambiguities or favors discontinuity and is therefore not highly legible can be quite stimulating for that very reason. In fact, most narratives which are considered to be readable—if not most narratives— tend to strike a balance between too much legibility and too little of it. In the classical detective story, for instance, the complexity of hermeneutic lines is often counteracted by the abundance of meta-narrative commentary, the coherence of characterizations, the strength of proairetic articulation. The distance between the fundamental question and its answer, between the enigma and its solution, may be great, but it is offset by the (relative) simplicity of the other problems raised. Similarly, in the so-called adventure novel, the difficulties which may arise from a complicated proairetic development are frequently compensated by the straightforward articulation of the text along other lines.

Finally, note that—as the above more than suggests— saying that one text is more legible than another does not necessarily mean that it is better (or worse). Legibility may be more or less valued by different people, in different

cultures, for different purposes. The same can be claimed
about readability: for there is no compelling reason to maintain that the interest a work evokes and the pleasure it
affords constitute sound measures of its worth. Indeed,
avant-garde writers have determinedly pursued the unreadable (or the minimally readable) not only by trying to un-
make sense rather than make it, but also by putting in
question the very notion that a text should be pleasing,
interesting, and entertaining.

* * *

The study of the legibility (and readability) of texts
provides a way of classifying them: there are complex and
simple texts just like there are complex and simple sentences;
there are texts which are highly legible along one axis (the
proairetic one, for instance) but not another (the symbolic
one); there are texts which become more legible as they
deploy themselves and others which become less legible.
Moreover, the description of a given text in terms of its legibility, by specifying how it accòmmodates some—but not
all—reading conventions, how it lends itself to certain interpretive strategies while defeating others, illuminates the
play of its intelligibility, its specificity, its *difference*. In the
final analysis, the study of legibility can even have historical
and anthropological import: by clarifying the conditions for
textual communicability, the premises in terms of which a
given text can be deciphered, it can help us understand why
certain texts are considered most legible or not legible at all
in various cultures and various ages.

University of Pennsylvania

NOTES

[1] See, for instance, Roland Barthes, *S/Z* (Paris: Editions du
Seuil, 1970); David Bleich, *Readings and Feelings: Introduction to Sub-
jective Criticism* (Urbana, Ill.: NCTE, 1975); Jonathan Culler, *Structur-
alist Poetics* (Ithaca, N.Y.: Cornell University Press, 1975); Stanley
Fish, "Literature in the Reader: Affective Stylistics," *New Literary
History*, 2 (1970), 123-62; Norman Holland, *5 Readers Reading* (New
Haven: Yale University Press, 1975); Wolfgang Iser, *The Implied*

Reader: Patterns of Communication in Prose Fiction from Bunyan to Beckett (Baltimore: Johns Hopkins University Press, 1974); Walter J. Ong, "The Writer's Audience Is Always Fiction," *PMLA*, 90 (January, 1975), 9-21; Gerald Prince, "Introduction à l'étude du narrataire," *Poétique*, No. 14 (1973), 178-96; Michael Riffaterre, *Essais de stylistique structurale* (Paris: Flammarion, 1971); Walter Slatoff, *With Respect to Readers: Dimensions of Literary Response* (Ithaca, N.Y.: Cornell University Press, 1970). Note that much of what I will say on reading applies to receiving and interpreting narratives which do not adopt written language as a medium.

[2]Cf. Eugene Charniak's interesting *Toward a Model of Children's Story Comprehension* (MIT Artificial Intelligence Laboratory, AI TR-266, December 1972).

[3]One of the weaknesses of Norman Holland's remarkable *5 Readers Reading* is a tendency to confuse reading and response.

[4]Of course, psychologists may be able to tell us how much information we can process at a time and to help us clarify the notion of maximal reading.

[5]See Roland Barthes, *S/Z*, pp. 81-83.

[6]My description of what a reader brings to a text is, of course, very incomplete.

[7]On the legibility and readability of texts, see Roland Barthes, *S/Z*; Jonathan Culler, *Structuralist Poetics*; and Philippe Hamon, "Un Discours contraint," *Poétique*, No. 16 (1973), 411-45.

[8]We would not want to say that one text is less legible than another merely because it is longer, even though length is not an insignificant factor. But a unit for measuring significant length has to be developed.

[9]On commentary, see Wayne Booth's *The Rhetoric of Fiction* (Chicago: University of Chicago Press, 1961).

[10]In a culture valuing the new, a text is not very readable on second reading unless it is relatively complex and allows for new questions to be posed (or unless we have forgotten it!).

KAY PARKHURST EASSON

"DESCRIPTION AS COSMOS": BLAKE'S SETTINGS IN *MILTON*

In order to defend John Milton's powers of visualization, Don Cameron Allen found it necessary to resurrect a
critical commonplace—"a poet's imagery is the reflection of
his satisfaction with his cosmology."[1] By recalling the relationship of imagery to world view, Allen shows, we can identify Milton not as a poet who in his blindness lacked a visual
sense but as a poet whose visual imagery, his use of words
suggesting color, shape, and motion, reflects the world he saw
and requests his readers to see. According to Allen, Milton
shapes a visualizable cosmos through his descriptive techniques. It seems that if we wished to comprehend the role
of visual imagery in the poetry of William Blake, John
Milton's "inheritor and originator"[2] we must follow Allen's
lead; we must attend to the commonplace in seeking to
specify the verbal practice of a poet who has been labeled
both pictorial and non-pictorial.[3] Blake has been said to
organize his words into pictures,[4] but it has also been stated
that he fails to evoke pictures in the reader's mind, that he
obliterates "the visual and objective aspects of the poetic
landscape."[5] Remembering that a poet's imagistic techniques derive from his cosmological perspective, however, we
can answer these apparently contradictory understandings of
Blake's poetry. Blake does not practice "imitative word-
painting,"[6] yet he does not obliterate the visual and objec-

tive. Blake evokes the world he sees through verbal descriptive techniques that are appropriate to his cosmology.

By focusing on Blake's poem *Milton*, we can begin the process of confirming that Blake encourages visualization through his verbal descriptive techniques. *Milton* is a convenient starting point not only because Blake uncharacteristically labeled it "descriptive,"[7] but also because *Milton's* content—it is about a blind poet learning to see so that he might open "to every eye" what he has seen (*M* 38:44, E138)[8]—encourages our sense that in such a poem there should be visual imagery. Thus while it is probable that Blake's techniques of visual description vary according to the particulars of the cosmos he creates in each poem, it is likewise true that the poetry reveals certain consistent cosmological features. Chief among these is the emphasis on visualization. Pointing out some of Blake's descriptive techniques in *Milton*, then, can initiate the search for a comprehensive view of his verbal techniques of description.

On plate 32 of *Milton*, Blake has drawn a map, and in the *Milton* text he gives verbal descriptions which fill the map's geography.[9] Considered together, Blake's words and design delineate settings for *Milton*;[10] these are settings outlined in the graphic images of plate 32 but completed only by the verbal images; the settings are Blake's dominate visual images in *Milton*, and, in one sense, they become the subject of the poem itself.[11] More precisely, the design on plate 32 is a graphic depiction of the territories which Blake verbally develops into a cosmography and forms into his cosmology. While the design on plate 32 provides visualization of a central ovoid shape surrounded and interpenetrated by four circles labeled Urthona, Luvah, Urizen, and Tharmas; while it shows that Urthona is in the North, Luvah to the East, Urizen to the South, and Tharmas to the West; while the ovoid shape is divided into two spaces, the upper labeled Adam, the lower Satan; it is in Blakes's text that we find the terrain which the map represents.[12] The map is incomplete. It gives the configurations and the relationships of the spaces. However, because neither its spaces nor their names bear immediate resemblance to ordinary geography, the map challenges its viewer to explication. Thus the map on plate 32 is not addressed immediately to the "corporeal eye" but to a rousing of the imaginative faculties. It is a Vision of

Fancy, yet Blake cautions us that we are mistaken if we say "that the Visions of Fancy are not to be found in This World" (E677). Blake supplies "This World" identities for the spaces of plate 32 in the words of *Milton*, as seen especially in his treatment of the center ovoid space.

Blake's descriptions of the ovoid space do not appear according to any pattern of chronology or logic in the text of *Milton*. Nor should they. They are all images Blake imposes on the ovoid shape. When a single image appears in the text, Blake focuses the reader's eye specifically on that image's field. But because the images appear randomly in the text, Blake constantly manipulates the reader's eye in and out, back and forth, to many fields of vision. With this technique, Blake calls attention to the interrelationships of his images. He fills the reader's eye with multiple identities for the ovoid shape. For the purposes of discussion, the images can be constructed into a series of identities; each item in the series is connected to the others by visual properties. The ovoid is an Egg, the Mundane Shell, a Concave Earth, the World, the Body of Man, the Brain and Skull, a womb, a tomb, and the eye.[13] Blake's descriptions are conveyed mainly through nouns, and the namings and the evocative effect of this nominative style are dependent on the ingredients of visual imagery—especially upon color values (translucence and opacity, light and shadow) and upon the values of shape (surface and depth, convexity and concavity). In looking at these multiple identities of the ovoid sequentially, we can further define Blake's presentation of them as "layered description." Thus the effect of the images upon vision may be compared to the operation of an overhead projector. Each identity seems to be on an individual plastic transparency. One transparency is placed in the projector, and its image is projected to vision. Then another transparency is overlaid upon it, and its image is added to the first until all the transparencies together create a comprehensive view of the subject. Although, as we have noted, the images do not appear in the text in such a sequence, both the actual reading encounter with the images and the sequential layering of them produce the same cumulative visualization. Hence, Blake conveys that neither sight nor the object of sight is singular. His words do not strictly imitate common reality. Instead, his words show the expansiveness of his vision and demand, rhetorically, expansion of vision within the reader.

The initial layer of visualization of the ovoid is that it is "the Egg form'd World of Los" (*M* 34:33, E133). Blake makes the egg the central image of his cosmos following the scientific assumption of his day that *ex ova omnia*. Yet, out of the rational data of science, Blake builds new assumptions to convey his understanding of imaginative life. Blake's egg/world, therefore, out of which come all things, is formed by Los, "the Spirit of Prophecy" (*M* 24:71, E120). That it is an egg allows us to see its three-dimensionality and its dual characteristics of sturdiness and delicacy. At first glance an egg looks hard and strong. Though relatively small, its textured surface appears substantial. Holding the egg to the light, however, we can see through it, a caution to us that its surface strength is deceptive, that its surface is indeed thin and fragile, a fact quickly confirmed if we grasp it too tightly. Blake capitalizes on these dual properties of the egg in each of his descriptions of the ovoid territory; hence, he seems to demand his reader's visualization of them. Consequently, in the next layer of vizualization of the space, our view of sturdiness and delicacy is intensified. Blake, using a synecdoche, where a part of the egg stands for its whole, frequently labels the ovoid the Mundane Shell. The synecdoche effectively delineates the perceptual habit of objectifying and thus strengthening the surfaces of objects. In making the surfaces the entirety of visual field, we neglect the dimensions of vision—the egg's translucent interior, for example. Therefore, despite its "mundanity" and despite that it is a "shell," the word connoting fragility, the Shell can become "an immense / Hardened Shadow of all things upon our Vegetated Earth / Enlarg'd into dimension & deform'd into indefinite space" (*M* 17:21-23, E110). With this description Blake requests that we understand that we are seeing merely surfaces; having been taught rational habits of perception, we erect "a mighty Incrustration" (*M* 37:53, E137) by taking shadowy and indefinite "portions of existence" as the whole (*MHH* 16, E39). And with this description, Blake relates the Shell not only to a small and ordinary egg, but also to the ultimately mundane, insignificant, and incomplete world we view when rational, physical existence dominates perception. According to Blake, the rational and scientific use of *ex ova omnia* has attempted to confine life to the egg-formed world within natural and physical boundaries.

Actually, as the next layer of description indicates, the Mundane Shell is "a vast Concave Earth" (*M* 17:21, E110), "a cavernous Earth" (*M* 17:25, E110), having a dimensionality which defies the rational and scientific view of the earth (even of all objects) as convex, as "a Globe rolling thro Voidness" (*M* 29:16, E126). Thus Blake, in this layer of description where the egg image is overlaid with the image of the earth, explodes our sight of a small egg into an astronomical image. Blake's amplification simultaneously demonstrates the limitations of rational views of the egg and the expansion of vision out of mundane and physical existence

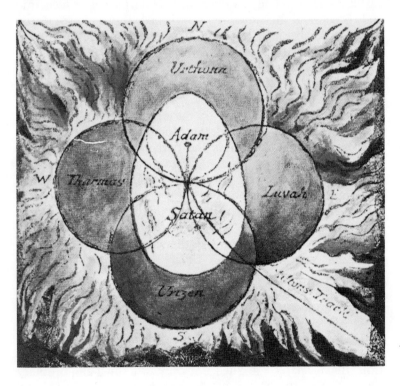

that is essential to vital, imaginative life. Blake shocks us into awareness that although we might have been taught to picture ourselves as placed firmly upon the surface of the earth, if the earth is concave, then we are somehow within it.

In the next layer of visualization Blake cycles our vision, as if he is adjusting the lens of a microscope and the focal point of vision, through the large image of the world back to a smaller image—the human body. In the process, he asks us to hold in mind the essential characteristics he has established for the egg and the world; thus the body must be viewed as concave with a surface that is both sturdy and delicate. Its interior can be dark, as in caverns, or translucent, as that of an egg held to the light. The Mundane Shell, consequently, can be visualized as the human skin, a container that can become the confines of human identity. The world John Milton explores in Blake's poem is his own body. He travels "in Caverns of the Mundane Shell" (*M* 20:42, E113)—and Blake identifies the Mundane Shell as Milton's fallacious shadow (*M* 37:19, E136)—in order to annihilate the errors of his own Satanic Selfhood and the Satanic world he creates and thus inhabits. Because Blake believes that the manner in which we view or inhabit our bodies influences the world we perceive as outside, Milton's Selfhood is simultaneously within his body and without as the erroneous world he projects. Milton could remain within his "Hells" and allow his Emanation (his work and his world) to remain "in torment" without (*M* 2:20, E95). In Blake's poem, however, Milton chooses to explore his inner hells, his Selfhood. As he annihilates his errors of perception, he liberates and transforms his work and world.

Blake objectifies Milton's Selfhood as Satan's Seat toward which Milton journeys while internalizing its locale, appropriately, within the "mortal brain" (*M* 20:36, E113). Again, Blake uses synecdoche to envision the limitations of Milton's body, his world, his Mundane Shell, when dominated by Satanic perception. The brain and its skull enclosure are a further layer of description for a world "of Labyrinthine intricacy" (*M* 17:26, E110). Since the brain can be understood as the seat of perception and of consciousness, we can effectively visualize it governed at times by Satan, by rationality. And since the skull, viewed from the top, has an ovoid shape and is a hollow case for the brain, the image connects to the central egg image and to the visual properties of other images. The brain and skull can be pictured as one more concave world we inhabit. Further, Blake locates the City of Golgonooza within the brain (*M* 20:39-40, E113). Golgonooza is the city of Los, of art and prophecy and imagination. Thus Blake uses the image of the brain and skull to envision the double goal of Milton's journey. Milton travels toward the four faculties of the brain, the "four Universes round the Mundane Egg" (*M* 19:15, E111).[14] And through his images Blake directs us to see the brain as containing both the Seat of Satan and the City of Golgonooza and, therefore, to see Milton's journey as a transformative process wherein Satanic consciousness becomes creative consciousness. *Milton* teaches that the eye, as emblem of all perception, in altering its Satanic perceptions alters all that it beholds. But Blake knows that identification of deceptive and fallacious "strengths" is necessary before the eye can truly see.

Blake's descriptive imagery has been seen to accrue associations. Blake requires that we connect his images by their visual characteristics. His frequent use of womb imagery can be seen as connected to the egg image, inasmuch as the usual anatomical shape for the womb in the eighteenth century was ovoid. Therefore, we can add the womb to Blake's layers of description. Both egg and womb, of course, generate new life, but the womb specifically images anatomical processes of the generation of new human life. The womb image also reminds us that each of the images of the ovoid space Blake provides is an enclosed form. In an archetypal sense, then, they are all feminine images. Positively viewed, each, like the womb, is a place of security and of nourishment. Also each is a "Temporal Habitation" similar to Blake's Beulah, a place of "mild & pleasant Rest" from the "fury" of creation (*M* 30:14, E128). Each of the places, consequently, is a source world for creativity—creativity of a body, of a work of art, of a cosmology—throughout a lifetime. When we are ready for "hatching ripe," Blake writes, we break the Shell (*GP* 6, E260); we awaken to creation. However, a female space can become not the origin of life but life itself. This comes about when Nature, what Blake calls vegetable existence, subdues Imagination. Then, there is "no Human Form but only a Fibrous Vegetation / A Polypus" (*M* 24:37-38, E119) enclosed by the Mundane Shell (*M* 34:31, E133). Blake describes such a world in one of his few "set" pieces of description in *Milton*, the self-revelation of the Shadowy Female (*M* 18:4-25, E110). Part of the effect of this description arises from its literary lineage—all the descriptions of warrior maidens from Camilla in the *Aeneid* to Spenser's Britomart and probably, in Blake's view, even Milton's Eve. But Blake's description can also be placed within the context of panoramic descriptions such as Homer's description of the shield of Achilles in *The Iliad* (8:476-616) and Michael's revelations to Adam in *Paradise Lost* (11:638-73), for these panoramic descriptions depict a microcosm. The Shadowy Female is a microcosm of the world manufactured by the mortal, natural, and Satanic eye, rather than by eternal perspectives. In one sense, her body is a womb generating female sorrow.[15] Her garment, then, is a Mundane Shell, a "mighty Incrustation," a Satanic covering, and a shield which she errects because she fears mortality.[16] Her garment and the body/world it covers are a reality; they are visualizable, and Blake makes each of the Shadowy Female's abstractions concrete by reification. Her garment is woven of sighs and lamentations; its border consists of "the misery of unhappy Families. . . / Wrought with the needle with dire sufferings poverty pain & woe." Famine clasps the garment together "with buckles & Clasps"; Pestilence is its fringe; War, its girdle. Her clothing is "Cruelty." She puts on "Holiness as a breastplate & as a helmet." With this description Blake gives a panorama of the oppressions which result from a reliance upon natural place—whether egg, earth, body, or womb—as microcosm. "Shut in narrow doleful form" man scarcely beholds "the great light" and converses solely "with the Void" (*M* 5:19-22, E98).

As a consequence, the womb becomes a tomb. Blake's descriptions of Satan and Satan's Seat especially lead to the tomb identification as an additional layer of visualization. In *Milton* Satan quarrels with the Divine Family and separates from them. He demands that all obey his "principles of moral individuality" and asserts that he is "God alone" (*M* 9:25-26, E102). Thus he fragments the eternal cosmos and falls from eternity. In his fall Satan's bosom grows "opake against the Divine Vision" (*M* 9:30-50, E102-03). His opacity hides him "from sight, in an extreme blackness and darkness." He sinks down "a dreadful Death," and—Blake writes—"the Separation was terrible; the Dead was repos'd on his Couch." We can now visualize Satan as an opaque, sculptured effigy reposing on a tomb, an image arising from the word "Couch." The tomb Blake describes is an actual kind of sepulchral monument, sculpted to resemble a bed or a couch upon which the effigy rests in the sleep of death, its head placed on a marble pillow.[17] With his tomb image and all the imagery of death which pervades the *Milton* text, Blake conveys that it is our very "fear of death," taught by Satan, his Priests, and his Churches (*M* 38:37-38, E138), that leads us to cling to the natural and rational body. To do so, Blake feels, condemns us to a living death. For this reason Milton must "go to Eternal Death"; he must enter without fear "the sepulcher" of his own Selfhood, the opaque Satan and his tomb. If entered, "the Void Outside of Existence," the death couch itself, "becomes a Womb" (*M* 41:37-42:1, E142).

Blake's frequent images of the eye in *Milton* and the ovoid shape the eye is given in anatomical illustration of the eighteenth century call us to layer upon the other images the visualization of an eye. For Blake, the eye is a synecdoche for the totality of perception and consciousness. Throughout his poetry Blake emphasizes that settings change identity according to perception of them. It is the eye, the "egg-form'd World," which creates all worlds in Blake's cosmology. Blake describes "every Space that a Man views around his dwelling-place" as "his Universe." If man moves his dwelling-place, then "his heavens also move" (*M* 29:5-12, E126). Visualizing the eye as the World is then crucial to understanding Blake's cosmology since Blake consistently sees the eye as representing and containing all that we are and all that we can be. "The clearer the organ," he declares, "the more distinct the object" (*DC*, E576). While we will not find the "sordid drudgery of facsimile representations of merely mortal and perishing substances" (*DC*, E576) in Blake's painting, graphics, or poetry, this does not deny that Blake uses the "perishing and mortal eye" (*DC*, E576) as a vehicle for visionary conception, just as each of his settings can be a vehicle for regeneration. No regeneration can take place if the Optic Nerve is hardened "into a bone / Opake," because we shut out "all the myriads of Eternity / All the Wisdom & joy of life" (*U* 14:28-29, E76). However, a view of existence as being "like the diamond which tho cloth'd / In rugged covering in the mine, is open all within" permits the "hallowed center" of our concave world—the eye itself and all it represents—to hold "the heavens of bright eternity" (*M* 28:34-38).

Don Cameron Allen states that John Milton's "visual imagery is likely to be based on a spatial sense rather than on local habitation."[18]   One of William Blake's responses to John Milton in his poem *Milton* is to provide local habitations for Milton's abstractions.   Satan, in Blake's visualization, is not an outside force ceaselessly in motion to thwart God's plan, but a marble effigy of the human body, the human body's own Selfhood in its own marble tomb. God is not "beyond the skies" (*M* 20:32, E113) but within the "wondrous & expansive" (*M* 20:28, E113) heart, brain, and body of man. It is through Blake's descriptions of Milton's settings Egg, Mundane Shell, Concave Earth, World, Body of Man, Skull/Brain, womb, tomb, eye—that we accurately visualize the worlds we inhabit. By his accurate descriptions of these images Blake combats the scientific view that whatever is real is independent of the human body. Blake asserts, contrary to science, that the prime reality out of which all other realities emerge is the Human Form Divine. Consequently, all his descriptive images have the human body as their common denominator. All the settings merge in Blake's cosmology so that there is actually one setting in the poem— the human body—but in the poem Blake discriminates the identity of each setting so that each lends a physical immediacy to the stages of John Milton's journey toward annihilation of his Selfhood. By his technique of description, Blake constructs visualization, thereby employing description in its basic function as a mode of analysis. Description, therefore, is not necessarily a mimetic tool but primarily a rhetorical tool, stimulating a reader to precise visual identification of the artifact being described. In this sense, Blake is descriptive. He uses description as a rhetorical instrument to direct

188

and modify his reader's visualization. As Blake names the
settings of *Milton*, he requires our visualization of them.
Naming the settings, Blake puts off "the Indefinite" (*M* 28:4,
E124) and creates the lineaments of "the Divine Revelation
in the Litteral expression" (*M* 42:14, E142).

Memphis State University

NOTES

[1] Don Cameron Allen, "Description as Cosmos: The Visual
Image in *Paradise Lost*," in his *The Harmonious Vision: Studies in
Milton's Poetry*, enl. ed. (Baltimore and London: Johns Hopkins University Press, 1970), p. 95. To record my debt to Allen's excellent
study, I have quoted a portion of his title in the title of this article.

[2] The phrase is derived from a passage in Virginia Woolf's *A
Room of One's Own* (New York: Harcourt, Brace & World, 1929), p.
113.

[3] Jean H. Hagstrum labels Blake "a verbal pictorialist" in his
"Blake and the Sister-Arts Tradition." W. J. T. Mitchell states that
Blake's poetry "avoids 'painterly' descriptions" in his "Blake's Composite Art." Both articles are in *Blake's Visionary Forms Dramatic*, ed.
David V. Erdman and John E. Grant (Princeton, N.J.: Princeton University Press, 1970). Mitchell expands his views in his book *Blake's
Composite Art: A Study of the Illuminated Poetry* (Princeton, N.J.:
Princeton University Press, 1978). Both Hagstrum and Mitchell offer
excellent and compelling arguments, and this article owes much to
their researches and to their incisive commentary. I agree at many
points with both Hagstrum and Mitchell. Perhaps, my basic disagreement with each stance arises due to terminology. Thus in this article
I try to clarify terminology in order to clarify Blake's descriptive
practice.

[4] Hagstrum ("Blake and the Sister-Arts Tradition," p. 85) states
that Blake's "verse is filled with verbal icons—that...his imagery suggests
or is organized into pictures or other works of graphic art." Blake does
occasionally do this, but it seems from his imagery in *Milton* that Blake
is less "organized," and hence less pictorial, than Hagstrum would perhaps allow. It is important to see that Blake's visualizations arise out of
a single image as well as out of a pictorial complex of images.

[5]Mitchell, *Blake's Composite Art: A Study of the Illuminated Poetry*, p. 21. By quoting Mitchell out of his rich context, I might unintentionally damage the line of his argument. I do agree with Mitchell that "the 'look' of Blake's scenery changes with every change in the mind of the perceiver" (p. 21). However, it seems crucial to me to identify that Blake is vitally concerned with both the visual and the objective aspects of landscape, even though he recognizes the realities of transformative perception.

[6]John Dixon Hunt, *The Figure in the Landscape: Poetry, Painting, and Gardening During the Eighteenth Century* (Baltimore and London: Johns Hopkins University Press, 1976), p. 153. Hunt discusses a trend in the second half of the eighteenth century toward a descriptive poetry which records scenery's human characteristics, as especially seen in Gray's "The Bard." Blake's practice is related to, but not identical with, this practice. If as Hunt says, Gray's bard is "endemic to his terrain," Blake's Milton is not "endemic" to the landscape. Milton's body and the way he perceives it, as I will show, *is* the setting of *Milton*.

[7]In his letter of 25 April 1803 to Thomas Butts (E697), Blake writes about the long poem (probably *Milton*) he has been composing for three years. The poem, Blake tells Butts, is about the "Spiritual Acts" of those three years and is "descriptive of those Acts." It is uncharacteristic for Blake to label a poem "descriptive." He usually uses the word "descriptive" in reference to his prose commentaries. Blake's failure to use the term for his other poems, of course, should not imply that they lack "description" in the sense of the term that this paper employs.

[8]All references to Blake are from E: *The Poetry and Prose of William Blake*, ed. David V. Erdman, 4th printing, rev. (Garden City, N.Y.: Doubleday, 1970); *M*: *Milton*; *MHH*: *The Marriage of Heaven and Hell*; *U*: *The Book of Urizen*; *DC*: *Descriptive Catalogue*; *GP*: *For the Sexes: The Gates of Paradise*.

[9]It should be noted that the illustration of plate 32 is Blake's only known schematic illustration. In the Commentary to the Shambhala Publications/Random House color facsimile of *Milton*, Roger R. Easson and I have proposed additional understandings of Blake's geography. In that commentary, we locate Blake's settings according to parallel schematic. This essay interrelates with and underlies that commentary. Needless to say, then, it owes much to Roger R. Easson.

[10]Blake's verbal and visual arts are, as Mitchell stresses, "two vigorously independent modes of expression" (*Blake's Composite Art: A Study of Illuminated Poetry*, p. 3). The map on plate 32 and Blake's verbal descriptions of it are, however, one instance of the fact that

Blake's graphics do, at times, bear an illustrative relationship to his text. The illustrative relationship, though, is not always one of direct illustration.

[11]Thus I disagree with Mitchell (*Blake's Composite Art: A Study of the Illuminated Poetry*, p. 22) that although "Blake frequently alludes to icons or artifacts" he does not do so "in a way that invites us to visualize them, or to think of their visual appearance as especially significant. . . ." Blake never makes [an artifact] the controlling image of a poem."

[12]There are four existing copies of *Milton*; thus there are four versions of plate 32. I have given the basic elements of the design. Changes in the design do not affect these basic elements although such changes may, of course, add to or modify our perceptions of how the basic elements should be related.

[13]These do not exhaust the number of identites Blake provides for the central ovoid shape. Because of space limitations, I have not discussed the Cathedral, the Country, the City, or the Sensorium.

[14]It is essential to recall here that the Universes, in Blake's view, are both around and within the Mundane Egg.

[15]And in this sense, she reminds us clearly of Milton's Eve.

[16]This idea of the garment as shield, raised because of a fear of mortality, is clarified below in the discussion of the tomb image.

[17]In our Commentary to the Shambhala/Random House facsimile of *Milton*, Roger Easson and I extend the implications of this tomb image.

[18]Allen, p. 106.

THOMAS O. SLOANE

BEAUTY'S SPOUSE'S ODD ELYSIUM:
BARTH'S *FUNHOUSE*

"Once upon a time": that is surely the storyteller's oldest opening gambit. But when it is used by novelists like James Joyce and John Barth, we do not expect it to lead to the storyteller's oldest out, in which everyone lives happily ever after. On the contrary, we expect it to open a journey in which something will be done with old gambits and new expectations.

> Once upon a time and a very good time it was there was a moocow coming down along the road and this moocow that was coming down along the road met a nicens little boy named baby tuckoo. . . .
> His father told him that story: his father looked at him through a glass: he had a hairy face.[1]

So begins James Joyce's *A Portrait of the Artist as a Young Man*. The final line of the novel, you will recall, is Stephen Dedalus's hopeful prayer: "27 April: Old father, old artificer, stand me now and ever in good stead." The climax of the book occurs when Stephen turns from a possible calling to the priesthood to accept his vocation as an artist. The book ends as he leaves to fulfill his new life. By contrast, John Barth's *Lost in the Funhouse* shows us an already dedicated artist who is struggling to write a novel, the very novel we are reading. Its climax occurs when the artist finds a certain answer, and its last line is "Wrote it." Secondly, in both novels the artist experiences the presence of another being, something ancillary, sometimes central to his calling, and always female. In her role as muse, her appearance is not extraordinary. From ancient times the male artist has always personified his muse as a female;[2] after all, the union between male and female is perhaps the most obvious though not the simplest emblem of creativity. Stephen's call, his angel of epiphany, came in the form of a young girl standing at the water's edge, but he also saw mad Ireland as mother figure, the female side of a parentage which he found virtually inescapable. In Barth's novel, the female in the artist's life is his muse, also his wife, his mistresses, both real and imaginary, his ideal of beauty, and in a crucial way his reader. There is a third comparison which can be made between the two novels, but I shall offer it later, after a closer look at the structure of *Lost in the Funhouse*.[3]

"Once upon a time": Barth's novel begins that way, too,. but the phrase is stretched out into a Moebius strip, which reads "Once upon a time there was a tale that began once upon a time there was a tale that began," ad infinitum— or, making entry at another point, as one may do with a Moebius strip, "There was a tale that began once upon a time there was a tale that began once upon a time," and so on, *in regressus in infinitum.* The Moebius strip is a chapter unto itself, entitled "A Frame Tale." By doing a Barthian inversion of the idea of a frame tale, we might suppose that it frames the entire book in its progressionless absurdity. In that light, the "Funhouse" of the title becomes The House of Fiction wherein the central protagonist, a writer of fiction, would seem to be forever lost. We can find evidence for this interpretation in the book itself. The line of reasoning might go like this: Once upon a time he—that is, we—could begin Once upon a time, but no more. Now we are suspicious of conventional beginnings, fearing that they are only gambits, for we have discarded that quaint belief that mere language can be made to yield truth. For example, in one chapter the protagonist states to his imaginary muse, mistress, reader:

> Once upon a time you were satisfied with incidental felicities and niceties of technique: The unexpected image, the refreshingly accurate word-choice, the memorable simile that yields deeper and subtler significances upon reflection, like a memorable simile.[4]

If the book is progressionless, it would seem to be not only absurd but nihilistic,[5] the force of its energy a catalytic conversion of novel into anti-novel, propelling an old-fashioned lover of beauty into far-outer space. But the book is not progressionless, as we shall see. Moreover, absurdity and nihilism are indeed omnipresent, but as dangers to the protagonist's efforts and to the author's strategies. They are not the point of the book. The point of the book, rather, is how novels get written, and because that point is dramatically expressed in terms of a writer-reader relationship, I should say that the point of the novel is finally *rhetoric*: the rhetoric of the novel in novel form. Accepting the full range of puns in that phrase I will offer it as my thesis.

I have called the book a "novel." It looks more like a collection of short stories, fourteen in all, counting the Moebius strip, the "Frame Tale." Barth subtitles the work "Fiction for Print, Tape, Live Voice" and makes a couple of points in his prefacing remarks: first, that the book is not a collection but a series, whose arrangement is significant,[6] and second, that some of the pieces were meant to be read aloud.[7] In order to determine whether the book is in fact a novel, let us review first the arrangement of the series, looking for that "stuff of all good novels," *time*.[8]

First, the Moebius strip. A frame tale is not necessarily a tale that frames. One need not invert the concept to locate the Barthian tone: a frame tale is, rather, a tale within a frame—like one of the stories told by the Canterbury Pilgrims—or, to move to a level of punning not inconsonant except perhaps in its crudity with the punning of this novel, it shows the author's tail in a frame (as in, his ass is in a sling). Once upon a time, but no more, there were stories beginning Once upon a time. Anyone who tries to follow that route can get his tail caught in a frame of meaningless conventions, in a confining, directionless pursuit of absurdity. Thus the Moebius strip is an introduction to an omnipresent danger. Of course, the danger would be most perilous to someone who has already experienced deeply the need to produce a novel, to speak, or to create.

That need both drives and harrasses the speaker of the second tale, entitled "Night-Sea Journey." The persona is a sperm who in his trip is beset with doubts as to the meaning of his act, doubts that "She"—that is, the shore who beckons—even exists, fears that nothing will come of his existence but more night-sea journeyers in an endless progression, like an absurdly eternal Moebius strip—or, seeing the sperm as a guise for the artist, like a cynical updating of Ecclesiastes' complaint that of the making of books there is no end. But the fears are modified by the mode of transmission. Barth tells us in his prefacing note that the piece is meant to be "quoted. . .by the authorial voice." Though no tapes are available at present on which we may hear the author's voice quote the sperm, nonetheless the advice allows us to imagine a certain communicative mode, one that I would argue is dramatically emblematic of theme: the sperm, and the creative urge which he represents, is a compulsion deep within the artist but answerable only to another compulsion, deep within "her," this is "you," that is "us," the artist's audience. Moreover, to be quoted by the authorial voice underscores a distinction between the author and his speaker, a distinction which as we shall see is emphasized at significant times throughout the series.

The third tale "Ambrose His Mark" has the look of autobiography—but no more so, when you think about it, than "Night-Sea Journey" has. (The two stories are hilariously linked in this one's opening line.) Ambrose is an adult narrator telling the tale of his birth. His family, failing to agree on a name, makes a kind of ad hoc decision to wait until, Indian-fashion, the boy finds his own name. This he does when as a nursing infant he and his sleeping mother are covered with bees, and it is later discovered that a birthmark near Ambrose's temple is in the shape of a headless bee. He is therefore called Ambrose, after the saint, who as an infant was marked for a life of eloquence when bees lighted on his mouth. But bees did not light on our Ambrose's mouth. They lighted on his eyes and ears. Moreover, they stung his mother's breast. The temptation is strong to equate Ambrose with Barth, whose name also begins with a B, and to use the stinging of the mother's breast to underscore the nihilism of of the work: language which should nourish us and give us perception has been poisoned.[9] Or perhaps we could say that, like Stephen Dedalus, Ambrose has been called, in this case from infancy, and not into a vocation of eloquence but consigned to an inarticulateness which, through the blessing of his eyes and ears he will experience most painfully—as the central protagonist in another guise will say later, "To see the truth is one thing, to speak it another." However, it is obviously the adult Ambrose who narrates this tale. He has therefore found *some* means of speaking, but his skill lies in creating beginnings, we realize, not conclusions. The story does not end. Moreover, as we progress through the series we find that in part it is the curiously unfinished quality of each of these stories which like a Moebius strip propels us on.

The fourth tale "Autobiography" is spoken by a disembodied voice born in the union of the author with a tape recorder. The voice is full of anguish—not surprisingly. We are meant to hear it proceeding from a tape recorder in the presence of the "visible but silent author," an unlikely event but one that in our imaginations shows us this situation: that wholeness of life which fiction requires is missing and whatever wholeness which is present but won't speak can't create fiction either. Ambrose's blessing has doomed him. The speaker of this story cries out to be turned off—but we don't turn him off, and neither does the silent but visible author. Our compulsions are still operative though doomed to go unfulfilled, and that would seem to be the point of this story, to dramatize the compulsions of fiction. The speaker has no persona, only his "fancy's own twist figure"—tape winding and rewinding through the recorder, in a figure 8 on its side, the ancient symbol for infinity, not unlike the figure of the Moebius strip, not unlike the letter B or the body of a headless bee, and so on.[10] All of these are associated with a certain kind of immobility—or paralysis, Barth would call it—which is particularly frustrating, for deep inside is an active principle.

In "Water-Message," the fifth tale, Ambrose is a boy of nine or ten. We begin to see some of the destiny to which he has been called. He is an imaginative youth, though his made-up stories are largely to protect him against bullies, sometimes to give him a sense of superiority, sometimes to help him feel he belongs. The water-message, which comes in a bottle washed up on the shore of the river, would seem to be both urgent and cynical, if we recall "Night-Sea Journey": breaking open the bottle and extracting the message, Ambrose finds it says only "To Whom It May Concern" and "Yours Truly" with blank paper between the lines. Another sign of Ambrose's destiny? Perhaps. If so, it's his task to fill

in the blank and his tragedy that he can't, at least not until
he learns something about the impossibility of messages that
are addressed to no one in particular and signed by no one in
particular. He notices instead that the paper, torn from some
cheap writing tablet, is filled with little flecks of wood. The
visual image recalls the game which the boys play, sending
staves of wood under and across the water, like submarines.
But whereas the game is imaginative, the paper merely awaits
and invites the imaginative act. Ambrose's stark perception
of the blank is his first glimpse of absurdity. As told by an
unnamed narrator, the story moves more toward closure than
any we've read so far.

The next tale is in the form of a petition (which is also
its title). We don't know the petitioner's name, for he signs
off only with "Yours Truly." But as a sequel, this is only a
partially anonymous attempt to fill in the blank. For the
story is composed of specific though curious details. The
speaker would have us believe that he's the smaller of
Siamese twins, joined to the back of his brutish brother in a
way that makes his own existence vile and disgusting. An
ostentatiously articulate writer, he's mute. Moreover, he's
unable to move except at the animal-like will of his brother.
The brothers are American, thirty-five years old. The petition, dated 1931, is addressed to "His Most Gracious Majesty
Prajadhipok, Descendant of Buddha, King of North and
South, Supreme Arbiter of the Ebb and Flow of the Tide,
Brother of the Moon, Half-Brother of the Sun, Possessor of
the Four-and-Twenty Golden Umbrellas." The petition urges
his majesty to bid his surgeons to divide the two brothers.
The differences between the brothers are extreme and signifi-
cant:

> We are nothing alike. I am slight, my brother is gross.
> He's incoherent but vocal; I am articulate and mute. He's
> ignorant but full of guile; I think I may call myself reason-
> ably educated, and if ingenuous, no more so I hope than
> the run of scholars. My brother is gregarious; he deals
> with the public; earns and spends our income; tends (but
> slovenly) the house and grounds; makes, entertains, and
> loses friends; indulges in hobbies; pursues ambitions and
> women. For my part, I am by nature withdrawn, even
> solitary: an observer of life, a meditator, a taker of notes,
> a dreamer if you will. . . . More to the point, what in-
> telligence my brother has is inclined to synthesis, mine to

to analysis; he denies that we are two, yet refuses to com-
promise and cooperate; I affirm our difference—all the
difference in the world! (p. 59)

To recapitulate, the story of Ambrose's birth (the third
tale) is followed by a story spoken by a disembodied voice
born of the monstrous union of the author with a tape
recorder (the fourth tale). Then the story of Ambrose's discovery of the blank water-message (the fifth tale) is followed
by the voice of a paranoid Siamese twin, sounding like a compulsive, frightened, hilarious, and doomed part of a schizoid
personality, or like a modern version of one-half of the medieval dialectic between Body and Soul, another kind of disembodied voice: the naked intellect. But in this case, the
intellect is something of a brat. For me, "Yours Truly" in all
these tales signifies the same persona, the protagonist in
various poses, who cannot deliver the truth plainly to
Ambrose in one tale but must in the next dramatize what
truth he thinks he has in capriciousness and outrage. In his
naked intellect pose, the protagonist is like a brilliant, willful,
and spoiled child begging not simply for attention but for
validation and reassurance. Moreover, according to Barth,
"Petition" would lose part of its point in any but printed
form, perhaps because an oral interpretation of the words
potentially unmasks the speaker or, if carried to extremes,
makes the situation so literal that its analogical nature might
be lost.

The seventh story is the title story and its beginning is
curious indeed:

> For whom is the funhouse fun? Perhaps for lovers.
> For Ambrose it is *a place of fear and confusion.* He has
> come to the seashore with his family for the holiday, *the*
> *occasion of their visit is Independence Day, the most im-*
> *portant secular holiday of the United States of America.*
> A single straight underline is the manuscript mark for ital-
> ic type, *which in turn* is the printed equivalent to oral
> emphasis of words and phrases as well as the customary
> type of titles of complete works, not to mention. Italics
> are also employed, in fiction stories especially, for "out-
> side," intrusive, or artificial voices, such as radio an-
> nouncements, the texts of telegrams and newspaper
> articles, et cetera. They should be used *sparingly.* If the
> passages originally in roman type are italicized by some-
> one repeating them, it's customary to acknowledge the
> fact. *Italics Mine.* (p. 69)

We are back with Ambrose again, now thirteen years old. But the narrator seems not merely to be telling Ambrose's tale but to commenting on fiction, its conventions, how it's created—everything but *by whom and for whom* it's created. The story in effect doubles back on itself, a characteristic which has been true of all the stories, including the Moebius strip. We begin to understand in this story that the funhouse isn't simply Ambrose's problem, but a dilemma of the voice within every mask in the book. The funhouse *is* the book, and our journey through the serial arrangement of the stories is as full of false starts, blind hopes, fakery, scariness, fears, fun and games as any journey through any funhouse. So that when the narrator says, "The climax of the story must be its protagonist's discovery of a way to get through the funhouse," we must realize that he's speaking not simply of Ambrose but of himself. Like all characters, Ambrose is only another ironic mask for the central protagonist—and so is the narrator—masks for a novelist who is trying to get his tale told.

Ambrose is irretrievably lost in the funhouse, full of vague dreams and fictions which he can't complete, can't sort out, can't make sense of. But Barth is not Ambrose. Ambrose personifies an artistic dilemma. He's one of several masks worn by Barth's central protagonist, whose search for creativity we trace throughout the series. Barth, that is the implied author, always makes it possible for us to judge his protagonist. Think of him as a sperm, for example: all head with a tail, a kind of naked intellect, analytical like the speaker of "Petition," like Ambrose unable to see himself as a whole person in a funhouse mirror because "his head gets in the way," resentful of being driven by vague compulsions which the intellect insists are meaningless.[11] Ambrose is left in the funhouse. He will never, can never, find his way out. But the protagonist's search continues.

In the remaining seven stories, all sense of chronology, the traditional principle of narrative *dispositio*, which was at least vaguely present in the first seven, has been tossed overboard. The eighth story is located in Tiresias's cave in ancient times. The ninth takes place in modern times near Niagara Falls and Lake Erie. The tenth is an anti-story, the total failure of the protagonist's creative efforts. The eleventh is a glossolalia of voices ancient and modern. The twelfth is spoken by a modern author between the hours of 9 a.m. Monday, June 20, 1966, and 11 p.m. that same evening. The thirteenth begins with a voice that gradually assumes the identity of Menelaus telling a tale of Menelaus telling a tale of Menelaus telling a tale—and so on unto the seventh level of a story-within-a-story. The final, entitled "Anonymiad," is spoken by a "nameless minstrel" from Clytemnestra's court, exiled to a lonely island, where he writes stories on animal hide, placing them in clay amphorae and sending them out across a sea to a future and destiny as uncertain as a sperm's. Obviously, it has become increasingly difficult to see the book as a series. The situation of the final story, "Anonymiad," is similar to the situation in "Night-Sea Journey"; in the absence of any assurance as to outcome, only the raw creative compulsion exists, and so it would seem that the Moebius strip does indeed "frame" the entire tale. And without any sense of temporal progression, the series could hardly be thought of as a novel.

However, behind the masks in the time continuum of the central protagonist, there is a progressive intensification of a certain feature which structures the series and turns it into a novel on novels: the central protagonist has been engaged in a dialectic with another whose presence he senses but sometimes doubts, just as he doubts his own presence. This dialectic begins to emerge as a dialogue in the narration: for example, "Who says so? Tiresias the prophet. What's he doing here? Conversing with Narcissus. How does he know—because he knows everything.Why isn't he in Thebes?" It's almost as if the narrator, lacking an audience, talks with himself. On the other hand, as the voice in the twelfth story so irascibly proclaims, an author creates his reader, just as he creates his story, just as he creates himself. We readers are drawn in partly because the narrator speaks our lines so well, partly because the very nature (and point) of this work is co-creation. Ingeniously, the two voices, narrator and narratee, become, fuse, slide into, reflect all dialectical pairings throughout the entire novel: speaker and listener, petitioner and addressee, male and female, lover of beauty and beauty's ideal self, sperm and egg. It takes two—and the pity and terror of that ineluctable necessity are dramatized in the personae of the eighth story "Echo": Narcissus, the primal and insufferable male ego; Echo, the epitome of the equally insufferable female self-effacement; and Tiresias, blind seer, who is both male and female and tragically neither. Tiresias recalls the horrible wail of the "Petition"-er: "To be one: paradise! To be two: bliss! But to be both and neither is unspeakable." Tiresias is but another version of the artist's agonies. However, the voice that narrates the eighth story is not Tiresias but a fourth persona, who is actually the protagonist, searching for a way out of the funhouse, a means of making the experience speakable.

The bleakest part of his search comes in the tenth story "Title." His utter failure at utterance is heard best near the end of the story. This is narration which sounds like frustrated dialogue:

> Go on. Impossible. I'm going, too late now, one more step and we're done, you and I. Suspense. The fact is, you're driving me to it, the fact is that people still lead lives, mean and bleak and brief as they are, briefer than you think, and people have characters and motives that we divine more or less inaccurately from their appearance, speech, behavior, and the rest, you aren't listening, go on then, what do you think I'm doing, people still fall in love, and out, yes, in and out, and out and in, and they please each other, and hurt each other, isn't that the truth, and they do these things in more or less conventionally dramatic fashion, unfashionable or not, go on, I'm going, and what goes on between them is still not only the most interesting but the most important thing in the bloody murderous world, pardon the adjectives. And that my dear is what writers have got to find ways to write about in this adjecive adjective hour of the ditto ditto same noun as above, or their, that is to say our, accursed self-consciousness will lead them, that is to say us, to here it comes, say it straight out, I'm going to, say it in plain English for once, that's what I'm leading up to, me and my bloody anticlimatic noun, we're pushing each other to fill in the blank. (p. 109)

But the despair of this story is offset by the happier failure to write a story in the twelfth tale "Life-Story": here "he" fills in the blank through sex, thus capping his pen, as it were. As we've known from the outset, the answer to the protagonist's search is "love," the name of that compulsion and call which the sperm's intellect would not accept but could not refuse. It is the means of the protagonist's way out of the funhouse, if he accepts it. If he does not, his world will be peopled with nouns. (Or freaks, as he's shown us in the story in which his co-creator was a tape recorder.)

The climax of the novel occurs in the thirteenth story "Menelaiad." The voice at the beginning of the story is that of the protagonist, the would-be author, the creator of fiction, the searcher for a way out of the funhouse. He begins by claiming to be Menelaus, in an effort to "grab" the reader; but having admitted his purpose, he also insists that he really *is* Menelaus, not just his voice, but all there is of him—like an "echo" of Menelaus, perhaps, or glossolalia. Menelaus's life story is peeled off in layers, in each layer of which someone has hold of someone else, and keeps hold of that someone else until the tale is told. The ground-situation of the tale is Menelaus's inability to accept Helen's simple answer as to why she picked him out of all the males who would have come running at her call: "love," she said. That's her reason, and her call. And through all Menelaus's journeys and travails because of her and on her behalf, fearing alike her sluttishness and her faithfulness, he ends up with only one answer, the only one we get in the entire book: "love." Menelaus accepts it. He has to. And so does the narrator. If we see the narrator as the protagonist of the novel, we know that he knows that Menelaus's answer only echoes the call which the sperm dreaded but could not avoid joining. The narrator in "Menelaiad" accepts his destiny far more calmly though no less grimly than the sperm accepted his: "...when as must at last every tale, all tellers, all told, Menelaus's story itself in ten and ten thousand years expires, yet I'll survive it, I, in Proteus's terrifying last disguise, Beauty's spouse's odd Elysium: the absurd, unending possibility of love." With that realization, the narrator rediscovers not simply his destiny, but also his identity and his voice.

Read in temporal progression, the story which it now becomes possible to tell is the one which concludes the series, "Anonymiad." Here a minstrel from Clytemnestra's court, who has long since forgotten his name, tells his story as a self-conscious narrator of the sort he calls "first person anonymous." Tricked by his mistress Merope and her new lover, he was stranded on a desert island with nine amphorae of wine, "Mycenaean red." Here this "lorn minstrel" creates fiction to master his abandonment.[12] He names each amphora after one of the muses, drinks all the wine therein, and in an act resembling love fills it with a manuscript, which he then seals up inside and sends adrift across the sea. A singer used to creating his songs in the presence of others, he invents writing on this island in order to achieve communication at a distance and in the perhaps not too vain hope that somewhere someone will invent the art of reading. Inevitably, despair overcomes him and he gives up the enterprise. One day, however, a bottle washes ashore with a message in it. He can't read it, of course, and admits that it may be one of his own returning upon him. But he also realizes another alternative meaning: the possibility of a non-Narcissistic kind of love, a kindred soul, a she, a you, a reader. The ninth amphora is emptied, the only other living being—a goat significantly named Helen—is slaughtered to provide a skin for writing, a poem is placed inside the bottle and set adrift—not a poem, really, more like a plan for a poem, ironically resembling the book we are reading. This was achieved upon emptying the amphora he named Calliope—whose inspiration in this case sounds less like epic poetry and more like distant water music in an amusement park. "There," says the minstrel, as the sperm himself might say were he in better relation to his destiny, "my tale's afloat." The speaker concludes with a tribute to Merope, in effect a moving appeal to a reader: "if some night your voice recalls me, by a new name, I'll commit myself to it, paddling and resting, drifting like my amphorae, to attain you or to drown." The possibility of love is the possibility of a you, a reader, a narratee for the narrator, that calling other who awakens in the author his own possibilities.

Have we come all the way through the funhouse only to realize *that*? The realization, it appears, is the theme of the book. The final line, which is a paragraph unto itself, is "Wrote it." The line completes a sentence in the preceding paragraph, to the effect that "a nameless minstrel / Wrote it." It concludes our journey through the funhouse for the two words "Wrote it" conclude the search of the novel's protagonist, for a means of writing. He found a way of writing by finding, and accepting, the possibility of love, and then he not merely accepted it but became it—became, in fact, the novel itself. But this is not necessarily Barth's way. Barth found a way of writing the novel by creating as a central protagonist a voice in search of a body.[13] When undertaken through the intellect, the search is foredoomed. The voice can only repeat past voices, ancient and modern, including some of those myths created by Barth himself.[14] But the realization of that doom and the overcoming of it, however pyrrhic, is the point of the book.

And it is the point on which we judge the central protagonist. The disparity between Barth, that is the implied author, and his protagonist is the source of the major rhetorical strategy in the book, as I have suggested, and for the name of the strategy I must use that shibboleth of New Criticism: irony. When you think about it, though, irony is really the only strategy Barth could have used—given his theme and his implied reader.

The participants in this drama may be divided into roles and charted on a continuum:[15]

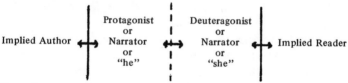

For the most part, it is the role of the narrator which provides the central protagonist's voice in the novel. Sometimes he is undramatized, as in "Echo" and "Menelaiad." Most often he is dramatized, as a sperm, as a Siamese twin, to name two. Characters, such as Ambrose and Menelaus, are also dramatizations of the protagonist, who is always on a quest for the means of telling his tale. The implied author, on the other hand, is detached from his protagonist's quest, for *he* obviously has found the means and knows the outcome. The protagonist is his surrogate, a coyly anonymous "Yours Truly," an implicit presence throughout, most visible and audible as the speaker of the final tale. In an important sense, the author and his protagonist are mirrored in the narratee and the implied reader—as if the continuum were folded in the center, on the dotted line. The narratee is most often undramatized, but at times "she" too is given a mask—as a mistress or wife, or as Merope—and at times we hear "her" voice during the narration. Always she is present, especially so when the narrator doubts that she is or agonizes

over her possible rejection or boredom. Because of the interaction between the narrator and the narratee, which is at
times voiced, the narratee in this novel is actually a deuteragonist, not simply an observer but a participant, like any
audience in a rhetorical transaction. So far as the implied
readers are concerned, we are not simply the end of the continuum but actors in the drama. We continually *judge* the
narrator, but we see that, in turn, he is our major index of the
implied author's character. They are near but apart. Similarly, we are near but apart from the narratee, our surrogate in
the process. The narrator-narratee relationship is an objecti-
fication of the very means by which we are drawn in and become engaged in the action of the novel—the very means,
too, by which we "real" people become implied readers. As
implied readers, our relationship to the work is like that of
the implied author: though we are involved with the transaction between the narrator and the narratee, though we may
closely identify with these two speaking roles, we never lose
our capacity for judging them. The chart shows the major
strategy of this work, as noted, irony. The term remains the
best one we have for near-identification, the process whereby
we sense discrepancies in our impulse to empathize.

"For whom is the funhouse fun? Perhaps for lovers."
For one set of lovers—the protagonist and his "she"—the trip
through the funhouse has been agony, the fear and confusion
of Ambrose irretrievably lost, the pain of Narcissus, Echo,
and Tiresias standing forever on the "autognostic verge," the
frustrations of a sperm unable to do anything but move toward an apparently absurd but ineluctable fulfillment. For
another set of lovers the funhouse is fun indeed. This would
be the implied author and his implied reader. The temptation may be strong to confuse the second set of lovers with
the first. But the two sets are easily distinguishable. For one
thing, their perspectives are different. The protagonist can
see only the next step he is about to take and can experience
only uncertainty about his accomplishment; the author and
his readers have the book in their hands. For another thing,
the very detachability of all the masks worn throughout the
book is made overt by the protagonist—for example, "Thus
we linger forever on the autognostic verge—not you and I,
but Narcissus, Tiresias, Echo"—one detachment inviting

others.[16] We play the role of the narratee and empathize with the narrator, but only within the limts set down by the implied author, who never lets us ignore the artifice, the masks, the pretense.

Commenting on the effect of *A Portrait of the Artist as a Young Man*, Wayne Booth describes the novel as allowing "deep involvement combined with the implicit demand that we maintain our capacity for ironic judgment."[17] This is the third comparison I would draw between the two works. For decades now we've seen critics assume an identity between Joyce and Stephen Dedalus. The mask is so thin that the temptation is strong to forget it and see only Joyce's face within and, poor Joyce, to assume that all Stephen's aesthetic credos are his. We stand to make similar kinds of errors in reading Barth's book. The mask is thin—indeed, sometimes the mask is not even tangible, the central protagonist only a voice—but that's to encourage our deep involvement. The mask is always detachable, and that's to insure our ironic judgment.

In sum, the ironic as well as the novelistic qualities of Barth's book are seen best in the development of the character of the central protagonist. Certainly the trip through the funhouse has been no fun for him, partly because he is intellectually wedded to the ideal in a relativistic age. Like Menelaus, he espouses Beauty only to be cuckolded by her. Barth would have us believe that his foibles are curious, ridiculous, anachronistic, sentimental, dismal, and profoundly comic, but at least temporarily worthy of that love which can be given only by "her," that is to say "us." If they are so worthy, the book's absurdity and nihilism are denied. His naïvete, his feelings of being divided into two or three persons, his interfering self-consciousness—those qualities which are dramatized in the various masks in the entire book and recapitulated by the narrator of "Anonymiad"—are finally overcome by a late-acquired honesty which gives him an ironic stance toward himself not at all unlike the ironic stance Barth and we have taken toward him from the outset. The honesty forces him to give up on almost every trick of the trade but possibility. And so "Anonymiad" places a seal on the ending of "Menelaiad." By the time we reach the final words "Wrote it," the discrepancy between Barth and the protagonist has greatly diminished. However, the arrangement of those words on the page makes them a kind of trope, tonally uniting the voices of the author and protagonist while emphasizing their differences in perspective.

In light of this progression, how could the Moebius strip frame the entire work? Barth intends us to read the stories serially, in the order in which they are arranged, but the Moebius strip denies all seriality. One may start and stop his progression on a Moebius strip at almost any point with the same effect, whereas the seriality of the stories not only underscores the irony but reveals the temporal progression of the protagonist's quest.

The function of the Moebius strip might best be considered rhetorically as a kind of proem or prologue establishing the "ground-conceit and the narrative voice and viewpoint" (p. 172). The Moebius strip is an objective fact, a thing which occupies space somewhere in the middle ground between the implied author and the implied audience; both can see it, neither is totally in it. This middle ground is the rhetorical situs of the ironic novel's text. Our "deep involvement," which an ironic novel can elicit, is gained later as the story line moves away from the curiosity of the Moebius strip and we hear voices and see patterns of behavior that encourage our participation. Too, the Moebius strip is largely an intellectual toy. It offers fun and games and dilemmas for such widely distributed audiences as the followers of the French psychiatrist Lacan and the readers of *Mad Magazine*. The Moebius strip, then, shows us that the book will be intellectually playful, though it does not rule out the possibility of seriousness. As noted earlier, it also shows us by the words on it what the funhouse is and how one can get lost therein.

To return to Barth's point about reading aloud, we should note that the book is subtitled "Fiction for Print, Tape, Live Voice." Barth's purpose, he tells us, in stressing the three modes of presentation was to turn "as many aspects of the fiction as possible—the structure, the narrative viewpoint, the means of presentation, in some instances the process of composition and/or recitation as well as of reading or listening—into dramatically relevant emblems of the theme." Of the fourteen stories, Barth urges us to hear five performed; of these five, three are meant to be heard performed by Barth himself: "Night-Sea Journey," which is meant to be quoted by the authorial voice; "Echo," in which again the authorial voice explicitly distinguishes himself from the masks he wears; and "Title," which is the most despairing part of the funhouse, where we see the protagonist fail in his struggles to write a book—and if it's Barth's voice we hear we know that the book he talks about is the one we hold in our hands. In each case, then, the authorial voice only emphasizes the discrepancy between the author and his protagonist.

But in spite of what Barth says, the whole book may profitably be read aloud by anyone to anyone, for that communicative process serves the theme by enhancing the book's identity as "self-conscious fiction." Self-conscious fiction is fiction that is overt about its processes: it explicitly tells the reader that this is a work of fiction, and the illusion of being created extends even to the implication that the "real" author and his "real" readers are fictive characters. Self-conscious fiction is a kind of drama that asks the questions, which of all the roles we play inside as well as outside literature are fictive and which are real anyway?

On the simplest level in Barth's *Funhouse*, the implied author plays the role of narrator; the implied reader, the role of narratee. On the most complex level, these four roles become four characters in search of a story. If Barth's strategies work in setting up this drama, we, too, we "real" people, vicariously join in the search, making entry first in our role as implied readers. But the idea behind it all is something more than merely eliciting our participation or getting us to play one or all of these fictive roles. The idea is to emphasize the point that the line between fiction and reality is fuzzy. As Barth puts it in his essay "The Literature of Exhaustion," published a year before this book: "When characters in a work of fiction become readers or authors of fiction, they're reminded of the fictious aspects of their own existence...."[18] *Lost in the Funhouse* constantly proclaims its self-conscious nature—as well as, in a typical countermove, complaining about it: in "Life-Story," the narratee's voice moans:

> Another story about a writer writing a story! Another regressus in infinitum! Who doesn't perfer art that at

least overtly imitates something other than its own processes? That doesn't continually proclaim "Don't forget
I'm an artifice!"? (p. 114)

Similarly, a few pages later the narrator delivers a Baudelair-
ian harangue against the narratee. Perhaps we have always
been aware of the fictitiousness of our roles as narratees,
however much harangued against and however admittedly
compulsive. But it was surely not until recent times, with the
tremendous resurgence of self-conscious fiction, that we have
once more had these roles *embodied* for us as "characters in a
work of fiction."   In this book, as in many others in the
genre of self-conscious fiction, whether we empathize with
the narrator or the narratee—or for that matter with the
implied author or the implied reader—we are continually reminded that all these roles are fictive and that our empathy is
elicited through contrivance and artifice. Robert Coover has
turned these implications into a program of social change:
"The world itself being a construct of fiction," Coover
said in a recent interview, "I believe the fiction maker's function is to furnish better fictions with which we can reform
our notion of things."[19] Barth's intention covers the ground
just preceding Coover's program: how is it possible in this
world to write fiction at all?
        Considering the self-consciousness of this fiction, an
oral interpretation of this book becomes a dramatically
relevant emblem not so much of the theme but of the book's
nature, its mode of existence, its ontological situs. The
central protagonist is a voice looking for embodiment in or as
fiction.[20] The oral interpreter begins at the other end of the
task, a person in search of a fictive voice, a speaker whom we
observe trying on masks of implied author as well as implied
reader, narrator as well as narratee, someone who seems to
be, like us, a member of the author's audience but who at
times seems to play the roles of implied author and his protagonist. The fictive self-consciousness could hardly be more
explicit, or more appropriate, for Barth's venture.
        Of course, oral interpretation, rhetorical analysis,
criticism itself—these are only avenues into the full life of the
book, which cannot be encompassed by any means not fully
as paradoxical or protean as its own nature. It is a book
meant for print as well as for voice, to be seen as well as

heard; it is a novel about a struggle to write a novel; it is the lay of the last minstrel in an age of Freud and McLuhan, not to mention "Lord Raglan, Carl Jung, and Joseph Campbell." It is, to go back to the metaphor used earlier, a lovers' quarrel. The lovers—the protagonist ("he") and his deuteragonist ("she") on the one hand, the implied author and his implied reader on the other—are continually involved in a kind of dialectic with each other, one that is finally resolved by "her" ostensible absence in the final chapter. "He" sends "her" the book, and so makes the final chapter a plea for "her" to return—to validate his presence, to give him a body as well as a name and a *raison d'être*. The implied author has his protagonist discover a way out of the funhouse through an ironic stance, and he would have his implied reader to be ironic, too. And insofar as "she" prefigures the implied reader, that reader is meant to be protean, adopting stances and poses, shifting as easily and as rapidly as "he" shifts, blurring the distinction between the dancers and the dance, and questioning finally where the fiction leaves off.

But surely more than a protean irony accounts for the force of this novel and for whatever success it has. Of all the many qualities suggested in my retelling of the plot, perhaps one has been most prominent and needs now to be made explicit: the novel overtly risks failure through paralysis, or, what is almost the same thing, a doubling-back upon itself in infinite regression. Each story moves dangerously close to stopping altogether. The sperm may get someone to put an end to "making" in midstream, the voice from the tape recorder could get its wish to be turned off, Ambrose is immobilized as he stands dully staring at the flat meaninglessness of paper like a character in an early Barth novel at the onset of paralysis. But none does become paralyzed. A force, embodied as a kind of conclusion between those fictions called "Implied Author" and "Implied Reader," drives us on. At the same time, however, this drive also moves each story dangerously close to a doubling-back on itself, to a turn and counterturn that can destroy the illusion in every fictive character and incident. The Siamese twin insists that the woman whom both he and his brother love is really two people; consigned to a cruel doubleness, he sees double, like an author finding that his words use *him*. Menelaus has to settle for the answer that the sperm knows is unacceptable. The narratee attacks the narrator and the narrator strikes back. "Yours Truly" has no message in one story and an outrageous one in the next. These contortions threaten to dispel whatever "partial magic" is created through character and incident.

We have been prepared for these risks by the Moebius strip (we've also been prepared for these risks by Barth's preceding four novels, a point I wish to recur to later): the strip itself as an objective frame is paralyzing enough; the repeatable words are a maddening *regressus in infinitum*. These qualities are given their most awesome form in the climactic story of the novel, "Menelaiad," a frame tale par excellence. Here the risks are taken most directly: the tale within a tale within a tale, etc., threatens to stop or become merely a virtuoso performance. In speaking of the frame tales in "Menelaiad," Barth in an interview suggested a model of the riskful movement of the entire novel, in which conclusionless stories propel us toward a climax:

> I thought it would be an interesting formal challenge to compose a work in which there were seven enveloped tales. Unlike the early practitioners, I decided to arrange them in such a fashion that each would be brought to the moment just prior to its narrative climax, then suspended for the introduction of the next. I wanted the whole thing cocked like an enormous firework, designed not only to be tripped in quick succession but so that the actual nature of the plot resolution of insidest tale would precipitate the resolution of the next one out, and so on. They would go off like a chain of orgasms.[21]

"Love" trips the mechanism. But then, at the conclusion of "Menelaiad," a victory of sorts is won through the protagonist's (and, indirectly at least, our) grudging acceptance of "love" as an answer—however endlessly bracketed it had been by quotation marks and however much one is prepared to reject the terms. The terms of the victory are stark: though traditional narrative art may no longer be possible, the motivations or compulsions for that art may yet remain. Thus we move to the last story, told by a lorn minstrel, a singer of tales inventing writing to fulfill—and from the implied author's perspective to certify—those motivations, that possibility of "love," the communion of an author with a reader.

Too, as I've noted, we've been prepared for the risks of paralysis and *regressus in infinitum* through reading the four Barth novels which preceded *Lost in the Funhouse*. *The Floating Opera* and *The End of the Road* on the one hand, and *The Sot-Weed Factor* and *Giles Goat Boy* on the other (the grouping indicates differences in texture and narrative tone, to say nothing of length) use frames and doubling-back, threats of (or actual) paralysis and compulsive continuance— all activated, to use words Barth employs in speaking of the first two novels, by "the discrepancy between the ideal of the rational life and the kinds of facts of our non-rational or counterrational nature with which we indeed live. . . ."[22] Or, later in the same interview: "Half of my bibliography is on the subject of paralysis—of one kind or another. I hate effeteness and paralysis. And yet I love the spiritual threat of it in the air. It's exciting" (p. 137). As his novels show, paralysis occurs when a choice cannot be made because the choser isn't present. So the protagonist searches for his self-hood, like Ambrose wondering if he will become a "real person" or Jake Horner seeking through "mythotheraphy" to ward off "cosmopsis" (in *The End of the Road*, a novel that, characteristically, offers no distinction between mytho-therapy and quackery)—always with the omnipresent danger that because the intellect motivated the search it will also paralyze the searcher, in a frame. As is customary in Barth, it is the intellect-induced frame which contains the potential for paralysis, like the allusions to fiction and myths, such as the implicit slouching toward *Pilgrim's Progress* in *Giles Goat Boy* or the parodistic outrages in *The Sot-Weed Factor*.[23] From this turmoil Barth is always at a half-insouciant remove. The central protagonist may, like a chambered nautilus, carry his past on his back, but the poet who invokes him finds the effort produces not "more stately mansions" but increasingly complicated funhouses. If the laughter is loud, it's also a little nervous at times, too. Where can all this lead?

Let me make one last start and stop. Though tempted by the whirligig route of the Moebius strip, I've begun to move slowly toward evaluation of my last few remarks. If that's my destiny, perhaps it's time not simply to accept it but to try to claim some linear responsibility for it.

I've tried to be largely descriptive. The points which I make which are different from those made by other writers whom I've read on this book are that it is an ironic novel and that it features the reader as co-creator. But in exploring *how* and *whether* something works, one is bound to wonder if it's worth all the fuss. I think Barth's novels are. He is one of our wittiest, most learned and clever writers. But his cleverness often only makes patent a sad fact: the art he is fashioning is ephemeral, use-up-able. In *Lost in the Funhouse* the protagonist well realizes that the only victory he gains is an "absurd, unending possibility." Barth writes the book and gains a reader—at least one kind of reader: surely the ironies through which most of these victories are won are effective largely for modern academics, who having hefted the load of Barth's bibliography—including Homer, Kierkegaard, Mark Twain, Borges, Camus, Cervantes, and Hans Vaihinger—would appreciate the daredevil way in which Barth makes a possible novel out of the impossibility of writing a novel.[24] It's possible only because as Barth admits, *we* make it so. He sends us something novel while complaining that the novel is impossible. He tries our patience with such relics as heroes, muses, laureates, genres, destiny, ideals, truth, and plot. And in doing so he caters to an audience that, like himself, is elusive, illusive, allusive, and a fourth term added to make the third seem less than ultimate. This is an academic audience of *this* moment amidst the exhausted literatures of our decade. Those of us who have read and loved Joyce's novel are best equipped to appreciate Barth's, as I have suggested; now I would add, we are also best equipped to sense the contrasting shortness of *its* life. Joyce's "Once upon a time" is a vigorous and confident assault upon artistic conventions. Barth's work bears all the makes of being novel # 5 by John Barth, and its labyrinthine ingenuity begs all questions about *his* calling. So when, as in any amusement park, we are left with the question, After the funhouse, where shall we go? Barth's answer is quick, Why to see the *Chimera*.

In place of values, answers, or even commitment, he sends us possibilities. (Indeed, he's even been called a "possibilitarian."[25]) In *Lost in the Funhouse* possibility is the author's happy hunting ground, the "odd Elysium" of the protagonist—protean, absurd, eternal, terrifying, but Barth would have us believe the only one immedaitely available. My point about the ephemeralness of Barth's work is that whether one is speaking of politics, rhetoric, novels, or the novel, the realm of the possible is always *of this time, of that place*. Little wonder, then, that Barth sees his *present* reader as his co-creator—a rhetorical program laid on us by the least impossible persona, the speaker of the final tale:

> Once upon a time I told tales straight out, alternating summary and dramatization, developing characters and relationships, laying on bright detail and rhetorical flourish, et cetera. I'm not that amateur at the Lion's Gate; I know my trade. But I fear we're too far gone now for such luxury, Helen and I; I must get to where I am; the real drama, for yours truly, is whether he can trick this tale out at all—not the breath—batingest plot in the world, but there we are. It's an old story anyhow, this part of it; the corpus bloats with its like; I'll throw you the bones, to flesh out or pick at as you will. (pp. 171-72)

University of California at Berkeley

NOTES

[1] James Joyce, *A Portrait of the Artist as a Young Man*, ed. Chester G. Anderson (New York: Viking Press, 1968), p. 7.

[2] Then, by that token mustn't Scheherazade's muse have been male? Barth plays that token in his latest game, *Chimera* (New York: Random House, 1972).

[3] Michael Hinden explores some of the similarities between these two books in "*Lost in the Funhouse*: Barth's Use of the Recent Past," *Twentieth Century Literature*, 19 (1973), 107-18. Hinden has provided one of the best available readings of Barth's book. My differences with his reading will become apparent in such matters as my insistence that the book has a central protagonist (someone who, for example, not Menelaus, speaks the "Menelaiad") and that Barth's significant "recent past" is the one he himself has fictionalized in his preceding four novels.

[4] The edition I have used is the one published by Bantam Books

214

(New York, 1969), though readers are warned to beware of typos in that edition. Another edition was published by Grosset and Dunlap (New York, 1969). The Bantam edition is readily available; the quotation appears p. 104.

[5]For Christopher Morris, the book is yet another expression of Barth's "nihilism," in this case centering on "the notion of language as an all-encompassing but autotelic medium, a Moebius strip which is wholly independent of everything outside it, even the speaker who uses it." Morris's reading is particularly illuminating if one may assume (as I cannot) that Barth is the speaker of the novel, its central protagonist ("Barth and Lacan: The World of the Moebius Strip," *Critique*, 17 [October, 1975], 69-77).

[6]In an early review of the book, Granville Hicks seemed unwilling to follow Barth's advice that it be read as a series, not as a collection, and offered the opinion that some of the "experiments don't seem to be getting anywhere," an opinion that might have been illuminating in accounting for the peculiar progression of the series (*Saturday Review*, September 28, 1968, p. 32). Recently, Josephine Hendrin in an important article (*Harper's*, September 1973, pp. 102-06) reviews Barth's six novels largely from a "search for identity" point of view, but ignores that search as a central structural principle of the *Funhouse* series.

[7]Gerhard Joseph argues that the book "complicates [Barth's] urge to blur received discriminations among genre by attacking the traditional expectation of fiction as the printed word" in *American Writers*, ed. Leonard Unger (New York, 1974), I, 139. A Barthian intention, to be sure, but one that does not quite take into account Barth's instructions on the speech medium.

[8]"The pressing actuality of historical time, or of an individual lifetime, or of both, is the stuff of all good novels, including self-conscious ones, the perennial subject that the medium of the novel—a sequential narrative use of unmetrical language extended at length in time—seems almost to require" (Robert Alter, *Partial Magic: The Novel as Self-Conscious Genre* [Berkeley and Los Angeles: University of California Press; 1975], p. 231). Alter does not discuss *Funhouse* as a novel, but I shall try to show that the temporal progression of its series would seem to fit the basic characteristics he has articulated. In this case, time is the "individual lifetime" of the protagonist, the progressive steps in his quest for identity.

[9]Morris succumbs to the temptation.

[10]The "lemniscate," a similar figure, is used in Nabokov's *Pale Fire* to emblematize a "circular reflective relation" (see Alter, p. 189). The two halves of the figure 8 reflect each other, distort each other, and are neither two parts nor one whole. In Barth, these reflections re-

produce each other, like mirror images stretching to infinity and so lead our "hero" to a sense of infinity, absurdity, nothingness, or at least nothing beyond maddeningly infinite mirror reflections, a sense that in a Barth novel usually precedes paralysis.

[11]Gerald Gillespie has captured the dangers of these compulsions in the following description: "The organically limited perceiver is detached from, yet chained to, self: 'In the funhouse mirror room you can't see yourself go on forever, because no matter where you stand, your head gets in the way.' This statement is equally applicable to the sperm, which thrusts its 'message' forward in the darkness toward a possible continuance through merger with the egg; or to the mind that, for all its infinite posturings, gets in the way by analyzing to pieces its own fiction and interferes with the organic process it fears as a captivity and delusion" ("Barth's 'Lost in the Funhouse': Short Story Text in its Cyclic Context," *Studies in Short Fiction*, 12 [1975], 230). But it would also seem that the timid soul is equally fearful of what might happen should the head *get out* of the way: absurdity, a projected future of meaningless reproduction and an equally meaningless *regressus in infinitum*.

[12]As D. Allen Jones points out, "The minstrel [progresses], successively, from sacred hymns and lyric poetry, literature's beginnings, to the contemporary, introspective, psychological novel" ("John Barth's 'Anonymiad,' " *Studies in Short Fiction*, 11 [1974], 363).

[13]Jac Tharpe, who continually keeps an eye on the serial arrangement of the stories, states ". . . in *Chimera* and *Lost in the Funhouse*, companion pieces like the first two novels, [Barth] writes to illustrate the idea that the style is the man. Style is man—*homo faber*, the heroic craftsman, who orders a chaotic funhouse" (*John Barth, the Comic Sublimity of Paradox* [Carbondale: Southern Illinois University Press, 1974], p. 11). Tharpe, however, posits no irony between Barth and his *homo faber*.

[14]For example: As the narrator of "Title" says, "The end of one road might be the beginning of another." Or as the narrator of "Anonymiad" says, "I imagined my *opera* sinking undiscovered. . . ."

[15]The chart is patterned after one in Seymour Chatman's "Story and Discourse: Contributions to the Theory of Narrative" (unpub. ms). The term "narratee" is used by Gerald Prince ("Notes Toward a Categorization of Fictional 'Narratees,' " *Genre*, 4 [1971], 100-05). The terms "implied author," "implied reader," "dramatized," and "undramatized" are used by Wayne C. Booth (*The Rhetoric of Fiction* [Chicago: University of Chicago Press, 1961]).

[16]Beverly Gray Bienstock sees the series as a search for identity—but not necessarily, as in the present article, of a novelistic kind:

"This is not a novel but a group of stories meant to be read in a prescribed order. While diverse in style and manner of presentation, these
stories have one basic element in common. They all revolve around the
search for one's identity amidst the tangled skeins of past, present, and
future" ("Lingering on the Autognostic Verge: John Barth's *Lost in the
Funhouse*," *Modern Fiction Studies*, 19 [Spring, 1973], 70). Bienstock's title and mine reveal the different centerings of our interpretations.

[17]Booth, p. 324.

[18]*The Atlantic*, August 1967, p. 33. On self-conscious fiction
as genre, see Alter (note 8 above).

[19]Frank Gado, ed. *First Person: Conversations on Writers &
Writing* (Schenectady, N.Y.: Union College Press, 1973), pp. 149-50.

[20]In this respect, his problem is not unlike Jake Horner's in *The
End of the Road*: "Articulation! There was *my* absolute, if I could be
said to have one. . . . To turn experience into speech—that is, to classify, to categorize, to conceptualize, to grammarize, to syntactify it—is
always a betrayal of experience, a falsification of it; but only so betray-
ed can it be dealt with at all, and only in so dealing with it did I ever
feel a man, alive and kicking." Or cf. Henry Burlingame in *The Sot-
Weed Factor*: "One must *assert, assert, assert*, or go screaming mad." Or
cf. any central protagonist in any Barth.

[21]Gado, p. 133.

[22]Gado, p. 117.

[23]On the matter of parody as a potential trap for Barth, see
Roland W. Noland, "John Barth and the Novel of Comic Nihilism,"
Wisconsin Studies in Contemporary Literature, 7 (1966), 239-57 and
Earl Rovitt, "The Novel as Parody: John Barth," *Critique*, 6 (Fall,
1963), 77-85.

[24]Barth's ironies, I've argued, are protean. I would also argue
that however protean they are "stable" (in the sense developed by
Wayne C. Booth) for a restricted audience. See *A Rhetoric of Irony*
(Chicago: University of Chicago Press, 1974), esp. pp. 39-40.

[25]See Tony Tanner, *City of Words, American Fiction 1950-
1970* (New York: Harper & Row, 1971), p. 259. Tanner closes his essay
on Barth by echoing Kierkegaard and worrying that eventually Barth
and certain other American writers "may find themselves hopelessly
'astray in possibility.' " The fears are realized by the narrator of the
"Anonymiad" and articulated in the following way: "Alas: for where
Fancy's springs are unlevee'd by hard Experience they run too free,

flooding every situation with possibilities until Prudence and even Common Sense are drowned" (p. 178). Barth's protagonists usually behave as if they are very aware of the dangers of drowning; it is his audience who may finally give up, astray in all these possibilities, too water-logged to stay afloat.